The Sonic Persona

The Sonic Persona

An Anthropology of Sound

HOLGER SCHULZE

Bloomsbury Academic
An imprint of Bloomsbury Publishing Inc

BLOOMSBURY
NEW YORK • LONDON • OXFORD • NEW DELHI • SYDNEY

WEST SUSSEX LIBRARY SERVICE	
201770843	
Askews & Holts	03-Apr-2018
302.2301	

www.bloomsbury.com

BLOOMSBURY and the Diana logo are trademarks of Bloomsbury Publishing Plc

First published 2018

© Holger Schulze, 2018

All rights reserved. No part of this publication may be reproduced or transmitted in any form or by any means, electronic or mechanical, including photocopying, recording, or any information storage or retrieval system, without prior permission in writing from the publishers.

No responsibility for loss caused to any individual or organization acting on or refraining from action as a result of the material in this publication can be accepted by Bloomsbury or the author.

Library of Congress Cataloging-in-Publication Data
A catalog record for this book is available from the Library of Congress.

ISBN: HB: 978-1-5013-0546-7
PB: 978-1-5013-0545-0
ePDF: 978-1-5013-0547-4
ePub: 978-1-5013-0548-1

Cover design by Louise Dugdale
Cover image: *Spreading Membrane* (2016)
Photography by Christine Amschler, Bayreuth, Germany & Rahel Müller, Switzerland

Typeset by Deanta Global Publishing Services, Chennai, India
Printed and bound in the United States of America

To find out more about our authors and books visit www.bloomsbury.com. Here you will find extracts, author interviews, details of forthcoming events, and the option to sign up for our newsletters

From Hermann von Helmholtz to Miley Cyrus, from Fluxus to the Arab Spring, from wave field synthesis to otoacoustic emissions, from premillennial club culture to post-democratic authoritarianism, from signal processing to human echolocation:

a research expedition to the sonic personae of humanoid aliens—their sensory corpuses, their auditory dispositives, and their elaborate precision of sensibility.

I'm going to prove the impossible really exists.

CONTENTS

PART ONE The materialization of sound:
A research history 1

1 Quantifying sound 3

   Pro tools and the phonautograph 3
   1863: Writing Helmholtz 9
   1929: Fletcher's weirdness 17
   1954: Experience by Beranek 23
   Projections in the pavilion 28

2 Materializing listening 31

   Destroying instruments, discovering ambient 31
   1962: Sound in flux 33
   1970: Baudry's dispositif 39
   2008: Beyond *Aufführungspraxis* 44
   Dispositives of surround sound 49

3 Corporealizing the senses 54

   Into darkness 54
   1985: Serres's *syrrhesis* 58
   1992: Tension in Nancy 66
   1998: Eshun and the senses 75
   New sensory materialism 79

PART TWO The sonic persona: *An anthropology of sound* 83

4 In auditory dispositives 85
The microphone as poem 85
Scarce signals 88
The Apparatus Canto 94
Dispositive's capitalization 101
In/Resurrection 107

5 The sonic persona 111
Sonic traces 111
Idiosyncratic implex 113
The sonic persona 120
Varying experientiality 126
Anthropology of sound 132

6 A sensory corpus 136
The material percepts 136
Corpus in situ 140
A generative sensorium 145
Corporeal epistemologies 150
The listening body 156

PART THREE The precision of sensibility: *A political critique* 161

7 The precision of sensibility 163
Nanopolitics 163
Sensory critique 166
Apparatuses naturalized 172
The precision of sensibility 178
Idioplex 183

8   Resistance and resonance 187
    zeige deine Wunde 187
    No response 190
    Erratic heuristics 196
    Noise as presence 200
    Persona resista 206

9   Generativity 212
    Cohesion 212
    Im Erwachten Garten 215
    Sensory syncope 219
    Synaptic Island 224
    Generativity 227

Sources 233
Tak. Danke. Thank you. 246
Index 248

PART ONE
The materialization of sound: *A research history*

CHAPTER ONE

Quantifying sound

Pro tools and the phonautograph

"Snap it to the grid!" So, my co-producer and good friend did what he had just announced. Both of us listened to this file again. Over and over. Both of us indulged in the fantasy the software offered of supposed exactitude as well as of a radical reduction of anything sounding to visual representations. For quite some hours now—on that hot and humid summer day almost two decades ago—we had been producing a radio feature for a Berlin public radio station. The station was definitely not the largest around; but nonetheless, it was a daring enterprise for both of us. Until then neither of us was really experienced with the production and transmission of major sound pieces. We did not produce it in one of the big recording or smaller production studios of the radio station, but at home, in front of the computer screen of my close friend, using the latest version of Pro Tools that had just been released in its so-called "Free" version. Like any post-production sound work in those days, we had to focus mainly on a rather simple 2-D visualization of the various channels and tracks we intended to integrate in our piece. For hours on end we looked at graphic details, followed and corrected lines and rectangles, adjusted cross sections, and made sensible selections to decrease or increase volume or activate other effects and plugins. There were only selected moments—sometimes longer periods—of exclusive *audition*, of extended *listening experiences*: like a stepping back from the canvas, from the designed page of a book or a newspaper, we granted our eyes a break and immersed ourselves, as deeply and as alienatedly as possible, into merely listening to our piece. It was slowly, incredibly slowly, growing and growing, ten seconds at a time. Quite intentionally, even forcefully, we switched from our highly focused stare at the depicted timeline and all those tracks and overlays, from an *imagined* sonic experience to an actual and physical sonic experience. We disciplined ourselves—so we thought—to subtract our ever-present strong intention to produce a great and stunning radio piece. "Okay: just listen now." And so we listened. We sat in our chairs, eyes closed, trying very hard to listen only to this artifact as if it were something completely new to us: just being transmitted to us, unexpecting listeners.

In these sequences of specialized and subtracted listening, these long and intensely focused layered seconds and minutes, we trained ourselves in a *listening practice* new to us. We were transferring our rather intimate practices of headphone listening, developed in times of adolescence and post-adolescence in the 1980s and 1990s while listening to our favorite records, to radio programs or sound pieces, to concert performances of various kinds between New Music, New Jazz, and regular popular music shows, to this new area and task of sounds and music projected in the clubs and discos in these decades. We tried quite hard to dismiss our individual biographical, personal, and highly idiosyncratic corporeal inclinations toward particular effects and excitements related to some sounds, samples, and snippets; and at the same time we still tried to retain and to strengthen our autodidactically well-trained ability to listen to every single, every miniature sound event very precisely, in-depth and in the context of the piece and all its structural transformations, references, allusions, continuities, and discontinuities happening right here, right now in the very late 1990s. A joyful meditation: a listening meditation.

The technology of sound production has become what it was intended to be, a widely distributed commodity. It is not at all a thoroughly new and exciting technology in all its glory, no longer surprising and not a novelty in itself. It is a tool, a very useful and versatile one. Being truly ubiquitously present, it has turned into the preferred imaginary space in which millions and millions of sound producers all over this planet, in all their diverse jobs and aesthetic traditions, in all their different project flows and production contexts, work on their individual sonic artifacts. All these producers imagine sound as an integral part of this software environment. Obviously there are many different software packages to produce and to refine sound, and many more of those since the 1990s; yet the main structuring elements, the main standards and formats of these tools, stay surprisingly unsurprising. Since 1989 the software suite of Pro Tools has been continuously adapted, expanded, refurbished, and relaunched to find its place in the realm of production software. In relation to the environment of musical aesthetics, production styles, and design preferences, the developers and key account managers at Avid Technology managed to promote this software—even more so after their acquisition of Digidesign—as the one and maybe only place of total access to all aspects, parameters, and transformations of any sound possibly being processed in an audio production. Naturally, this cannot be true. Albeit in the early twenty-first century, this is exactly what is expected from a digital commodity; while no one software package can do everything, that is nonetheless what is expected of it.

This book is not a book on Pro Tools. It is a book on the historical, anthropological, and political traces that relate practices of listening and practices of sounding to each other in a mutual interdependency that surrounds us and that shapes and limits, transforms, and freezes the individual sonic experiences of *humanoid aliens* like you and me. Thus, I trace the historical roots of software like Pro Tools that can be found—as a surprise for some readers—in the invention of the so-called *phonautograph* or similar devices for sound recording and reproduction in the heart of the nineteenth century. This "cultural origin of sound reproduction" (Sterne 2003) might seem as far as can be from contemporary technologies. Yet, its anthropological and epistemological concepts, its ontological predeterminations of what sounding and listening could be or should be, are present and taking effect in both massively commodified pieces of technology: Pro Tools and the phonautograph. The latter is an astonishing apparatus that occupies, in the history of technological inventions of recent centuries, a remarkable point between *no longer* being an organic or mechanic extension of a humanoid's senses and *not yet* being an inconceivable or even invisible algorithmic representation of sensory signal data processing. The phonautograph is not a musical instrument; it is not a mechanical hearing aid; it is not a piece of automated performances of musical scores; it is surely not immaterial like a piece of software that allows for recording, generating, manipulating, processing, transmitting, and reproducing any sound event audible to humanoids and their state-of-the-art microphones or other audio sensors. The phonautograph is a refined object of desire, physically impressive and in part handmade. It incorporates automated elements as well as the affordances to use specific storage media to record and to play back the recorded sounds. It consists of an (internal or external) writing device that inscribes sounds on a material surface. It also consists, therefore, of a removable, interchangeable, and quite plastic object on which these sounds can be inscribed; finally, it consists of a reading device that amplifies these sounds and projects them into a spatial environment in which listeners might be idling or awaiting the one and only sacred transmission. The master— historically gendered in an androcentric culture—might then speak to us.

For an anthropology of sound—like the one I am proposing here—the most exciting part of the phonautograph, though, is not easily visible or palpable. It is to be found in the aforementioned succession of materials, mechanical tools, and objects as convincingly conjoined by its many co-inventors on various continents and various research cultures: in a succession and relation of materials solely intended to assemble various listening and sounding dispositives of a humanoid's body. The ear, the tongue, the finger, the larynx, the vocal chords, the tympanic membrane—you will find all of these and many more either in this exact succession or in a slightly adapted one in listening and sounding devices being built by humanoid aliens in recent decades. As a distant relative of the phonautograph, software like Pro Tools still today refers to this original corpus of nineteenth-century knowledge about the senses, the process and reach of listening, and the role of a standardized and non-specific body that listens and makes sounds. Our machines that hear for us resemble a bricolage of listening homunculi: *May the apparatus be humanoid!* In recent research, especially with a focus on the interdependencies between the sciences and the arts, this fact has been taken as an argument for the immense auditory knowledge of researchers and developers in the nineteenth century. This form of knowledge is thus anatomically and physically—let alone aesthetically, pragmatically, or politically—a deeply anthropocentric, solidified (if not paralyzed) form of knowledge: even more so as explored through means of laboratory experiments with various dead corpses of animals and extracted organs as research objects and major references. The knowledge represented in such artifacts, be it a mechanical tool or a piece of software, I argue, is not mainly developed out of the specific material and dynamic requirements of the auditory—but out of arbitrary requirements of a historical period of research, of industrialization, and of a kind of technoscientifist imperialism taking over Western societies indulging in an industrializing frenzy. In the early twenty-first century, you and I are living in the materialized fantasy of nineteenth-century imperialist and nationalist research squads.

The main anthropological question driving my inquiry here as a researcher in the field of *historical anthropology* therefore reads as follows: What are the historically and culturally specific assumptions about this strange and alien entity called "The Human" as present in the recent history of sound technology and listening practices? How was it possible that pieces of soft- and hardware, Pro Tools or the phonautograph and their manifold descendants and unlikely twins are now occupying sound cultures on a massively large, even global and transcultural scale? Is it possible to imagine a different and even more valid concept of listening and sounding that resembles more contemporary concepts of technology, corporeality, and personality? And what would be the political, social, and institutional consequences of such a thorough transformation and remodeling of contemporary sound cultures? As I remember my friend and I, arduously crafting our first larger radio piece, we were in touch with rather early beginnings of ubiquitous sound recording and sound reproduction. In the course of our constructing activity, in refining this artifact, our individual *sonic personae* as well were refined and remodeled following the technological dispositive present at this time. My way of listening and my collaborator's way of listening, my sense of audio aesthetics as well as the sense of my friend, have crafted a sort of *longue durée* of the history of technology and of anatomy as present in the software apparatus we were working with. Our shared and piously rebellious minutes of audition, though, seem to fall out of this dispositive—

or are they even affirming and supporting it in a sense? How do you and I actually manage to live with all these scientific dispositives predetermining an actual situation of sonic articulation? How do humanoid aliens cope with a sonically preconceptualized world as individual, sonic personae?

So, what is a *humanoid alien* at all? And what is *historical anthropology*? The background and the main research strategies of historical anthropology I am working with and within now have a history of almost four decades; and this history will also help me in actually introducing the notion of the humanoid alien I am experimenting with in this book. Historical anthropology represents a non-disciplinary endeavor to research the differing transformations and conceptualization of this strange and alien entity called *The Human* across cultures and eras. Coming from cultural history and ethnography, performance studies, literature studies, and visual as well as sensory studies, from philosophy and various areas of regional studies, researchers came together, in the early 1980s at the Freie Universität Berlin, to review and to rework the age-old and often hopelessly essentialist, Eurocentric and androcentric, decidedly bourgeois, ableist, and Western research tradition of anthropology. Until then most of the approaches to anthropology branded as *philosophical* or *biological* were apparently mainly interested in preserving an existing social, habitual, biological, and philosophical state of how to think about "The Human Being." A being who would resemble, rather unsurprisingly, mainly the lifestyle and the habit of its white, male, professorial or aristocratic authors. From such more normative approaches came the notion of anthropology being a deeply affirmative, a rather elitist and a largely non-critical field of research and of reflection. In the 1970s whoever would have dared speaking about *The Anthropological* would have been immediately under strong suspicion of promoting an only loosely camouflaged *Western Suprematism*. Contrarily, the Berlin researchers of those years, such as Dietmar Kamper, Hans-Dieter Bahr, Gunter Gebauer, and Christoph Wulf at the Interdisciplinary Center for Historical Anthropology, would be interested in the quirkier, the weirder and exotic, the idiosyncratic and more troublesome questions concerning anthropology. Together with colleagues not only from Western Europe or North America, but also from South America, from the Middle East, from East Asia, China, Oceania, and Africa, they founded the international, peer-reviewed *Paragrana*—with topics such as: *Selbstfremdheit* (vol. 6: Self-Strangeness), *Muße* (vol. 16: Idleness), *Töten* (vol. 20: Killing), *Fuß* (vol. 21: The Foot), and *Unsicherheit* (vol. 24: Insecurity). And the second volume ever to appear in *Paragrana* was on the issue of *Das Ohr als Erkenntnisorgan: The Ear as an Organ of Knowledge* (Kamper, Trabant and Wulf 1993). This focus on the auditory and the sonic, on listening and sensing is a direct result of the constant interest of this research strand of historical anthropology for the corporeality and the sensory experience of individual creatures on this planet. Exactly this focus on the auditory and the sonic, on listening and sensing, represents the constantly provoking interest of this research strand for corporeality and sensory experience. After an assumed *End of Man*—Western, white, middle-class, academic males, I feel urged to add—and in the advent of an intensely globalized, mediatized, commodified, and heavily networked period of the late twentieth century, a fundamental reflection seemed fascinating again: What varieties, what forms of excess, transgression, and invention, what potential is there, in this creature one might be tempted to call now rather a *humanoid alien*?

I introduce the notion of the humanoid alien in this book and will be experimenting with this concept throughout the following chapters. It allows acknowledgment of the intrinsically non-standardized, inherently plastic and transformative character of you, of me, of the persons and creatures around us. They and we might show more or less humanoid and anthropoid traits in our looks, habits, our physics, our expressions; but it would be hard to deny the endless differences between her, them, him, you, or me—even more so in our everyday practices, self-perceptions, our bodily specificities, body enhancements and selected deficits, visible symptoms of earlier diseases, our professions or passions not often evident in each moment of our action or inaction. In contrast to the metaphysically petrified and largely androcentric, Eurocentric, heteronormative, and normophiliac concept of *The Human Being*, the much more malleable and divergent concept of the humanoid alien allows us to actually study in *everyday life* the minor and often neglected relations between humanoid aliens and sensory occurrences: the obsessions these aliens find in imaginations they like to indulge in the materialist aspects of various cultural practices, and the desires to promote a social situation supportive for such idiosyncratic needs, an urge to political action. Such an anthropology intends not to superimpose an imaginary norm of humanoid behavior—but to open up an endless series of variations of evermore strange and alien extravaganza of how *aliens like me and you* might perform, perceive, and experience. The study of humanoid aliens performing, perceiving, and experiencing sonic and sensory conditions constitutes an *anthropology of sound*.

This present inquiry, therefore, starts in the first part of this book, "The Materialization of Sound," with a historical exploration and critique scrutinizing selected aspects in the development of science and technology and history of sound since the nineteenth century. The main interest lies here in extracting the underlying anthropological concepts predetermining the main research efforts in order to quantify, to materialize, and finally to corporealize listening and sounding. The second and main part, "The Sonic Persona," takes these anthropological concepts and proposes a thorough rewriting and resignifying of technical, corporeal, and personal processes of listening and sounding. The historically arbitrary anthropological concepts of listening and of *The Human* are taken into our presence and a projected future, a time in which it might finally no longer be appropriate to standardize one listening homunculus—but to assume a multitudinal variety of humanoid aliens in all their highly idiosyncratic and deeply situated, corporeal differentials of sensing and experiencing. The third and final part, "The Precision of Sensibility," presents a series of exemplary sensory critiques on the levels of individual, corporeal sensibility, of social and political transformations, and of a critique of single auditory artifacts. The crystallized matter of technology is liquidated: a soft membrane of liquefied gold seems to be spread out on a puddle in the woods: this artwork, *Spreading Membrane* (2016), by Rahel Müller and Christine Amschler, envelopes this whole book. The nine chapters of this book in their entirety undertake a critique of contemporary approaches to the senses and to technology from a *hearing perspective* (Auinger/Odland 2007) crucial to an anthropology of sound. How will we live with sound?

1863: Writing Helmholtz

Not merely music but even other kinds of motions may produce similar effects. Water in motion, as in cascades or sea waves, has an effect in some respects similar to music. How long and how often can we sit and look at the waves rolling in to shore! Their rhythmic motion, perpetually varied in detail, produces a peculiar feeling of pleasant repose or weariness, and the impression of a mighty orderly life, finely linked together. When the sea is quiet and smooth we can enjoy its colouring for a while, but this gives no such lasting pleasure as the rolling waves. Small undulations, on the other hand, on small surfaces of water, follow one another too rapidly, and disturb rather than please. (Helmholtz 1885: 386)

An inspiring narration, no doubt, a metaphysical, maybe even a pataphysical one. In a few words the author sketches in a poetic manner the manifold layerings and movements taking place in water, in an ocean, in a sea. He takes us with his narration into a description of movements and layerings constituting a sonic experience. An insightful narration. Mustn't such a great narration unavoidably lead to a new and situated exploration of the senses' activities in humanoids? The senses at sea, the senses at the shore? Don't we almost physically grasp a provocative model of sensory performativity that takes place in the author's immersive narration of waves rolling, crushing, tumbling over one another, erasing and amplifying their impact and their vectors? The ambition driving this narration surely was not easy to perform for the author, Hermann von Helmholtz. The chasm between epistemic imagination and research practice is a wide one. To make things worse, the strongest cultural trend of the mid-nineteenth century seemed first and foremost to be a utilitarian and instrumental theory of the senses. A research practice was demanded that followed on the one hand the guidelines of the vast amount of accumulated capital and on the other hand the newly, pretentiously founded nations expanding into globally militarized empires. Helmholtz felt urged to decline these demands. Soon he engaged with a wide variety of cultural movements—with late romantic artists, composers and poets, with philosophers thoughtfully criticizing the dialectics and inner contradictions in any strife for enlightenment that were so obviously starting to erect powerful new social structures in order to discipline the new workforces. He even engaged with newly formed political movements, such as the communist movement, to support them in establishing a prolific way of educating all the aspiring young humanoids of these years: not only the educated male, European students from higher, financially well-endowed and ambitious dynasties or still-influential aristocracies. Helmholtz wanted to support education on the senses, on technology on all levels—especially concerning the education of female and immigrant students, the latter arriving from lands afar being called "The Colonies." He knew deeply that these were disturbed and dislocated humanoid aliens like himself—seeking refuge, salvation, even an epiphany in immersing themselves into the details of listening, of sensing, of experiencing the empirical world.

Helmholtz' ambition was stunning: His dedication to influence the research done on nature, on living creatures and their interrelations and interpenetrations on all levels and aspects resulted in a true opening of new horizons. He succeeded in connecting the hitherto unconnected in a sometimes wild but always inspiring and fascinating establishment of new concepts of the senses. Helmholtz was deeply aware that his ambitions were quite contrary to the historical trend of his times; yet being an ambitious and gifted, materially rich and psychologically strong person, he took all this personal capital and directed its forces against a frightening trend of his times: a trend toward imperialist militarization, toward the technological advancement of weaponry, and the transformation of the Earth's face to merely a resource for future battlefields, for transporting fighting divisions, and for firing off weapons in order to fulfill the desires of warmongering politicians and entrepreneurs. He was arrested over and over for his ambitions, and he truly had to face the cruelest and meanest adversaries. It was his cleverness and also his political trickery that led him to inspire established colleagues, young researchers and artists, outworn politicians as well as upcoming thinkers, poets, leaders of rising political movements toward social and political welfare. At the core of his exciting approach toward the discontinuous streams of the sensorial stood the idea: *How is one to understand the senses in their genuine and erratic dynamics?* How to avoid an all too simple anthropocentric projection onto things effectively outside of a humanoid's influence? How to conceptualize the senses and the aliens living through and with these senses without any reference to a higher structural order? How to think about the senses without applying the ancient idea of writing the one book of nature as so many prophets before him tried to do, in vain?

Yet, alas: All of this Hermann von Helmholtz did *not* do. A fresh and deviating start of an alternate science in accordance with an alternate political, aesthetic, and social history did not take place. Probably such an alternate history would also have eliminated any need for alternate histories in itself. It did not happen, though. You who are reading these lines, and me continuing to write this section, we live in a different, a far stranger and more alien and, to say the least, truly abnormal world. It might be interpreted as a dystopic one, but for sure this world took quite a different course than the one imagined on the previous pages. A course where the hegemonic cultures in research, politics, and economy destroyed an incredibly large and unimaginably diverse number of individual lives, particular cultures and subcultures, a vast range of rich and promising cultural traditions. These present times rely on the killing of earlier possible worlds. This present time does allow me, nevertheless, the conceiving, the writing, and even the publishing of this book. It is, moreover, also highly probable that my previously imagined world of a more integrated and highly complex exploration of the senses would have destroyed various other traditions and cultures as its very consequence.

How did von Helmholtz, then, essentially undertake his project of exploring the senses? What followed this great and promising first start cited at the beginning of this section—to understand ever better the nature of the waves in oceans, in the air, on land, and in nature in general—and in every special, individual, material case? Unfortunately, from a historical and not an imaginary perspective, one has to witness a slow but cumulative reversal of this initial interest in the complexity of sensory phenomena. Helmholtz himself pushes this inspiring narration, this *sonic fiction*, aside. In the following sentences of the cited source at the beginning of this section, Helmholtz laconically excludes all of the richness just laid out by him as too complicated to research and not actually a valid object for a scientific inquiry. The affective impact of sounding phenomena gets epistemologically marginalized. In consequence, von Helmholtz is suppressing one of the very reasons that made him become a researcher in the first place: the sensory affections and intense individual experiences which he just proved to be incredibly inspiring and touching, moving and joyful. Helmholtz performs a symbolic castration on these pages: a castration of the whole of joy, of desire, and of corporeal lust indulging in sensory experiences, standing at the seafront, the ocean before him. How distant, not too close, the liquids are flowing and playing; following a path and leaving it again. Playful and somewhat aleatoric. There is a sort of freedom and liberty in listening to this, in sensing this. I indulge. I digress.

Helmholtz' symbolic self-castration of an individual sensation of sound is, unsurprisingly, in accordance with dominant scientific paradigms of the time: a paradigm of rational, systematic, and methodological research in experimental research cultures. This paradigm has been installed by making use of the writings by Immanuel Kant in order to establish a presumably anonymous, generalizable, and ahistoric research practice with outcomes of a similar nature. A supposedly total abstraction of desires, obsessions, affects, and imaginations of individual researchers seemed to provide a necessary ground for a political order that many researchers could agree upon—just to realize many decades later how this paradigm exactly represented the dialectics of enlightenment. Research in times of newly founded nation states, of newly installed national academies, and of imperial ambitions to globally impose the results of national research efforts was an intrinsic part of European nation building. Being a researcher in this time might have been camouflaged as just a personal effort to gain knowledge about how the world tumbles and tips; but the empirical side of it, the daily tasks of representation and establishing, of promoting and of publishing research already in the nineteenth century, required a researcher to be an executive manager, a spokesperson, and a sales promoter of his (almost never: *her*) own research efforts and his own research business. Around the year 1860, the major work cited before—*Die Lehre von den Tonempfindungen als Physiologische Grundlage für die Theorie der Musik (On the Sensations of Tone as a Physiological Basis for the Theory of Music)*—was yet to be published. Helmholtz' first wife recently deceased, his second marriage yet ahead, a thirty-nine-year-old father with two kids, holding his third professorship in Heidelberg and ongoing in his efforts to expand the reach of his research. An ongoing effort that would eventually lead after yet another decade to more strictly political activities. Recent research in the history of the sciences did point out that one of his major goals was indeed to invent and to establish a new, a more empirically founded approach to music, to sounds, to listening. Therefore, his seminal *Lehre von den Tonempfindungen* set in with one of the traditionally boldest claims possible in research: the claim to fuse hitherto separated fields of research. A fine example for the rhetorics of interdisciplinarity:

> In the present work an attempt will be made to form a connection between the boundaries of two sciences, which, although drawn together by many natural relations, have hitherto remained sufficiently distinct—the boundaries of *physical and physiological acoustics* on the one side, and of *musical science and esthetics* on the other. (Helmholtz 1885: 1; emphasis in the original)

The author claims to make an unprecedented leap; A leap away from a premodern, precritical speaking and writing about sounds and music in which mainly an individual's joyful or fearful experience with sounds and their supposedly immaterial nature was at the core of all articulations and thoughts. Paradigmatic for this rejected premodern approach to music as part of the arts as well as part of para-religious experiences is an example of late-eighteenth-century writing. This example, by the luxuriously emphatic and undisguisedly religious name of *Herzensergießungen eines kunstliebenden Klosterbruders (Heartfelt Effusions of an Art-Loving Cloister Brother)*, was written by two German authors, Ludwig Tieck and Wilhelm Heinrich Wackenroder. Tieck and Wackenroder expose in their (only partly ironic) text the style of speaking about the arts and about music that dominated in premodern times: a way of rhapsodically, libidinously, and joyfully poetic dancing about sounds and musical experience. A way of speaking about sound that was doomed by later readers and researchers as merely arbitrary, badly subjectivist, and irrelevant because it might just be mainly personal, anecdotic, and arbitrarily affect-based. Before any advent of musicological, let alone acoustic research, such a form of writing was endemic—as it occasionally might still be today:

> Art is to be called the flower of human emotion. The Universal Father, who holds in His hand the earth, with all that is upon it . . . . He sees the traces of the heavenly spark which, having emanated from Him, passed over through the breast of the individual into his little creation, from which it then glows back again to the great Creator. The Gothic temple is just as pleasing as the temple of the Greeks, and the raw war music of the savages has for him a sound as lovely as artful choirs and church songs. (Wackenroder 1971: 109)

This becomes even more obvious when strictly speaking about musical experiences and its emotional benefits:

> It is the only art which reduces the most multifarious and contradictory emotions of our souls to the s a m e beautiful harmonies, which plays with joy and sorrow, with despair and adoration in the same harmonious tones. Therefore, it is also music which infuses in us true serenity of soul, which is the most beautiful jewel that the human being can acquire; – I mean that serenity in which everything in the world seems to us natural, true, and good, in which we find a beautiful cohesion in the wildest throng of people, in which, with sincere hearts, we feel all creatures to be related and close to us and, like children, look upon the world as through the twilight of a lovely dream. (Wackenroder 1971: 180f)

This style of writing was the archenemy, the detested and rejected form of non-critical and anti-rigid approach to sonic experiences in the eighteenth and nineteenth centuries. It was rejected by the younger researchers, as they regarded it to be just uneducated, trivial, and generally a lower form of speaking about sounds, a merely *schwärmerisches*, that is, a quixotic meandering and dwelling on personal impressions and random illusions. Such writing definitely does not adhere to the Kantian concept for any proper research in the sciences: it does not erect a rigidly, terminologically, thoroughly defined and unified, organized system generated by an educated humanoid's capability of reasoning in a combinatory, logical, and hierarchically prioritized manner, that grants a rest from the regression to merely arbitrary empirical judgments in some unconditioned ground (Kant 1781). This quixotic writing might in contrast only rely on unreflected assumptions and hopes, desires, and anxieties, like articulations by humanoid aliens like you and me quite so often do. Kantian epistemology, though, is hegemonic in nineteenth-century research in Germany, as well as in other European and American research communities. Helmholtz then, being a researcher in his early forties, had by then studied medicine as a more applicable discipline than physics; and he had taught anatomy at a Berlin art school and traveled to various places for teaching physiology: the German revolution of 1848 apparently neither crossed, nor hindered, nor fostered his further progress in research and teaching. It was in Heidelberg, when Wilhelm Wundt was his assistant, that he undertook the research for his book on tone sensations, a research effort that already had started a decade earlier in the context of his general interest in signal transduction in animal and humanoid creatures. His ongoing contact and apparent desire to come closer by means of research in understanding humanoids' bodies and how they act and react, sense and sound, is also in accordance with the efforts of fellow researchers, both older and younger scholars such as Johann Wilhelm Ritter, Georg Elias Müller, or Carl Stumpf (cf. Erlmann 2010). All of these noble adventurers into the microscopic territories of nerves and cells, electric currents and habitualized reactions, almost desperately wanted to contribute to the aforementioned leap in research: a leap from self-sustaining imaginary edifices toward a reference to specific empirical details, observable, documentable, and reproducible reactions by sensing, reacting, and listening bodies. The major blasphemic itch is still present in these efforts as they all tried to take from the "allgemeine[n] Vater" (Wackenroder/Tieck 1797: 100), the *all-seeing, all-caring godfather and lord*, the "Erdball mit allem was daran ist" (ebd.), the *globe and all therein* from *HIS* hands, the hands of The Lord. Researchers in the nineteenth century represent an impressively energetic, liberating, and exhibitionist style in inscribing the new bourgeois subject as the only relevant approach to life and the cosmos: the religious sanctum, heavenly choirs, and otherworldly substances and journeys are abandoned by them in order to promote this very (European, male, bourgeois, educated) subject's autonomy: a will to power, will to knowledge, and will to occupy new, hitherto supposedly uncharted territories—by a new, now bourgeois *HE*, "The New Lord." They made an effort to materialize the sensory apparatus of humanoids in using rather iconoclastic laboratory instruments such as framing and measuring, copper wire and spools, mechanical relays and artfully arranged, soldered, and bolted experimental settings:

> Nerves have been often and not unsuitably compared to telegraph wires. Such a wire conducts one kind of electric current and no other; it may be stronger, it may be weaker, it may move in either direction; it has no other qualitative differences. Nevertheless, according to the different kinds of apparatus with which we provide its terminations, we can send telegraphic despatches [sic], ring bells, explode mines, decompose water, move magnets, magnetise iron, develop light, and so on. So with the nerves. The condition of excitement which can be produced in them, and is conducted by them, is, so far as it can be recognised in isolated fibres of a nerve, everywhere the same, but when it is brought to various parts of the brain, or the body, it produces motion, secretions of glands, increase and decrease of the quantity of blood, of redness and of warmth of individual organs, and also sensations of light, of hearing, and so forth. (Helmholtz 1885: 149)

Sensory experiences of humanoids *are* material. With this approach to research they need not anymore be described as immaterial and ephemeral, not anymore as merely angelic or spiritual: they are physical. Sounds are corporeal. Hearing and sensing sounds is conceptualized as a process in electric circuits. Circuits that can be drawn, rewritten, and executed. A materiality that can be translated into writing, into written traces, symptoms, and signs: a new writing culture has been established, a new *Aufschreibesystem* (Kittler 1985). Research in nineteenth-century natural sciences was therefore on the one hand leaving a tradition of ephemeral writing and fantasizing behind, of imagining and immaterially conceptualizing a sensory experience; and in a truly dialectical move, writing as the major research practice of retrieving, presenting, and embodying results is restored again. The just-abolished tradition of writing sound returns as the repressed other in an even more institutionalized and epistemologically crucial position. The obsession with writing in humanoid cultures had to prevail (Tkaczyk 2015). The listening body was not taken as main reference and method, main approach and dispositive, but again a secure and well-known set of *anthropocentric* concepts of writing the senses, of inscribing and thus manifesting and generating evidence. The body is again not any body, but the body of *The Human*: and this idealized, androcentric, and useful body is to be conquered by research and by writing. It is to be explored and dissected, dismembered and thoroughly squeezed and pinched in order to produce insight, to generate a mechanically written account. Helmholtz and his colleagues worshipped Kant's *Über-Ich*: They were the good boys who were able to discipline—obeying Kant's orders—their original desires and ambitions for the sake of rigorous and honorable science. These young and provocative researchers produced evidence to be able to sublimate their *juissance*: they engaged in the new methods, settings, and technologies that would allow them to approach the senses—yet, this new approach granted access to the senses at the cost of separating sensory organs from living humanoid or non-humanoid aliens or non-aliens. To be precise, *Living* creatures were not observed—but parts of *carcasses* were dissected and prepared. This process in place exemplifies almost ideally how material writing culture executes scientific *reification* as described by Ian Hacking (Hacking 1983): This reifying is a process that not only develops but also *invents* a scientific entity as such in a convincing manner. This invention takes place when Helmholtz finally writes on sounds and the progression of pitch as if they were already known and objective and petrified entities. Though he is effectively proposing and only claiming a working definition here:

> Melodic motion is change of pitch in time. To measure it perfectly, the length of time elapsed, and the distance between the pitches must be measurable. This is possible for immediate audition only on condition that the alterations both in time and pitch should proceed by regular and determinate degrees. (Helmholtz 1885: 252)

"To measure it perfectly" (*vollständig zu messen*) is affirmed, and as such also solidified as a major research practice in this paragraph. It is legitimized by the necessity to observe this progress which is already "regular and determinate" (in regelmässigen und fest bestimmten Stufen). The axioms of *perfect measuring* and a *regular progress* of pitch in a mechanically written account effectively predetermine everything that is to be known and to be explored in listening and sounding. The borders of this scientific paradigm are the borders of the researcher's world. Helmholtz, being a professional pianist and dedicated music lover, and thus to a crucial extent thinking sounds via keys and notes, via fingers and chords, models listening and the whole of the auditory realm after the utilitarian concept of the human ear as known and explored in the nineteenth century. He is intrigued and fascinated by the instrumental logic he claims to find: in full accordance with the long history of Western anatomical analysis and epistemology he turns again to a dissected and partialized, to an instrumentalized human body. The corporeal opening at least potentially possible in Helmholtz' research framework is again being closed toward a utilitarian focus and an affirmation of established musical and performative principles. Helmholtz' phonautograph is essentially writing and reading proof of the acoustic truth in Western music and Western anthropology. *The Human*'s body and the new apparatus prove the correctness of Western aesthetics. Actual corporeality is being trumped by a predominant research dispositive. Anthropocentric and Eurocentric concepts prevail. Actual waves vanish under concepts.

1929: Fletcher's weirdness

Listening is a material, a physical, and a bodily activity. Consequently, this groundbreaking insight was rather prolifically promoted into all realms of society so eagerly connected to the natural and the technical sciences. Research on the dissected carcasses of animals generated a useful knowledge that was easy to apply by newly founded industrial corporations. Whereas researchers in the nineteenth century started to explore the bodily realm of listening and to apply technical metaphors, this effort was fundamentally transformed in the twentieth century. The opening question, *What is listening?*, as explored by Helmholtz and others, now turned into, *What are the limitations of listening?* To follow this continuous stream of epistemological desire and all the energy it fuses into society, it is helpful to take the next crucial steps after Herman von Helmholtz—toward a range of inventions and applications that you and I are still using today. One of the most influential and prolific technocultural artifacts in the last decades was without a doubt the newly invented data compression formats, especially for audio coding. It was the format MP3 that paved the way to all possible means of rapid, massive, and huge file sharing all over the electrified and networked world around the millennium. As Jonathan Sterne pointed out (Sterne 2012), the fundamental algorithm of this compression relies mainly on research done in the 1920s by the physicist Harvey Fletcher and published in his volume *Speech and Hearing* (1929), still influential today: a treatise that indeed provided the listening concept used in developing the MP3-compression algorithm. Sterne writes:

> I interviewed JJ Johnston, an engineer who worked at AT&T Bell Labs and developed one of the first working audio perceptual coders.... During our interview at his home, Johnston took me downstairs to his bookshelf and we talked about where his various ideas came from. Johnston showed me a copy of Harvey Fletcher's 1929 edition of *Speech and Hearing* (his may have been the 1953 version), and we discussed how ideas and methods in that book shaped his work in the 1980s. (Sterne 2012: 29)

It was this research—almost a century old as of today—that laid the foundation upon which every recent sound experience one would have with an MP3 file is built. Humanoid aliens in the early twenty-first century tend thus to listen through the historical ears and the aged technology, through the rather outdated listening concepts and research cultures of the early twentieth century. You are effectively time traveling if you listen to an MP3 file. In the late 1920s and early 1930s Fletcher served for the AT&T Bell Telephone Laboratories as a principal investigator on the limitations and the potential of speech recognition. These laboratories—as well as the corporation AT&T as a whole—belonged since the early twentieth century to the investment banks of John Pierpont Morgan and some of his associates. By their quite clever actions of trading and selling, buying and rebuying additional institutions, departments, and equipment, the Bell Labs, as they were abbreviated, grew to be a dominant player in the market of industrialized communications research (Sterne 2012: 42–4):

> AT&T's interest in maximizing the capabilities of its infrastructure was not simply a technical matter of improving service or equipment—it was directly tied to its status as an aspiring monopoly. (Sterne 2012: 43)

As a monopoly, the whole character of research transformed successively as it became more and more tied to the main business of this company: financial activities and market expansion. Not only AT&T but also the Bell Labs had to serve this purpose. Though the individual and detailed outlines of research remained at the hands of the researchers, the institutional framing, the guiding approach to research, and the subsequent style of researching were shaped according to the company's main business. Therefore, the goal of Fletcher's research in speech recognition was the following:

> By measuring the minimum bandwidth needed for intelligible speech and then building filters to limit calls to that bandwidth, the company was able to effectively quadruple the capacity of phone lines by 1924. (Sterne 2012: 45)

This research issue might sound quite fundamental and almost irrefutable: to measure the bandwidth that English-speaking humanoids (supposedly upper middle class, white, mainly male Americans with academic background) necessarily need to understand any transmission of spoken word. Doesn't this research issue just represent a strictly earnest interest in the capabilities of humanoid listening and in the necessities of technology to transmit humanoid speech? Maybe. Yet the results of this research were instrumentalized without hesitation in a way that follows the overarching business strategy—a strategy for maximizing profits in the communication business:

> Where a phone line once transmitted one call (and sometimes also a telegraph message), it could now transmit four, each filtered into its own band. Where AT&T could once bill for one call, it could now bill for four—with minimal modifications of infrastructure and no price increase. (Sterne 2012: 45)

The research Fletcher oversaw, initialized, and took responsibility and accolades for connects the physiological and physical research on sound propagation and speech recognition to the demands and business models of a large telecommunication company. Therefore, its methods and approaches remain quite obviously not untainted by the actual values, the entrepreneurial long-term goals and projected profits in the near future of this company. Though it would be quite far-fetched to claim that Fletcher's research would be thoroughly defined by the obsessions with financial acquisition and institutional growth that characterize the actions of J. P. Morgan, it is equally naive to assume that this atmosphere would have been totally irrelevant for his work. The research results and their use speak a clear language: the claimed factual reduction of quality, of richness and of depth in sound experience was immediately being translated into a richness in revenues: Fletcher's research did not provide in its end a richer and more complex and intense listening experience—but it provided better and more profitable options for commodifying mediated communication. Maximization of profit and a more efficient use of bandwidth are not only implied, but also expressively pursued research goals here. Communication businesses and communication research of this kind served and still do serve foremost the capitalization of the company. Anything else is dependent on this major goal.

One could interject: But how could he have pursued alternate research? Did he actually have any options and possibilities to pursue research that would *not* have been centered around the efficiency of bandwidth use? Similar to the alternative biography and research history of Hermann von Helmholtz, in the beginning of the last section an alternative research question for the professional research practice of Harvey Fletcher could have been the following: How could it be possible to transmit the most dynamic and complex, the most multisensorially, improvisationally and musically impressive performance by making use of the most advanced contemporary technology? How could it be possible to technologically reproduce all sensory and bodily, however subtle, aspects of a musical or sonic performance? Yet, a maximization of quality, of subtlety, and of impact in *sonic experience* (Augoyard and Torgue 2005) was definitely not the goal of Fletcher and his colleagues. Not only this, but it was also the *minimization* of quality that they sought. Specific desires of humanoid aliens concerning listening would have only hindered this process of reduction: How low can the quality of speech transmission be that the relevant users and listeners (as said before in this case: English-speaking and supposedly upper middle class, white, mostly male Americans with academic background) can still roughly understand what is being said? As a result, the researchers at Bell Labs continued the exploration of the empirical, material, and physiological emanations of sound. They, too, wholeheartedly moved away from the assumptions and deductions of earlier sonic writings in premodern times; they also proceeded in the methods of the experiment, in constructing material research setups to observe effectively how humanoid aliens actually *listen*. Yet—as already observed with Helmholtz' approach—the more specific historical and ideological framework of this highly influential research in acoustics probably could not have been critically and historically reflected at the time: the same way a reflection of this very present today is hard to reflect as if from a distance. Over a century later, it becomes nevertheless quite obvious how primary decisions in research on listening and sounding were dependent on and mainly followed an economic and social development. This development—of which the research at Bell Labs is an integral part—translates into an instrumentalization and exploitation of corporeal characteristics in humanoids; and subsequently into a highly consequential narrowing, a limiting and restricting of possible listening concepts in research, in development, in home entertainment. Concerning the corporeal politics implied in this research, Sterne again detected the main rupture in Fletcher's research: "It aimed to render the user's ear an object of its own administration" (Sterne 2012: 45). The ear for Fletcher and for this strand of communications research is being regarded as a truly useful and quite exploitable organ that can be administered and—if you will—actually cultivated and farmed like a given common good. In reducing the quality of a sound reproduction, the researchers implicitly (and to their defense: often involuntarily) decided to regard the corporeal joy and excess in listening, all the multisensorial, situational and relational effects of indulging in a listening experience, as irrelevant. The body of the listener is conceptualized as a receiving apparatus—and as such it is, to say the least, reduced to one selected activity and one sensorial capability. As in communication research at that time, the research at the Bell Labs does not on any level of its experimental outline or its resulting presentations make a major distinction between the wide variety of individual bodies, of biographies, and of social statuses, of ethnical heritages or of the idiosyncratic inclinations to listening: All bodies are the same. All aliens are the same. *The Human* as an abstract and ideal entity is just an object of research. Nothing else. The tailoring of the sensorium to fit the necessities of technological developments is evident. Or, as the philosopher Mario Perniola would put it: The humanoid sensorium and the technological apparatus constitute a mutual *sensologia* (Perniola 1991), a *sensology* that provides the framework of what can be sensed, what can be thought, what can be conceptualized or discussed. The approach of *sensologia* is quite fruitful as a concept to analyze contemporary ideologies at work; its ramifications and its consequences in the form of a *Sensory Critique* will therefore be discussed in the third part of this book, "Generativity," especially in Chapter 7 on: "The Precision of Sensibility."

The aforementioned major research decisions made by Fletcher and his colleagues translate moreover into aspects of listening concepts that are relevant for sensory politics and communication politics on another note. Though this research is so extraordinarily proud of its foundation in actual material, empirical, and physiological studies, as this marks a big development if not progress from earlier approaches, it actually oversees some of its major limitations in research. Only in recent years, a quite vivid discussion began on those inherent limitations, especially in the field of *experimental psychology*. Here the main argument discussed is that the experimental setup as well as the selected probands in the history of experimental psychology were and are mainly: *weird* (Henrich/Heine/Norenzayan 2010). With the word *weird*, the authors refer not to potentially disturbing flaws in the empirical basis—but to an acronym they proposed, in a quite sardonic denial of the common claim of objectivity in referring to an empirical basis. *Weird* are, according to these authors, exactly those societies from which most of the probands in empirical research come—societies that are: "Western, Educated, Industrialized, Rich, and Democratic (WEIRD)" (Henrich/Heine/Norenzayan 2010). The authors argue:

> The comparative findings suggest that members of Western, educated, industrialized, rich, and democratic societies, including young children, are among the least representative populations one could find for generalizing about humans. (ibid.)

It does not happen frequently that one can find in research one simple sentence that almost immediately renders earlier research efforts by millions irrelevant in a second. This is one of those sentences. After having read this sentence, most research projects are either rendered completely meaningless—or at least they are in dire need of being restudied. To future readers of the late twenty-first or mid-twenty-second century, I hope it might seem quite surprising if not disturbing: but the fact of this truly marginal quality of empirical research in Western research cultures of the nineteenth and twentieth centuries has largely been ignored as too marginal in itself. A ridiculous ignorance by standards of the twenty-second-century research, I wish to assume. One actually doubts if the protagonists of such research activities ever actually reflected on their own individual and quite extraordinary position of power in their particular cultural and historical context? It might not be too exotic to assume: Such thoughts only rarely crossed their minds; they surely never made it into any serious research proposal or article in an academic journal. Even these days—writing such a cocky critique against canonical researchers and their findings—it is strangely enough, almost never a *demanded* aspect of research to reflect on the social, corporeal, cultural, and historical specificity and limitation of a proposed or introduced research project in itself (it might only be required if exactly *this issue* is at the core of one's research question). All this research that claims and boasts about its global relevance, its systematic impact, and its endless generalizability, all this research is even more so a limited articulation of this particular cultural if not subcultural strand these days. The more one claims its abstract and eternal (read: *ahistoric*) value, the more it is actually driven by quite personal obsessions and rather arbitrary interests. Surely, the book you are reading right now can be of no exception.

The weird and hegemonic societies that still today provide the foundations for the main locations, the central technical equipment, the environments, and the funding for most of the empirical research, technological development, and, sadly, also the cultural research these days; these societies are more and more recognized as being actually marginal. The weird societies of the so-called "West" (still a strange and absurd geographical denomination of entities that are rather surely not mainly defined by their geographical location, but by their self-ascribed opposition to an other in the *Southern Hemisphere*, in the *Orient*, or in any other culturally constructed area brought into opposition; cf. Said 1978) are not representative, they are not characteristic at all to what any alien humanoid now or in history or in the future could experience, perceive, perform, or desire. These weird cultural agglomerations represent a rather thin layer that—and this becomes more and more obvious these days—covers up only haphazardly all the incredibly luscious diversity and multitude of experience, all the ways of living, all those myriads of momentary sensory practices and forms of self-reflection that else could be found on this tiny, tiny world. The research setup considered representative in these cultures finally resembles in almost no aspect the everyday experience of a mobile, mingled, distorted, dynamic, and corporeal listening to a multitude of sound events, interlocking, interweaving, and layered, in various and surprisingly changing quality and urgency. The empirical basis as well as the research method itself resembles more, I dare to conclude, the possibilities of the technological means at that very historical time and its cultural preferences. The historical specimen of the empirical research of Fletcher and his colleagues at the Bell Labs therefore can and need rightly be regarded as a thoroughly weird freak of science history. It cannot—by standards of today—be claimed as being representative for the whole of all humanoid aliens in pre- or post-history and all of their listening experiences. Yet, in continuation of Helmholtz' research, one still finds the symptoms of a materialization of listening in its forms of quantification as well as a deeply habitualized obsession with academic writing culture, manifesting quantification. This ongoing project of quantifying sound by means of a materialization of the events, the effects, and affects sound results in, this project is connecting the nineteenth century with the twentieth century. The research of Harvey Fletcher is therefore taking the foundations for a sensory quantification as laid out by Hermann von Helmholtz to a new level of instrumentalization and of capitalization—and of perversion, if one will. This commodified perversion of quantifying sound is an inherent quality of the desire to quantify. Yet, it has not been completed with the works by Fletcher alone.

1954: Experience by Beranek

I am standing on the street. What do I hear? I may hear humanoids approaching and moving away; I may hear cars and trucks, bicycles and motorbikes. I may hear men or women with a pram; I may hear the well-known noises of younger or older aliens, sounds of approval and disapproval, sounds in which they explain language-like and—a bit more lengthily—anything they wish to convey to their attentive listener. I may even hear my own body moving: I may be able to hear the textiles I wear, as they wrinkle and fold or rub on themselves; I may also hear any sonic traces of corporeal activities of my inner organs, my stomach, my muscles, bones, teeth, sounds of swallowing, of heartbeat, of nervous activity, and of my paranasal sinus. I *may* hear all of this. But maybe I just don't. It could be that I do not hear most of it; maybe I only hear the wind rushing through the streets, maybe I am disoriented by strange echoing effects that make noises from far away suddenly seem to be happening just behind me—or perhaps I am disoriented by effects of reflection and of abatement that almost erase some sounds or articulations just in front of me. The buildings all around me might have such strange effects: They *do* shape the instantaneous space of reflection for all sound waves emitted and vibrating through this public place. In almost every moment of their lives, humanoid aliens are situated in such instantaneous spaces that shape the auditory. And still: those spaces are only rarely planned to have exactly *these* specific auditory effects on the people living there or passing by. Though there are impressive examples in cultural and architectural history that prove that an audile design of such artifacts is possible: The Sanctuary of Asklepios at Epidaurus, for instance, on the Peloponnese peninsula in southern Greece recurrently is mentioned; also the Great Hall of the *Musikverein* in Vienna, the Kresge Auditorium at the Massachusetts Institute of Technology in Cambridge (e.g., in Serres 2008: 85–106; Beranek 2004: 173–6; Blesser and Salter 2007: 146). Would it not be a bit arrogant and just plainly false to state that *no one ever* cared for how the architecturally built world really sounds? Are these buildings not proof enough that *there is actually* a long and instructive history of audile building and of room acoustics? These edifices are indeed impressive pinnacles of what is truly possible as soon as humanoids being engineers, designers, architects, and builders reflect on the specific use, the situational necessities and the contextual references of an auditory space. They truly are impressive: As the great electrical engineer, entrepreneur, and influential acoustician Leo Leroy Beranek showed, for example, in his seminal work on *Acoustics* in 1954, the principles by which concert halls are perceived as astonishing or merely acceptable can be translated into physically proven and even quantifiable formulae to process given data. Continuing the achievements of Fletcher in the 1920s and Helmholtz in the 1860s to materialize sound events as quantifiable entities, Beranek took their effort an essential bit further: into space. Helmholtz' inquiries mainly focused on sensory perception and tone sensation in organs in the carcasses of various animals that he used as stand-ins for humanoid anatomy as it was known in the nineteenth century. Then Fletcher focused his research on the limits and necessities of electrical transmission of spoken words as recorded by carbon microphones with single dynamic membranes and transduced by copper cables in the early twentieth century. It was Beranek who expanded these early, necessarily quite narrow-focused materializations of sounds into buildings, rooms, and architecture—that is: into open space.

The work of Leo Beranek is nothing short of a truly great achievement for the sciences in its efforts to remodel a perceived version of reality into precise and operable formula and models. Though the issue that troubles contemporary sound studies here—and especially an anthropology of sound—is: how are these models founded and by what patterns of description, by what imagery and by what implicit anthropological concept of the listener do they operate? Science history, and especially the strand of Science and Technology Studies, assumes and proves that scientific endeavors and their results are—like any other cultural practice alien humanoids might perform—*never* completely free of social and historical context, of individual and group-centered interests, of rather non-scientific obsessions, ambitions, fears, and desires. The aspiration for objectivity, for abstraction, and for the economic application of knowledge *is* a truly idiosyncratic and a deeply weird one, a joyful and insightful one nevertheless (writes this author of an academic book, quite unsurprisingly). The intention in going back to the actual framing of scientific work by cultural, historical, sociological, but also by biographical and psychological factors is not to neglect the effort and the major cultural contributions these researchers have made; rather it is to understand the impact and the ramifications of these efforts: all the consequential developments in the sciences and in the public sphere that humanoid aliens like you and me might be inhabiting today, that we might have incorporated, and that might be sources for various inner contradictions and unresolved problems in contemporary societies. In the words of Beranek himself, in his 1954 preface to *Acoustics*:

> Wherever possible, the background of the electrical engineer and the communication physicist is utilized in explaining acoustical concepts. (Beranek 1954: V)

He states this goal to incorporate for the first time supposedly *the background of the electrical engineer and the communication physicist* exactly as the main difference to other acoustical models and textbooks:

> The book differs in one important respect from conventional texts on acoustics in that it emphasizes the practical application of electrical-circuit theory in the solution of a wide variety of problems. (Beranek 1954: V)

This explicit emphasis by Beranek might be read as just another topical figure of speech in acoustic research since the mid-nineteenth century: stressing the ongoing effort to found acoustics on practical (read: *material*) explanations to problems that occur in his field—and not on para-religious self-sustaining imaginary edifices. The empirical focus of research is put again and again in harsh contrast to the earlier focus on written rhapsodies of sound. A claim of practical feasibility and focus on the concrete, the material, the quantifiable, is a recurring trope in arguing for acoustic research. Nevertheless, the way acoustic problems and constellations are presented in the textbook by Beranek is predetermined by the knowledges of electrical-circuit theory at this specific time. Here Beranek again moved away, in accordance with a certain tendency already observed in Fletcher's work, from a closer adherence to the erratic corporeal movements and reactions of a humanoid, living, and perceiving body. Helmholtz is almost forgotten here in his actual experiments: He serves now mainly as a distant forefather, more a symbolic patron saint than an actual teacher or even role model to inspire new research. The effects of sound events and auditory perception are thus not explained and analyzed in respect to a wide range of humanoid aliens in their highly individualized, biographical backgrounds and physiological details, their cultural and historical remanence; these effects in contrast are explained by Beranek as if there would not exist any such malleable aliens with their soft, wet, and amorphous ties to biography, physiology, culture, and history. All there are are electrical circuits—in the models by Beranek. They seem sufficient. This major strand of research—as represented in the history of acoustics—capitalizes on ingenious reduction.

At this historical point the parallel universe of acoustic theory is almost fully elaborated and ready to serve its purposes. It is not only founded on the works by Helmholtz or Fletcher but mainly also on the work of the physicist Wallace Sabine. Around 1900 Sabine proposed the first ambitious descriptions of how sounds propagate in architectural environments. The way he undertook his research is quite telling of the hidden prerequisites of acoustic research and various carefully camouflaged inner contradictions in its epistemological foundations—contradictions to be found in research practices by Beranek, Fletcher, and Helmholtz. Sabine was—as Emily Thompson documents (Thompson 2002: 33–44)—an ingenious listener with an apparently abnormal precision in listening to reverberation times. His individual, corporeal idiosyncrasy provided him with the sensorium to generate what later was turned into a generalized reverberation formula. Contrary to a common misconception, his research therefore started out with a *bodily precision in sensibility*. It was not a piece of technical equipment, not an incredibly precise measuring instrument, but it was his own, very personal and truly idiosyncratic way of experiencing sound that provided a starting moment. This corporeal foundation of research can, supposedly, be found in research projects and their researchers again and again—and probably the one writing and claiming this on this page right here would be no exception to this. Nevertheless, being a researcher in times of imperialist scientific ambitions to put knowledge to practical use and application, Sabine's personal listening practices led him to a translation of an individual listening capability into functions of a measuring instrument and into a generalizable reverberation formula. The functioning of these subsequent material and conceptual tools has been proven in almost all recently built, acoustically excellent concert halls. It is quite surprising, though—and again: *weird*—that it was the sensibility of one humanoid alien with extremely idiosyncratic sensory capacities that provided a set of tools to effectively *prevent* any further refinement of sensory idiosyncrasies in other humanoid aliens. The result of subsequent measuring instruments and measuring outlines, even the reverberation formula was a surrendering of humanoid sensibilities to technically written translations of measurable effects. Humanoids delegated their sensibility in an *interpassive* way (Pfaller 2003) to machines, to apparatuses, to equations. Experience was to be neglected. The rather devastating results of this surrendering can be observed in the manifold examples of edifices that claim to adhere to reverberation standards—but provide quite unbearable locations in respect to individual and situated listening experience. The calculated reverberation time trumped the situated listening experience. In the words of Darryl Cressmann:

> Adopting this historical perspective, Sabine's reverberation equation transformed our understanding of how music behaves in enclosed spaces, but it did not change how music should sound in these enclosed spaces. (Cressmann 2015)

In the end, the highly experienced, extremely sensitive, and situationally aware researcher, Wallace Sabine, provided the grounds for an ongoing and tragic fallacy in the history of acoustics. A fallacy that would be unthinkable in the field of optics or in the field of genetics: the fallacy to take an empirical and thoroughly probabilistic description of a phenomenon as sufficient to extract normative, aesthetic, and even social and ethical guidelines for design, for cultural forms, for humanoid behavior. At this point it is time to turn back to the work of Leo Beranek:

> Because this text deals primarily with devices for handling speech and music, gases (more particularly, air) are the only types of elastic material with which we shall concern ourselves. (Beranek 1954: 3)

Relying on Sabine's formula and instruments, Beranek can indulge again in the joyful reductionism of material experience to a set of circumstances that are easier to model. They provide in turn the sources for newly developed measuring and writing instruments. A "tiny cubic 'box' out of air" (Beranek 1954: 3) seems to be enough to understand exactly all relevant edifices and spatial listening situations he is interested in. This reduction neglects all the minor ornaments, protrusions, and irregularities (let alone the activities of performing and idling humanoids and non-humanoids) in the so-called *shoebox* of the Wiener Musikverein, for instance. This reduction is also guided by an interest that is—needless to say—again focused on a rather weird selection of venues for artistic, and to be more precise, *musical* performances in the Northern Hemisphere, focusing on the European tradition of musical aesthetics and performances. If buildings from Tokyo, Buenos Aires, or Hong Kong are discussed, the reason for their construction is mainly to serve performances of music following the European tradition, serving also the instruments, the ensemble-structure, and the sonic experience as established in the European musical tradition of concert performances. The extreme and stunning selectivity concerning the vast amounts of, to put it bluntly, non-European traditions, aesthetics, and performances is almost never addressed in his writings. The fact of the superior relevance of these aesthetics and performances is simply out of reach and out of the question in the epistemological concepts underlying this research. Yet, the formulaic and reduced abstraction in this major strand of acoustics essentially prolongs the premodern assumption of sound as almost immaterial, transitory, not physically present and altered by corporeal irregularities and erratic performativity. Any meaningful concept of *experience* is actually nonexistent in Beranek's work. Beranek confirms this critique even in his own words:

> The word "acoustic," an adjective, means intimately associated with sound waves or with the individual media, phenomena, apparatus, quantities, or units discussed in the science of sound waves. (Beranek 1954: 9)

Here you have it: effectively the word *acoustic* in Beranek's interpretation does *not* mean any auditory experience of any individual or corporeal listening encounter by humanoids or aliens in any physiological appearance whatsoever. The field of acoustics following Beranek is thus exactly limited to the predetermining scientific concept of *sound waves*; as soon as one speaks of other concepts (e.g., *audile techniques, sonic bodies,* or *sonic skills*), another terminology becomes more adequate. Beranek claims in this passage with all scientific rigor and askesis the limited but nevertheless profound status of his research: a quite impressive and unusually reflective statement on the limitations of a researcher's craft. This exact limitation, nevertheless, provided him and his colleagues at his own company, BBN Technologies, with all the terminology, the arguments, and the means of presentation to convince his trade partners to buy his company's products: products of military technology and network-technology. The acoustic research of Beranek—like the research of Fletcher—is as strongly driven by effectivist and reductionist theory models present and praised in the realm of developing military weaponry in the twentieth century. The discipline for which Beranek wrote his classic textbook is, consistently, never concerned with *living* humanoids expanding and refining their listening and sensing abilities in specific, minuscule situations of everyday life and experience. This discipline of acoustics is concerned mainly with restricted situations in which the scientific concept of sound waves can be applied sufficiently to describe subsequent effects on rather immovable carcasses with no agency, no intention, no tension: A theory of dead models for dead bodies in pressurized air. It is safe to assume: Reverberation is not space. *Experience* by Beranek is a research trademark. Effectively, it is nonexistent.

Projections in the pavilion

We enter this building. It is dark in here. We are disoriented. Light is hushing, lightning strikes; color fields move across the walls, they lie over each other: new colors emerge. Ancient faces, archaic masks appear. Sounds can be heard; they sound spooky to us—daunting and haunting, ghostlike. Archaic souls trying to judge, to warn us. Are we in a prehistoric cave? Is this a post apocalyptic scenario after the extinction of most of the humanoids living now? The annihilation of all known history? This impression gets even stronger as we manage to decipher the projected titles of this literally audio visual presentation: "Genesis," "Matter and Spirit," "From Darkness to Dawn," "Manmade Gods," "How Time Molds Civilization," "Harmony," and "To All Mankind." The unashamedly anthropocentric ideology of global and social progress is as present in these titles as could be. Apparently, after the hitherto gigantic genocides and mass murders in and around the Second World War, especially driven by conflicts and ideology generated mainly in Western Cultures, this praise of certain qualities in humanoids was needed to restore faith in them—even if their substantial lack was so convincingly performed just a decade ago. Abstract claims to make up for a lack of material evidence. After millions of carcasses piled up, such an apotheosis of Western culture as the pinnacle of history and advanced technology seemed to be necessary—in a dialectical sense. This apotheosis was the Philips Pavilion, presented at the World's Fair in Brussels, 1958. It was conceived by a stunning trio: the architect Le Corbusier, the composer Edgard Varèse, and—as an integrating figure on the level of programming—the composer and architect Iannis Xenakis. Yet, all concrete remains of this building and its installation are lost.

A few years ago a sensible reconstruction of this space—the visual, architectural, and sonic arrangement—was produced as a *Virtual Electronic*

Poem (Lombardo et al. 2009). This virtual reconstruction now makes it possible to effectively experience this pivotal work for electroacoustic and multisensory installations in the mid-twentieth century. After having read so many praising and glorifying mentions of this work in studies on musical and media history it is, to say the least, a truly vexing experience to see and to hear an approximation of this work for the very first time. This work being one of the cornerstones of modern architectural and electro acoustic aesthetics is—judging by this reconstruction at least—a strange breed of existentialist-avant-garde-humanist pathos mixed with an equally existentialist evocation of prehistoric civilizations and their apparent authority. On the one hand, it represents the perfect example of what Johanna Gampe has described so convincingly as a *Sonario*: an "interactive scenic, spatial sound installation" (Gampe 2014: 13), in which the sonic is inherently constituted as spatialized, scenic, and interactive; on the other hand, its specific strategies of spatialization adhere almost unbearably to premodern if not preclassical concepts of *The Human*. The textual and the visual aesthetics of this work are—in harsh contrast to the incredibly advanced *Poème électronique* by Edgard Varèse—surprising if not disappointing. It is in turn not a surprise that most historical accounts refer to this pavilion mainly for its musical composition or for the architectural experiment it represents. The performance as a whole can in almost no way be regarded as an expression of avant-garde art at its best, but a document of the post-Second World War shock still trembling and moving the arts at this point of history. A weird, post apocalyptic hybrid of humanoid artifacts.

A naive observer might have guessed that the collaboration of three geniuses, three proud and ambitious geniuses, could have resulted in an even more seminal work. But with three super-egos in the mix, their individual ambitions, pride, and rigor apparently left little room to breathe for a subtler collaboration to take place effectively. There is no documented sign of a more intricate, responsive, and interacting level of collaboration between those three—as it might, for instance, be observed in advanced theatrical productions of today in which a director, a composer, and a sound designer, a visual artist and a scenograph indeed try arduously to find a more improvisational or combinatorial crossing of their aesthetics and working strategies. Such a thorough collaboration was apparently no perspective for the three geniuses at work here. To the contrary, more traditional hierarchical principles prevailed, such as seniority, authority, territorial warfare, and merit: Le Corbusier, near the end of his career then, became the main, truly authoritarian director (even temporarily expelling his main assistant Xenakis from the whole project); Varèse rather cleverly implemented his own more fragile musical aesthetics into Le Corbusier's strong and eccentric spatial framework; and Xenakis took the chance of applying an almost classic hustler move of twentieth-century artists: hiding behind the role of being *just an assistant/engineer/technician/craftsman*—who essentially makes all the major decisions. His aesthetics is overall the strongest and the most inspiring and prolific aspect in the whole pavilion: it is *Xenakis's pavilion* today—much more than Le Corbusier's, betrayed by his own anthropocentric rhapsody. Xenakis managed to work dynamically and responsively with a given structure; a structure that apparently has been sensorially paralyzed by the technological overload provided by the ordering party, the Philips Corporation. Its purpose was overshadowed, and it apparently also burdened the work of the artists: to provide a "spatial-color-light-music production" (in the words of artistic director Louis Kalff; Treib 1996: 2) as a state-of-the-art showcase for their advanced technological products. This paralyzing is a quite common result in early media art periods if technological means are more tentatively explored than mastered. The hubris of the artists is too often—and unsurprisingly so—being conquered by the cocoon made of machinery and apparatuses as provided by sponsoring corporations. This aporia of the technological materialization of sound grants a perspective to one major effect of the strife for quantifying sound: in the course of focusing on the technological reproduction of a convincing simulacrum of the artistic or aesthetic or scientific idea behind it, many more subtle and visceral aspects get lost on the way—aspects that were crucial for the concept in the first place. A more static, stable, and indestructible setup of the work is cherished, many forms of dynamic tensions and instabilities, of plastic and mingled aspects of the work, are delicately bypassed. The writing of technical blueprints and work assignments, of briefings, checklists, and debriefings suddenly stands at the core: the cultural forms of obsessive academic and engineering writing culture are too easily bypassing any corporeal arguments (as encountered in this chapter in the work by Hermann von Helmholtz). Moreover, a weird selection of cultural references and associations is taking place (as in the *weird* selection of probands in the studies by Harvey Fletcher). Finally, the joyfully reductionist abstraction of all living anthropoid aliens retains just simple, empty, and stable models, void of all humanoid stains and tensions (as already noted regarding the research by Leo Beranek). The final work is now perfectly in sync with values of dehumanizing and quantifiably stabilizing a large production process in intercontinentally operating corporations. The work by Xenakis, Varèse, and Le Corbusier has become the work of the Philips Corporation. The corporation decorporealized this sonario.

CHAPTER TWO

Materializing listening

Destroying instruments, discovering ambient

This is an execution. It is not merely a symbolic killing or an erasure, an annihilation of a truly powerful and pervasive kind, paternalist tradition in all its details, its materializations, and its structural constraints. It might be more convincingly interpreted as an act of exorcism—or is it more a burning of witches? "The piano is a taboo. It needs to be destroyed" (Thwaites et al. 1963, S. 64). This exclamation by Nam June Paik in the early 1960s represents far more than just the usually mischievous and improper treatment of a musical instrument now known from various avant-garde movements. At the very beginning of this literally and materially destructive artistic practice, the artists, instrumentalists, composers, and activists engaging in and promoting the destruction of instruments considered themselves to be establishing new forms of musical compositions in doing so. In one of the earliest and truly exemplary performances and compositions by Nam June Paik, *Etude for Piano*, one could have witnessed how the supposedly mindless, aggressive, and provocative actions of the performer and the composer were actually exploring and refining musical performance. Paik was one of the artists who expanded the realm of composition from the written score into the merely physical and profanely material sphere of the instrument, of the performer, and of the experienced situation of performance. This situation of the first performance was materially shaped by the exhibition rooms of the *Galerie 22* in Düsseldorf. The small piece—of just about ten minutes length—was loaded with references to avant-garde artists like Marcel Duchamp, Kurt Schwitters, or Antonin Artaud, as it ended with a forcefully executed destruction of the strings of the piano as well as the discombobulation of the whole wooden-steel corpus of the instrument. A quite complex, surprising, and a truly dynamic series of singular and mingled sound events could be heard. Yet, it still was an instrumental practice that was excessively turned into an unusual and anti-traditional way of generating sounds. The opening and the breaking loose of the specific piano-corpus hence was turned into an opening of the realm of possible sounds, possible *sound practices* (Altman 1992; Maier 2012), possible concert listening habits. Did I hear the sound of wood cracking? Of clutching at steel? Squeaking and crunching of lacquered surfaces, of polished bolts, of fine strings? I follow these sounds, these destructive and oh-so-joyful ambient noises. One tends to listen more closely, more attentively to these. They are truly a form of *noisy jouissance*.

From afar in the historical distance one might project onto such a performance merely a kind of deep anger and violence. A kind of structural and systemic anger, an aggression, and an urge for change is quite obvious and historically coherent in these destructive happenings. Yet the destruction of these fine (or not so fine) artifacts for musical performance not only introduced an agglomeration of sounds quite new to the acknowledged performances in a concert hall or a gallery space. These sounds actually transformed these art spaces in their very material substance as locations also for listening experiences. Sounds that might have been surprising as well as annoying, hurtful as well as joyful, intricate as well as brutal. Out of these very violent and yet at the same time highly sensorially refined acts, something else emerged. What emerged relied basically on the destruction of a previous, an ingrown listening practice: this practice was mainly attentive to very specific sounds in a trained and articulated way that has been refined before by historical traditions, slowly fading, evading. Hence these strange and weird, these newly, violently happy sounds—they could have seemed as the labor pains of a sonic aesthetic to come, a nascent sonic aesthetic. Listening from now on would not anymore be directed toward a single performer and his singular performative sonic acts—but to a whole lot of various soundspheres, territorial and environmental sounds occurring at a given location, in a specific, social, and material situation. Hand movements and actions with tools; everyday sounds of construction and destruction. Some people some years later might like to tend to call this: a *soundscape*? Or just: *sound art*? *Klangkunst*? The social and political as well as the deeply economic and ecological critique inherent in this whole artistic movement might have been lost on the way in the excruciating commodifications of the globalized and monetarily obsessed postmodern art world. Though taking a time leap back into these years in the midst of the twentieth century has become possible by a recent performance recording.

In 2004 the BBC Symphony Orchestra performed a concert in the Barbican Hall London with pieces by Aaron Copland, Henry Cowell, and Charles Ives, transmitted live during primetime on a Friday evening: *Live at the Barbican*. One of the pieces was John Cage's 4'33". On the very surface, both pieces by Paik and by Cage seem to represent opposing musical aesthetics of *Neue Musik*—in the genuine interpretation of European if not

German music culture. Yet, the contrary is true. Both performances of *Etude for Piano* and *4'33"* are generated from exactly the same equally aggressive and imaginative core: the urge to transcend the well-established and well-trained apparatus of rehearsing, performing, of attending, applauding, of conversing and lecturing on music. *4'33"*'s first performance took place in the Maverick Concert Hall, a wooden edifice from 1916 in Woodstock. It was performed by David Tudor on August 29, 1952 as one of twelve pieces. Since then, the explosive, punk impetus of this piece might have been forgotten. But the staging half a century later with a symphony orchestra brought all of it back. In listening and following the recording of this live transmission, it becomes intriguingly obvious how a whole institutionalized cultural and technological apparatus of education, training, of monetary investments, of research funding and developing extravaganza, of airtime, of engineers and technicians, of musicians and cameramen, of producers and assistants, is gleefully wasted in less than five minutes. It is a visible and slightly audible destruction. Maybe in KLF's burning of one million pounds in 1996 one can witness a similar burning down of a whole production apparatus for institutionalized music and composition. The sound of this annihilation is not audible if one listens merely to the sound of musical instruments. One can hear their destruction as an institutionalized restraint. Quite similar to Paik's piece, one suddenly listens to a much larger universe of ignored sounds outside musical instruments, a multitude of incredibly tiny noises, *petite perceptions* (Leibniz 1765). The ambient noises of architecture, of people gathering, of the humming and hissing of technology, of irritating insects or disturbing coughs or sneezes—all these miniscule sounds constitute a sound performance from now on. *Ambient music* is actually performed as a result of the destruction of instruments, of institutions, and of the idling apparatus. As soon as the apparatus burns, its environment becomes abruptly audible. One can breathe again. Sound pieces turn into listening pieces.

1962: Sound in flux

Knowledge of the anatomy of listening and of the physics of sound was rather unstable and insecure over long periods of history. There were ongoing efforts to gain secure insights and indices on how a humanoid alien can listen and on how sound emerges, travels, and arrives, how it is in the world. Hence, this evolved to a major task of researchers in the nineteenth and twentieth centuries—as laid out in the previous chapter—to secure some more precise insights into listening and sounding. Most of the time the composers and musicians, the doctors and nurses had more vague and idealized assumptions at hand to imagine how one listens and how sound acts. Hence, the quite typically humanoid assumptions of sound being a truly ephemeral and transitory, an unworldly and outer-human property. Yet:

> bababadalgharaghtakamminarronnkonnbronntonnerronntuonnthunntrovarrhounawnskawntoohoohoordenenthurnuk! (Joyce 1939: 3)

After the groundbreaking experiments of the nineteenth century on physical and on physiological effects of sound and their massive, almost imperial dissemination into industrial production, into social welfare, into commodity production, and into the education system, one could assume that it had become almost impossible to retain any vague and mystified assumption on sound and listening. But knowledge travels at a very, very slow pace—even in times of prolific education for all age levels, all social strata, and of open and continuously updated libraries and databases. Individual knowledge of a humanoid alien, personal values, ideas, models, and assumptions concerning all areas of life might more often than not stay frozen at the state they had after the first two, maybe three decades of such an alien's life. To learn that sound is as material as Hermann von Helmholtz described it, and to accept that listening might then also be material in a similar way, is a form of *auditory knowledge* (Sterne 2012; Volmar 2015) that is only recently becoming more common. Aside from specialized professions like audiologists or sound engineers and their *sonic skills* (Bijsterveld 2018), the assumption that music and sound are ephemeral, bodiless, and mainly a cerebral and computational activity is a still dearly cherished idea that more than a few humanoids consider desirable. This assumption is poetic in a tragic, aberrant way. Sound was never immaterial for actual musicians, intensely trained instrumentalists, experimenting sound engineers, or concert organizers confronted with thoroughly physical and material issues. For practitioners and for performers, for craftsmen and for engineers, it seemed to have been perfectly clear: listening is an activity. The properties of this activity are material in various layers of the body of the listener, of the performer or performers, of the walls and the floor, the furniture or the machinery; listening as an activity is situated in material and personal, sensorial and performative, as well as technological and historical relations to a given listening environment; finally, such listening activities are thoroughly performative in all the aforementioned areas. Listening and sounding alike are material, situated, and performative activities. This auditory knowledge of practitioners, this practice-based theoretical approach to sound and listening, is nevertheless still a seemingly new aspect for theorizing sonic and musical performances in the second half of the twentieth century.

Musical and artistic secession movements in Europe and in North America since the late nineteenth century engaged in the disruptive and generative activity of promoting sound as a performative act. The inclination to explore sounds in all their material and situated, performative aspects grew in many different cultural environments until the shocking and fundamentally disturbing experience of the First World War: a thorough rupture of civilization that confronted so many artists, listeners, composers, researchers, engineers, and developers with an experiential environment made out of seemingly unbearable noises, hurtful sights, and excruciating forms of dismemberment (Volmar 2014 et al.). This disturbing horror that—in all its humanoid ambivalence—fueled the avant-garde movements of the late 1910s and 1920s was only outdone by the subsequent horrors of thoroughly industrialized and globalized violence as part of the ideology of national socialism in Germany and its allies in a number of other European and non-European countries. Hence, in the 1950s, political, social, and art history is full of renditions of these progressively advancing experiences of violence, of annihilation, and of horror. Not a few artists and artistic movements of those decades took the first drop of nuclear bombs as a next, terrifyingly logical step toward total annihilation of all life on this planet.

This far too brief historical recap might seem to some readers of this book irrelevant for research on sound and listening. Yet in the case of artistic movements concerning sound, it is crucial. Avant-garde movements of the twentieth century developed in close relation to political and societal occurrences—and these relations have themselves explicitly become part of selected artworks or related writings on poetics and aesthetics. It is mainly unthinkable to speak of modern art and modern composition and *not* to speak of the experiences with politics and war these artists had:

> I let it be known to my friends, and even strangers, as I was wandering around the country, . . . that what was interesting me was making English less understandable. Because when it's understandable, well, people control one another, and poetry disappears—and as I was talking with my friend Norman O. Brown, and he said, "Syntax [which is what makes things understandable] is the army, is the arrangement of the army." (John Cage in a radio interview, August 8, 1974; also in: Cage 1979: 11)

This famous reference by John Cage to Norman Oliver Brown's theory of the militarized language, as well as similar radically pacifistic statements by other artists, is indeed basically inconceivable without the warfare and the continuous genocides on all continents of this planet in the nineteenth and twentieth centuries. Otherwise it would seem a weird, paranoiac assumption to state this. After the First and Second World Wars, such a statement, however, was perfectly clear. Cage drew an almost too logical conclusion: such negative anthropology might have seemed the only convincing interpretation of military culture so very present in all layers and aspects of humanoids' lives and actions. Brown was a colleague and collaborator of Hayden White and Herbert Marcuse and worked mainly in a Marxist and psychoanalytical tradition that proved so generative for advanced theory in the twentieth century—between the artistic and philosophical works by Philippe Soupault, Antonin Artaud, and André Breton, as well as Gilles Deleuze and Félix Guattari. As a consequence, Brown seemed not to be so content with what he read as an overly naive thread in Cage's work (Perloff 1994):

> So what we're doing when we make language un-understandable is we're demilitarizing it, so that we can do our living. (John Cage in a radio interview, August 8, 1974)

Cage—as well as other avant-garde artists of the 1960s—was still thoroughly motivated by a genuine US pragmatism. The parallel globalization of genuine products of the US-rooted material popular culture fostered this approach to critique and to pacifism even more. Consequentially, the various goals of avant-garde aesthetics culminated in yet another, again apparently overly optimistic, naive, maybe even shallow effort, to take effect in everyday life and in politics: How could it be possible to *demilitarize culture*? How could one achieve the goal of establishing a less violent and a deeply pacifist social life—from medicine and early education, up to professional life, to commodity production, to research and development, to politics and the arts? One of the movements, beside Zero in Germany, Arte Povera in Italy, Internationale Situationniste in France, was the stunningly globalized Fluxus movement. Fluxus is truly an international movement as well as being radically decentralized and disseminated over many artistic fields and subcultural areas. Whereas other avant-garde movements found their spiritual leader, their propagandists, their section heads for the various art forms, and their hidden hero and/or saint (Schulze 2000), such an entrepreneurial organization was not overly present in Fluxus. It started after first uses of the word Fluxus by George Maciunas in 1961 on the occasion of founding a new artists journal with festivals of New Music in German cities such as Düsseldorf, Köln, Wuppertal, Wiesbaden, and later also in Copenhagen, Paris, Amsterdam, Den Haag, London, and Nice. The various installments of this Festum Fluxorum, a celebration of flux, fluidity, and dynamics, consisted mainly of exhibited artworks and performances often by the more famous and internationally known Fluxus artists, completed with artworks by local heroes. The core concert performances by Joseph Beuys and Wolf Vostell, Robert Filliou, George Maciunas, and Nam June Paik set the tone. These performances made a strong effort to dissect formerly essentially connected and interrelated elements of artworks and artistic performances: the location of a performance does not need any more to be an institution of disseminating art; the means of an artistic performance do not anymore need to be known and established in the known institutions for disseminating art; and even the protagonists of performing artistically need not necessarily be educated in conservatoires or art schools. Characteristically for such a movement of liberation and of dismembering the (as some might like to say) rotten, artistic corpse, most of the core items of an art form are still in place—yet only anecdotally and symbolically broken up. The performance spaces in Fluxus are maybe not always concert halls, but they are very often galleries and project spaces that still genuinely belong to the art world; the instruments are not anymore traditional ones, but new ones that still allude to older ones, or destroyed and strangely reassembled older ones; the performers may not be educated in the actual genre they perform—but in another genre or sphere of artistic practice. Sculptors, painters, and directors are hence performing as sound artists. In consequence, the whole Fluxus movement is to be understood as one further and truly crucial step in the modern process of deconstructing aesthetic principles in relation to the art world.

This performative deconstruction as a Cagean (or Brownian) demilitarization takes place on many levels and in various, particular ways. A crucial performance of Fluxus, such as *Motor Vehicle Sundown* (1960) or *Water Jam* (1962) by George Brecht, as well as other performances, expands first of all the whole concept of composition as well as the limits of notation: almost every thinkable, dreamable action by anthropoid aliens or by machines or by animals or by infrastructures or by natural and astronomical processes can turn into an intrinsic part of an artistic composition. Not even the sky is the limit. A performance such as the *Alphabet Symphony* (1962) by Emmett Williams brings this basic operation of decontextualizing to its logical and radical end: in this performance and composition, not even the artistic repertoire, nor the way of selecting and organizing is predetermined. Williams provides merely a rough framework to determine a certain repertoire, a selection process, and an organizational structure. This randomization of the artistic work goes so far that he leaves almost every element in it to the actual performers to decide (Schulze 2000: 134–9). In this direction, various works of Fluxus were intended to demilitarize and to undirectionalize the artistic process. From Stockhausen's *Klavierstück XI* (1956) to Ferdinand Kriwet's *Apollo Amerika* (1969) to John Cage's *Europeras* (1987–91), all possible constituents of an artwork could—from Fluxus onwards—be made aleatory. Not even the artistic field, the genre, or the medium, was rigidly determined anymore. A piece like Williams's *Alphabet Symphony* can generate a sound art piece as well as a visual assemblage, a happening, a collage, or even a theater piece, a piece of video art or software art. The material, the situation, and the performative acts of art are in flux. The sensorium and the sensations are in flux.

Being a performer or a listener, spectator, partaker, or even consumer of such a dynamized work of art, you will encounter various obstacles and aporias. You might experience the well-known doubt and fear of being part of a thoroughly irrelevant, arbitrary, and negligible performance. This troublesome experience is rather common as soon as one leaves a more intentionally structured work for a less intentional, more improvisational and combinatoric artifact. What one experiences here is basically the fear of losing control, of being a passive object to external forces playing with you in unforeseeable ways. In the actual working process, this rather abstract fear will dissolve more and more—but maybe through phases of increased and panicking fear. Are you now just a visitor from the outside—or are you a main protagonist of this performance? Or are you both—and lost at the same time? As a performer or as a visitor, one will undoubtedly experience one's own limitations and capabilities of acting and intervening: a surprisingly generative force in this situation. In partaking in such a performance—no matter if as actual performer or as actual visitor—one's whole sensory experience has to readapt. One's whole concept of what such an artifact could be is in dire need of reordering. This reordering hurts humanoid aliens. It hurts as it is a thoroughly new corporeal activity one has to learn: The body as a performative agent has to adapt in quite uncomfortable ways. It is a surgical operation one is performing upon oneself—with an anesthetic measure at hand only rarely. This operation represents the dialectics of modernity present in Fluxus: a dynamization of core items; a stressing of the contingency of all aspects in cultural performativity and in cultural artifacts; and finally, the aleatorizing of all these aspects. This aleatorization can in turn be experienced as freeing, liberating, or expelling one from traditional cultural ties—yet exactly this untying can in turn also be understood as one of the major characteristics of modern Western culture and its genuine capitalist excess. Fluxus can thus be interpreted as highly ambivalent, as the various research efforts explored in the previous chapter: on the one hand, it represents a transformative and generative movement of contemporary and future musical and performance practices; a movement that stresses the corporeality, the materiality, and the constructedness of any sonic act and any listening practice. On the other hand, it must also be regarded as a somewhat involuntarily force contributing to the accelerated capitalization and proceduralization of already dynamized cultures. Individual ties in history, biography, in training, or in belief seem less and less plausible and less and less relevant in the course of this accelerating movement. What might be a joyful play for some on the wealthier parts of this planet, and in the more gifted strata of society, needs precisely to be understood as a threat for other, more precarious areas, professions, and sociological strata in this world. Aside from these truly ambivalent and partly scary and disturbing results of the postmodern dynamization of societies, of lifestyles and professions, the main contribution of avant-garde movements like Fluxus to contemporary developments in sound and listening is the questioning of the role of any apparatus, any dispositive, any seemingly given and previously unquestionable societal, technological, and habitual structure. If there is a structure stable enough, hegemonic enough, powerful enough—it might be necessary to deconstruct it, to destroy it, to annihilate it. It seems to be extremely useful and generative—and this is one of the major lessons of Fluxus—to work against the utilitarianism, against the supposed functionality and effectivity of contemporary cultures. This fundamental opposition against the main values and major artifacts of one's present can be regarded as a driving force of a productive transformation. In order to reinvent the apparatus, one might have to destroy it. The apparatus of listening and sounding hence was under massive performative and material attack in the arts before it was effectively dissected by the philological and historical tools at hand in the humanities and in cultural and media research. Avant la lettre, Fluxus was apparatus theory and media critique—in actu.

1970: Baudry's dispositif

A strange dream. Edgy and weird, my eyeballs feel squeezed, I am sitting rather uncomfortably. The creatures and personae occupying this location seem alien to me. At least I seem to recognize the ideal figures they seem to be modeled after—but I am having a hard time focusing on their colors and forms, on their arms and legs, their accessories. Have I lost the ability to integrate everything my eyeballs receive into one coherent, spatial representation? I am lost, overloaded, and I realize how I cannot measure up to this presentation. I feel nausea. The same goes for the sounds I hear. I am quite familiar with the various ways in contemporary cinema to make a location as convincing as possible just by the sound design. But in this case, all my experience, my bodily memory, is in search, helpless, lost. My nausea gets even worse. I hear sounds that I actually sense but do not really hear. I feel deeply insecure: do I effectively hear these sounds? Or do I just register some bodily reactions, sonic answers by some other spectators here in the audience? In this dark place, full of seats seemingly prepared for a pilot to sit. The eye of the subject, *l'oeil du sujet*—as Jean-Louis Baudry calls it in his crucial article from 1970, *Effets idéologiques produits par l'appareil de base (Ideological Effects of the Basic Cinematographic Apparatus)*—is being generated, it is being shaped, determined, weaponized, and maintained by the cinematographic machine in this movie theater.

Half a century after Baudry's article, this transformation by an *appareil idéologique* called cinema is hardly to be reduced merely to the moving image and the co-moving eye. The *soundtrack*, the *sonic traces* (Burkhalter, Grab and Spahr 2013; Schulze 2013), the noises and musics are as much a sensorial and a mediated, a thoroughly constructed artifact (Flückiger 2001; Schulze 2012) as the visual track, the shapes and the colors, the images and pictures were. Or in the words of Baudry:

> Between "objective reality" and the camera, site of the inscription, and between the inscription and projection are situated certain operations,

a work which has as its result a finished product. (Baudry and Williams 1974/75: 40)

If translated into contemporary terminology of sound production, this crucial quote would read as follows: Between the recording device and the audible reality, between the storage of a recording and its playback, a process of editing takes place—only at which end the final sonic artifact can be found. What one hears or sees or *senses* constitutes—following Baudry—a transcendental subject: *le sujet transcendentale* (Baudry 1970, S. 20–22). The concept of *sujet* has a double meaning here: it means on the one hand that the object that the listeners (or spectators) hear (or see) in the end is not at all present in its final shape in the actual situation of recording; but it is an object that only in the process of production gets to be thoughtfully imagined, conceptualized, and computed by the means of technology— it is transcendentally generated *after* the recording. Yet this means on the other hand that, according to Baudry, this process of subsequently generating an audiovisual (and I might add: a kinesthetic, an olfactory, a gustatory, a multisensorial) object of individual sensory perception, that this process of perceptual generativity in itself constitutes the perceiving subject: the humanoid, sensing alien. Baudry follows with this argument not only Immanuel Kant and Edmund Husserl but even more so, Sigmund Freud. Referring to Freud in the beginning of his article, Baudry excludes apodictically the mere possibility of *any* immediate perception inside of such a technical apparatus. In accordance with contemporary media theory, this means a media product is in its pivotal framing parameters mainly constituted by the apparatus and all its specific forms of production—not an *auteur* or *Genie* on the director's chair. This apparatus constitutes the so-called *dispositif* or dispositive.

A dispositive consists, further following Baudry, as a whole of a technical as well as a habitual side—that both are irresolvably intertwined. They constitute each other mutually and continuously; to focus only on one side of the apparatus would qualify as a misunderstanding of this concept. The apparatus of cinema, for instance—as depicted in a diagram in Baudry's original article and referring to the state of moving images at that time— consists not only of the screen, the celluloid, or the filmed object. Essentially, it consists of the integral process of framing, of cutting, of reordering by montage, by recording (also by recording and cutting sound), and by projecting onto the screen; it consists also of a certain building made to house these screenings, a certain order of seats, of curtains, of an established process of buying the tickets, of waiting and buying drinks or snacks, of entering finally the screening hall, and of the process of lowering the lights, of starting the cinematic experience with previews and commercials. It is this ritualized and thoroughly organized process that allows spectators to indulge and to joyfully regress in a somewhat masochistic, kinesthetic, and even introspective state of an externally guided, rapidly exciting, and experientially rich imagination. A guided, a skillfully crafted dream. The phenomenon of *hyperrealism*—later diagnosed by Jean Baudrillard (Baudrillard 1976)—is to be found exactly in this forcefully prescribed, this ritualistic series of actions and bodily positions: the cinematic prescription, one could say, generates first of all the spectators' receptivity to be then heavily treated by the installed entertainment weaponry of sound and image projection. The *dispositive of cinema* includes all of this: the processing of the filmed material, the preparation of material and of spectators, the position of the spectators, and the cultural practices before, during, and after going to the movies, even extending today to a globalized movie industry, an overarching merchandise culture, and all the textual and audiovisual publication formats of advertising and critique around movies. As soon as you or I decide actually we would want to watch a certain movie—be it in a movie theater or in a home movie setup—we are actually already part of this dispositive. Hence, the various contemporary forms of distribution called *piracy* need also be regarded as integral parts of today's cinematic apparatus—though involuntarily. An apparatus does not consult its constituents for approval. A dispositive hence is to be regarded as the largest and most inclusive form of organizing, predetermining and executing mediated experiences of cultural productions. Examples for dispositives outside the cinema (Brauns 2003) can be found in forms of theater, of the musical, of choir singing, of opera productions, even of entertainment parks, of television or radio programs, of gaming, of VR-caves, or of instruments to experience augmented or enhanced reality presentations; one can quite reasonably include here also the dispositives of going to the restaurant, to a natural resort, or going to a holiday resort. In this most daring expansion of the apparatus-concept, it becomes a general framing for interpreting any material culture manifest in commodified artifacts and their continuous everyday consumption. This pervasive ubiquity of the dispositive is its genuine quality and its most disturbing effect on humanoid aliens.

The dispositive for presenting a movie or equally a sound piece is actually, following Baudry, a technically reconstructed head and armor: it is a fortress consisting of rigid shields against unintended behavior of listeners and spectators in order to actually make the ballistically calculated trajectories of light and sound meet the intended membranes and nerves of the humanoid receptacles installed as listeners and spectators—that might still act as irritating targets and implicit enemies of this fortress. The technical dispositive of a media theater is a fortified shooting stand for shooting audiovisual, perceptual rays and waves in the direction of its spectators and listeners: a castle to secure the functioning of media technology. Only in the innermost spaces, the darkened chambers of these castles, is an actual process of sensorial perception allowed to take place. One sits in a closed head and brain machine, "no exchange, no circulation, no communication with any outside" (Baudry and Williams 1974/75: 44). The black iron prison is shutting down. The ways in which a perceivable artifact can enter this castle seem thus to be as labyrinthine as the adventures of an honorable knight in search of a beloved lady he intends to court—a lady who seems to be hidden in the darkest corners of such a castle. This castle is the apparatus of mediated humanoid perception:

> The prisoner in the tower loves the gaoler's daughter. . . . The love stories which so astonish our supple, naked bodies, painless and nearly mute, were stories of knowing, long ago. Just as the call of love circulates through the corridors, grilles and vaults of the chateau-body, haunting them, so do sense data pass through the obstacles placed into a kind of statue or automaton with twenty layers of armour, a veritable Carpathian castle, their energy purified as it makes its way through successive filters towards the central cell or instance, soul, understanding, conscience or transcendental I, to which very few gaolers hold the key. (Serres 2008: 144f.)

A humanoid's body seems to be as much an apparatus as any cinema, any theater, any concert hall: At least, if one follows Michel Serres when he summarizes this truly *weird* (Henrich/Heine/Norenzayan 2010) tradition of Western thought. Still, today, in the early twenty-first century, this strange and unsettling if not deeply flawed tradition provides the conceptual foundations for perceptual theories materialized in any audiovisual media technology. The loudspeakers and recorders, the cameras and projectors, are materialized emanations of this theory of perception that strangely enough resembles an alien humanoid's performative acts of perception to a closed apparatus with distinct and fixed entry points for input and output electrical currents. These technological artifacts, though, have in turn then even been used by researchers as common models to conceptualize humanoid sensibility. A strange but recurrently established historical feedback loop of epistemology can be observed here: First inventing reduced models of culture, of sensing, of existence; then materializing these models in new, even more reduced artifacts; and finally taking these reduced artifacts as convincing new models of existence, sensing, culture. Models that in turn—what a surprise—prove to be reduced to mere functions; and trigger the evident conclusion: might Humanoid aliens just be similar to reduced artifacts? The fallacy and the rounding errors are resounding.

The *Beloved Lady*—of which Michel Serres speaks in the passage cited above—is actually representing a humanoid's consciousness, his (and again, only rarely: her) sensibility, subjectivity, a transcendental subject. To get access to this subjectivity, to this Beloved Lady of Consciousness, is a major goal of research and development efforts in the natural sciences and in the engineering sciences. These sciences *desire* to possess and to utilize such sensibility, this romantically adored Lady. Yet, there is one axiom, one assumption made in this research dispositive that previously put exactly this adorable and desired sensibility in a dark and hidden dungeon of fortified technology. It is this main assumption that represents a fundamental ground of Western epistemologies of distance and of abstraction in order to qualify as proper research. This basic assumption ignores quite willfully a basic fact that any researcher, writer, and scholar, any artist, composer, and performer, being an anthropoid alien, essentially relies on: It is the fact that sensibility is—horribile dictu—already a quite complex given trait of everyday life, in every single performative act a humanoid might execute in a given situation. At the same time as the body of a scientist is claiming that sensibility, consciousness, the Beloved Lady, is hard to find—at this very moment, his body is actually the area where his (in case of the patriarch history of the *weird*—read: Western, Educated, Industrialized, Rich, and Democratic— sciences only rarely: her) individual sensibility is to be found, if not overly present in research all the time. There is a scientific rigor of ignoring the subtle corporeal sensibilities in research that only forcefully generates this research gap by erecting the fortified castle of mediated perceptivity—an artificial obstacle that would not exist *without* this epistemological and ontological claim in the first place. It is hence the actual process of scientific research that places The Beloved Lady of Consciousness in this hidden and cryptic dungeon. Maybe just to heroically free her from this cruel fate the liberator himself imposed on her? Maybe just a too masculine fantasy of courtship around a far too passively waiting other? Maybe—dare I say— such an approach to research is relying too much on an outdated, almost prehistoric narration of aristocratic courtship cultures? Sciences are deeply and intrinsically gendered (Harding 1987), and with Serres's metaphor, the fundamentally gendered quality of epistemology as a whole is explicated. Yet, this dated and gendered dungeon of technology, hiding a desired sensibility quite artfully in some sort of paradox self-sabotage, is equally present in every traditional or IMAX-cinema, in a search for the *sweet spot* of a Dolby 5.1-, 7.1-, or 13.1-surround-environment, it is present inside the massive weaponry of speaker arrays in waveform synthesis (WFS). Entering these machines to hear and sense for us, one is entering the *Dungeon of Subjectivity*—which nevertheless grants us the historically relatively perfected illusion of mediated transmission (Sterne 2003). Surely future generations will laugh out loud about contemporary illusions of perfect mediated projections, ignoring the intricate bodies of sensing humanoids. Baudry's dispositive explicates the Black Box of the Platonic Cave by way of Serres's Castle: an adventurous, a cryptic and cathartic, a melodramatic model of how subjectivity and perception are mutually constituted artifacts.

The unconscious of the apparatus is disclosed: The *Black Box* is being materialized as a dark chamber of media technology—inaccessible for the uneducated masses. Such a concept of *The Human* requires hence an anthropology of the senses as sinuously problematic and implying massive detours, deceptions, and lies. The legitimation for the superiority of this epistemological knowledge is the invention of major obstacles and intrinsic aporiae in the first place. This skillful invention of fundamental dilemmata is the stage on which heroes can perform their heroic mission to enlighten the world and its uneducated masses. A humanoid's perception is—on this stage—implied to be an ongoing struggle, a fight with one's own and surrounding illusions, even a heavily invested courting of *Madame La Vérité, The Beloved Lady*. But what if this imagined and desired Lady is in the end nothing more than a strategic, a corporate and power-driven mock-up? What if this courted Lady is merely a promotional mascot as part of the marketing for a globalized arms manufacturer and arms dealer corporation by the name of *Truth Inc.*? Such a more or less unconscious desire toward a perfectly mediating machinery that generates effects of realness, of immediacy, and of presence is a core motivation of recent developments in the field of sound reproduction. The High Fidelity of Sound strives toward a Maximum Fidelity to the desired *Lady of Truth Inc.* Though this effect of a supposed realness is aging: each younger generation of humanoid listeners and spectators is evermore confronted with evermore new and more reliable and even more real generations of machineries to reproduce sound. Each generation of listeners has to adapt to new perceptual techniques (Sterne 2003) connected to new perceptual apparatuses. Otherwise one would not be capable of enjoying all the sonic artifacts projected in the most recent castles of technology. Humanoid aliens do effectively learn seeing, hearing, reading; they learn perceiving by way of these dispositives—incessantly. Listening is therefore indeed a practice, a material and a situated one. Listening thus has been materialized in the course of the second half of the twentieth century; it can only be called ignorant if a listening activity is still today being described as merely an imaginary, an insecure and solely subjectivist, an arbitrary and ephemerally passive state. If one does so, one affirms a premodern ordering of the senses and one also negates the vast amount of auditory knowledge and of sonic skills evolved in recent decades. Listening is part of material culture. The actors, the materials, and the artifacts in this process of listening are continuously affirming, evolving, and remodeling the listening apparatus, the *auditory dispositive* of which they are part.

2008: Beyond *Aufführungspraxis*

As soon as I entered the space, I sensed that there was a performance in progress. I could not say why I sensed this. But I did. What could have been the possible indicators, I ask myself in retrospect. The humanoid aliens in this location did not actually look like musicians; they did not wear a specific outfit, they did not even hold onto specific musical instruments. Nor did they stand on a stage, or behind microphones, or in a sort of choreography of concentration and musical communication. They were scattered around the place. And still, there was something I sensed. I had the immediate sensation of an intense and reflected, rehearsed and previously conceptualized performance. Such a sensation is not just an individual illusion or an esoteric assumption. Actually it is a rather material detection I might have registered in this very instant. Maybe it started with a specific bodily tension of some people standing too close to me in this location? A tension that seemed to radiate with a sort of externally directed and internally trained *tension of performance* (Schulze 2012: 77–83). Though one might not be able to define right away and exhaustively the characteristics that make up such a tension of performance, it is quite obvious in the actual situation, when humanoids are not simply in their own thoughts or just following their duties and tasks over any given day. Various subtle details are quite different as soon as an alien humanoid is externally directed by a strong and focused urge to convey a certain performance, an idea, an action, or anything else—and he or she has been training for such an instance for a number of hours, days, even months in order to perform this trained sequence of actions in the best and most appropriate way possible. There is something sculptural, something uplifted, and an air of transfiguration around these personae, then. Yes: the more or less humanoid aliens then have immediately become *personae*. They are on stage (even if there is no physically perceivable stage at all). German cultural theorist and popular culture analyst Klaus explores this phenomenon by way of the fundamental materialist if not monist presence of humanoid aliens in one connected physical space. He does so in a work he wrote in reference to the media theories of Vilém Flusser:

> We are figures of light and water, of a series of acids and a few minerals, and articulate ourselves in waves. All of our body cells constantly receive not only food, but light and waves, media stimuli and stimuli from the air, including a tremendous amount of stimuli emanating from other bodies, from other persons. It is only for the grossest of these stimuli that we have a consciously developed sensorium. (Theweleit 2007: 26; transl. HS)[1]

Theweleit quite laconically states here that the body of a humanoid is part of the mediated nexus of gases and liquids, acids, minerals and particles, of

---

[1] "Wir sind Figuren aus Licht und Wasser, einer Reihe von Säuren und ein paar Mineralien, und äußern uns in Wellen. Alle unsere Körperzellen nehmen ständig nicht nur Nahrung, sondern Licht und Wellen auf, mediale Reize und Reize aus der Luft, darunter eine ungeheuere Menge an Reizen, die von anderen Körpern, von anderen Personen ausgehen. Nur für die gröbsten dieser Reize haben wir ein bewusst ausgearbeitetes Sensorium." (Theweleit 2007: 26)

streams and waves, frequencies and various rays. Any volume on the planet we know and live on is full with all of these, at least with some of these. Humanoids are never in an empty, vacuum space. This is for Theweleit a sufficient foundation for any perception of moods or atmospheres, inclinations or obsessions in other aliens around:

> We immediately perceive the "whim" of persons when they enter the room; especially from people we know well. But when we say: "He or she was 'loaded,'" then we are sure of that, also of people we know little or not at all—and how does that work? "Attention! Exploding now!" We perceive part of it with our eyes, attitude, facial expressions. Maybe we can "smell" the rage here (without notice). But the person also "radiates." Certain cell structures of their body send: anger. And certain cell structures of our body, which are receptive to it, warn us: "caution, explosives." (Theweleit 2007: 26; transl. HS)[2]

Another person can be radiating *anger*. Theweleit argues this to be rooted in a thorough bodily inclination down to the last cells and cell structures. Therefore, to assume an ongoing connectivity between physical actions and individual sensibilities is not impossible or eccentric—but rather a logical and deeply materialist consequence. There is an actual, not solely a metaphorical, connection between actors and materials, humanoids and their artifacts. It is one continuum—also between performativity, materials, technology, concepts, and meanings. A performance practice or *Aufführungspraxis* can never be independent from its artifacts, its media technologies, its material listening practices. But what may sound trivial and unquestionable in my previous sentence is actually not an established practice in the analysis of a musical performance. The focus on a humanoid performer as such is still the dominant aspect for analysis, for training, for critique, review, and revision of a performance. It would still be quite unusual if not weird to find in the critique of a concert performance a lengthy reference to the specific sound engineer and specific speaker setups and the use of microphones in describing and criticizing a common, everyday performance. This does happen, of course, with advanced and experimental media art performances, but they are globally the rare exceptions to the rule. Also, one would not

---

[2] "Wir nehmen sofort die 'Laune' von Personen wahr, wenn sie den Raum betreten; besonders von Personen, die wir gut kennen. Aber wenn wir sagen: 'Der oder die war aber 'geladen,'' dann sind wir uns dessen sicher auch bei Personen, die wir kaum oder gar nicht kennen—und wie geht das? 'Vorsicht! Explodieren gleich.' Einen Teil davon nehmen wir mit dem Auge wahr, Haltung, Gesichtsausdrücke. Vielleicht 'riechen' wir auch hier (ohne es zu merken) die Wut. Aber die Person 'strahlt auch aus.' Bestimmte Zellstrukturen ihres Körpers senden: Wut. Und bestimmte Zellstrukturen unseres Körpers, die dafür empfänglich sind, warnen uns: Vorsicht, Explosivstoff." (Theweleit 2007: 26)

expect to read in such a critique a reference to the *aural architecture* (Blesser and Salter 2007) of the concert venue and its specific historical as well as physical effects on the specific type of performance taking place there. Again, this does happen with advanced sound art performances, but these qualify as globally rare exceptions to the rule. The material and technological side is still effectively being considered a more accidental property to a musical performance: any humanoid performing seems to be more important for the result of the performance than all the thousands of lines of commodified software code written or all the dozens or hundreds of cables, of hardware machinery, of speakers, microphones, and amplifiers being connected to effectively make this performance appropriately audible for us listening aliens in the audience. In research this insight slowly seems to be acknowledged as common sense—but in the discourse between musicians and critics, in the more traditional writings in musicology, this still seems to be a really far-fetched if not exotic assumption. Hence, the German Jazz musician, musicologist, and media researcher, Rolf Großmann, proposed in 2008 in a crucial article to change this. In his article, *Verschlafener Medienwandel* (Overslept Change of Media), he writes:

> In the medium, this would be my necessary and unquestionable insight: the world always appears as being tailored for the senses. (Großmann 2008: 8; transl. HS)[3]

A medium, therefore, presents the world by definition in a way that is from the start shaped *for the senses* of a specifically intended audience. Any idea of mediatization as a *transparent transmission*—a quite pervasive obsession that will be discussed later in this book (in Chapter 4: "In Auditory Dispositives")—must immediately implode if one accepts Großmann's dictum. It is a fundamental insight of recent media theories to leave the idea of transparent transmission behind; yet in audio technology and its holy grail of signal transduction, the idea of a perfectly clear signal (or at least a feasible signal-to-noise ratio) is still dominant. Großmann makes it impossible to stick to this. The consequences of this introduction of major insights of media theory in the analysis of musical performances are manifold. The common denominator of all these consequences is but one: What Großmann proposes here is nothing less than a thorough *de-anthropomorphization of artistic (in this case: musical) practices*. In recent history of the deconstruction of literature, the arts, design, and music,

---

[3]"Im Medium, so die notwendige und selbstverständliche Einsicht, erscheint die Welt immer bereits als eine auf die Sinne zugerichtete." (Großmann 2008: 8)

this seemed to be a recurrent motif. Yet in many cases it also seemed to be restricted to a discourse in critique and to the field of studies that did not really touch and transform artistic practices. Thus the eternal rhapsody of the author, composer, or artist merely being a medium and a weak tool of higher forces and inspirations never seemed to actually push the modern history of the arts outside of forms of anthropocentric production, of revenue, of authorship, and of production assignments and intellectual property. If there were machines or algorithms involved, if there were aleatoric or combinatorial structures being used for producing an artwork, typically it was in the end a male, white, socially accepted artist who got the credit—neither the piece of software, nor a climate condition, nor the actual programmer, the sound engineer, the nameless young composer who actually did the score arrangement. Bluntly put, only if societies would be granting intellectual properties to things or animals or immaterial entities, or if societies would be willing to pay revenues or royalties to those things, animals, or immaterial entities—only then might we essentially dare to speak of leaving anthropocentrism behind. *Only then.* Before these factual, these material consequences, any posthumanist or post-anthropocentric claim will be under suspicion to serve foremost the individual distinction of exactly the person speaking in the field he or she intends to advance. A function of rhetoric, not an actual goal. A lip service with no consequences.

Großmann's goals are far more realistic and more empirical. In his article he proposes, with various examples from technological history to actual musical performance practices, to leave behind the anthropocentrist description and focus of analysis solely on composition and instrumentalization. He offers instead to focus more on the intricate relations between and among technological apparatuses, material artifacts, performance spaces, bodily techniques, and various other practices and artifacts. This approach therefore converges with the characteristics of Jean-Louis Baudry's *Effets idéologiques produits par l'appareil de base* (1970) discussed earlier. Großmann offensively applies Baudry's concept of the apparatus for musicology, and he manages to evoke a thoroughly transformed and evolved practice of studying sound and music. The field of sound studies in general and of an anthropology of sound in particular can find in Großmann's article a foundational outline for a methodology and terminology, of research subjects and research interests. The main characteristics of an *auditives Dispositiv*, an *auditory dispositive* as proposed by Großmann, also bear close resemblance to a number of other neighboring concepts of post-anthropological media constellations. The concept of *affordances*, as proposed by psychologist James Jerome Gibson (Gibson 1979), might be useful to explicate the almost intuitive fit that some proposed audio media dispositives can inspire in their targeted consumers, their users, and listeners. The concept of the *vibrational nexus* as proposed by Steve Goodman (Goodman 2009) is capable of explicating the thorough and continuous sensorial connection between any apparatus, its humanoid servomechanisms, and any sonic performance—as already alluded in the previous references to Klaus Theweleit: "Man becomes the servomechanism of his technical products" ("Der Mensch wird zum Servomechanismus seiner technischen Hervorborbringungen." Großmann 2008: 7, transl. HS). Humanoid aliens even tend to become auditory servomechanisms of mediated emissions. Finally, the concept of an *actor-network* as proposed by Bruno Latour further explicates the assimilating quality of an auditory dispositive that actually includes all its actors in a pervasive process of a *sonic-actor-network*, a process that could be understood as a *sound cultural transmission*, in application of Régis Debray's mediological concept of cultural transmission (Debray 2000). All these approaches converge in seeking a thoroughly *non-anthropocentric* understanding of social and mediatized actions and interactions. This does not mean that anthropoid aliens are radically erased and are not allowed to appear in descriptions resulting from such research; the contrary is true. Such research ends through a mere reference to an abstract and unfounded collective truism of *The Human* and exchanges it for a very specific, radically concrete, and miniscule exploration of individuals. Throw out *The Human*—but bring in multitudes of aliens! A multitude of aliens that is almost imperceivably implemented into a myriad of machines and microorganisms, of gases and particles, of software agents, of plants and mushrooms, of heat sensations and smells, of sensorial percepts. "We are figures of light and water, a series of acids and a few minerals, and we articulate ourselves in waves." ("Wir sind Figuren aus Licht und Wasser, einer Reihe von Säuren und ein paar Mineralien, und äußern uns in Wellen." Theweleit 2007: 26, transl. HS) An anthropology of sound following these approaches and assumptions will be a fundamentally de-anthropomorphized anthropology: *a non-anthropocentric anthropology*.

Dispositives of surround sound

In this very moment, I sit and I listen. What do I listen to? I have to recognize it first. What I listen to right now is not trivial in any way. Do I listen to the environment in this large, rather technical room? Do I listen to the humming and the buzzing of all the machines and the cables in here? Do I listen to my own heartbeat, the high-pitched, continuous whirring in my head? Or, do I actually, candidly, listen to this one song that keeps popping up in my mind today—like an earworm, somewhere in the back of my inner ear? Picked up from our neighbors below or from a shop I was walking by? What do I hear actually? What do I listen to? I listen to this room. This room is a research environment that is also used for an artistic presentation, for aesthetic experiences. I am standing in a technical space. A space that provides one of the most recent inventions in surround sound reproduction, called WFS. I walk into this room as I would walk into any other university venue. Yet then I realize: I did not actually walk in here. I walked into another, a second auditory space—very different from the space I am physically occupying right now. And I am struggling. Quite similar to the efforts in dealing with mediated transmission of spatial vision in 3-D, the mediated transmission of spatial sound also poses at first serious problems for a person not familiar with this form of media transmission. It is a weird, an unsettling experience. A decorporealizing experience that takes one out of his or her habitualized performativity and sensitivity through and in her or his body. I need to use— no: first I need to *learn anew* how to use my sensing body, my listening body, in here in quite a different way. Though I really like this challenge, though I really have the ambition to be capable of enjoying or just merely perceiving the actual sound art piece presented in here—I still struggle. Smiling about the struggles of my own sensitivity, my ability of aesthetic integration of unforeseen dynamic sensory events. The process of adapting my perceptual habits to those required here, in this, for me, now completely unusual technical environment and its sound emissions, this process might take a long time. It was definitely not completed as soon as I felt more comfortable in this space, finally merely listening and paying attention to the sound piece presented. Even as I forgot that this whole listening experience was new for me, I still had to adapt, to learn, to adjust and readjust my aural focusing, my selectivity concerning unusual acoustic artifacts, to let myself be guided by the *sonic affordances* (Maier and Schulze 2015) of this sound reproduction technology.

This sonic environment does not reorder a listener's attention habits in exactly the same way a Dolby 5.1 or a stereo environment would. In that case, remembering my first experience with Dolby 5.1, the main trouble was the sudden deep bass continuously being dropped, as well as the surprisingly manifold sound events attacking my focused listening from unusual directions; but this was quite manageable after some time, since no one sits immobile all the time in the perfect *sweet spot* between stereo speakers anyway: the experience of speakers in unusual angles from one's ears is a rather common one. Maybe it is even more weird now if speakers are actually directed perfectly to one's earlobe? For once I feel strangely fixed, really attacked, and on auditory observation, then: the focus of a *Panacousticon* (Schoon 2012). Similarly, the adaptation process to stereo sound setups was even more simple, it seems to me. After years of listening to just a single speaker of a 1970s kitchen radio, television, or a portable record player, the first experiences with a hi-fi stereo or even headphone listening were almost too much to bear. It needed a slow but continuous form of *auditory desensitizing* to not be totally scared and overpowered by the sheer impact of all these sounds and noises, the complexity and clarity of sound reproduction. Though, obviously, I learned to listen to it;

I learned to love it. In all these cases, though—and similar with WFS—this new technology made me a disciple who had to ignore selected bits or aspects of perception and to focus more specifically, often weirdly to me, on other aspects. It is a truly hurtful reordering of habitualized perception. It is also clear that all of these culturally learned forms of perception are in no way perfectly transparent or the maximum listening experience. All are— and the individual resistance to and the joy in learning proves this—all are enveloping one in a new routine, in new habits of sound reproduction: new *perceptual techniques* (Sterne 2003). New technologies are often promoted to be the ultimate ones. Science and technology studies have recurrently pointed to the fact that the idle goal of high fidelity resembles more an urge to transform current technological and ideological constellations into yet another form of sensory representation. In this sense, the phonautograph and later the gramophone indeed were the highest fidelity achievable in their times—as was the transistor radio for consumers in the 1950s or the MP3-format in the early twenty-first century. It would be rather arrogant and ignorant to state that these formats and auditory dispositives would have no power to evoke a lasting sonic experience in their dedicated listeners. A new auditory dispositive is being established in all of these cases: It gets implanted into my sensing and my hearing body. It is a form of sensorial and habitual surgery, inserting a new piece of technologically enhanced hearing aid (Papenburg 2012) into a corpse. Thus, once one managed to assimilate this new habitual hearing aid into one's body, one will for sure experience completely different forms of auditory events: auditory events one never before had experienced. The auditory dispositive of WFS is therefore at the same time an example and an exception to various dispositives of surround sound. It is different from the ones mentioned before in that it changes the relation of a listener to its sound environment. Whereas with more static sound reproduction technologies, like stereo or Dolby 5.1, the physically experienced sound environment obviously stays in place rather unaltered— just with inserted new sources of mediated sound. Though one might still see the same walls, the same furniture, the same displays and speakers, the same other listeners, what is being heard has thoroughly been changed, at all single spatial spots in this location. My listening experience is swapped, but my visual and my visually induced kinesthetic experience might mainly stay the same. But what about the auditorily induced kinesthetic experience? Suddenly I tend to move differently, to react in another way, to seek and to fear other sound events. My movements transform; I feel the urge of moving quite differently. What shall I do? The room has changed:

> However, the influence of the reproduction room on spatial perception has been dealt with less thoroughly, although it is considered by this author to be one of the main reasons for an impaired spatial perception in WFS. (Wittek 2008: 201)

As this quote points out, the experiential conflict between the actual physical projection room in which a WFS system is being installed and all its acoustic properties—including the physical appearance as well as all the habits and performative acts of people visiting this room—is hardly being addressed with all needed urgency. This conflict, thus, is a fundamental and conceptual one. A conflict that arises also, though with a different impact, in listening to stereo or to Dolby 5.1. The ambition of radically transforming and improving a spatial listening experience brings these technologies ever closer to a fundamental contradiction of any mediated sound reproduction: the physical properties of the location in which a sound reproduction takes place will necessarily contradict, sometimes frame, but typically also ridicule and destroy the efforts to evoke a precise spatial sound reproduction. This aporia of spatial sound reproduction is revealed in all its potentially destructive impact as soon as the properties of the reproduced sound environment come ever closer to the previously recorded sound environment. Effectively, one is then listening to two sound environments at the same time. This is only superficially the case with all the older technologies of spatializing sound, as in those cases only new sound sources are being added to the present physical environment. With WFS, the haptically, kinesthetically, and audiovisually perceivable environment receives a second, only auditorily perceivable environment. An endless array of virtually generated sound sources is occupying this environment—not only two or six or more speakers, like in earlier sound reproduction. This new auditory dispositive of surround sound requires from a listener to learn how to hear two materially dominant sound environments that are at the same time comprehensively covering each other and intersecting each other on all points in space. The *vibrational nexus* (Goodman) to the spatial environment hence is a double one: a sinuously problematic one. Also, new *sonic actors* are introduced into this network in a form of the virtually endless number of speakers; as well, the cultural forms of transmission and receiving are being transformed: How can one learn and achieve the ability to actually listen *materially* to this layered structure? Obviously, one can. But what perceptual efforts of revising one's earlier habits and idiosyncrasies are to be made?

It is a form of *sensory critique* I am performing in this final section of the chapter. This analysis of a WFS setup is not focused on historical, on mathematical, on electroacoustical or even artistic aspects of such a form of sound reproduction. It is focused on the brutally material and sensorial effects it has on at least one listener—who gained confidence in articulating these effects after various and recurrent discussions with other experienced consumers, users, programmers, and engineers working with this technology. Obviously this form of critique has strong similarities to a phenomenological description, to an ethnographically *thick description*, and also to accounts in sensory ethnography in general. Added to these similarly corporeal, individual, and sensitive accounts of a situated experience is the potential to critique. As I will discuss in more detail later in this book (in Chapter 7: "The Precision of Sensibility"), this perhaps unusually personal and often intimate form of critique, by way of a concentrated, educated, and versatile sensorial experience, is actually relying on some of the oldest research strategies proven effective and insightful in analyzing artifacts. This sensory critique concerning surround sound systems hence might be contributing to ongoing discussions of other bodily forms of auditory perception, especially outside the two bluntly visible earlobes of humanoids and their visually hidden, individually molded apparatus of the inner ear. In terms of humanoid corporeality, it may be that a thorough and pervasive spatial sound reproduction is either genuinely impossible or it requires more spatial points of a humanoid's body than just the two pinnae (outer ears) for sonic affect. Actual vibrations, olfactory and gustatory sensations, kinesthetic and visual sensations, are not to be ignored as major influences to how one perceives a spatial environment auditorily. The situation of listening extends vastly and excessively the mere transduction of selected, proper signals. A listening situation is more of a ravel and less of a traffic plan. After the developments in the twentieth century in the arts and in research that have materialized listening—as shown in this chapter—through Fluxus, through dispositive theory, through media studies, and through new forms of sound reproduction, after all this long and winding process of thoroughly, ubiquitously, and intensely *materializing listening,* this materialization now, in the early twenty-first century, seems to demand also another degree of *materializing sounding* in regard to the sensing body.

CHAPTER THREE

Corporealizing the senses

Into darkness

You enter an area that might look strange to you. The buildings take strange forms. The pathways on which you might find your destination are hidden and sometimes tiresome to walk on. You might want to go there with your closest friends—but they might not be interested in going to that venue. You asked other friends, more comfortable with such venues, but they are not in town. As soon you enter this building, full of noise and only some people idling, you start to explore it. Or are you slightly scared, waiting paralyzed in the entrance? In this case, you might suffer the age-old and quite civilized idiosyncrasy of preferring to stay a spectator and not a participant: the latter position seems too exposed, too risky, too scary, and dangerous for all aspects of your life. You might be uncovered, and you might even be altered substantially by what happens here as a result of your participation. Yet, as long as you stay just a spectator, you might not grasp anything about what's really happening. This dilemma constitutes almost an axiom for any new and slightly more immersive and more performatively demanding environment you might encounter these days. So you proceed. And this is the best you can do. As a core conviction in your own personal existence, but also as part of your habit as a curious person—maybe even a researcher? Encountering something hitherto unexperienced is part of what you are doing, right? As you proceed further into this space—be it a closed architecture, a bunker, or a more open venue, an open-air location maybe, a lakeside, a beach, a hilltop—you might get ahold of another sensation grasping your mind, your senses, your inner organs, your outer extremities. This sensation is at first a tactile one, or at least it seems so. Do you sense how some vibrations travel over the floor into your feet? Can you feel the beats in your intestines, in your bones? Do you also sense a certain heat of all the people moving and shaking, grooving and walking on their spots? This space is full of a specific heat some humanoids exhale as soon they are working their bodies heavily. It is a physical process—a process that might extend to something at the same time that is not at all physical anymore. It is a cultural event. A thoroughly *rhythmic event* (Ikoniadou 2014). This event happening here is a dancing event in its most sonically imaginable meaning. Dancing is happening here—not only by the moving bodies of all the humanoid aliens who are gathered here. In writing this, I recall myself in various moments, situations, extended nights and unsuspected daytime moments in which I entered the realm of dancing—and in which various bodily practices entered my habit. In many of these cases—be it in 1999 in Berlin, in Nuremberg in 1995, in my hometown Baden-Baden in 1986, or in 2003 in Berlin, also in 2009, 2010, or several times in Copenhagen in 2015 or 2017—the predominant form of dancing happening in such a place was not familiar to me. Yet in many of these cases, just being in this place, just opening my sensorium for an empathic notion of what was happening at this place—right here, right now—just this corporeal presence made me easy prey for an apparently new form of dancing getting hold of my body. I remember early dancing experiences as an insecure, thoroughly doubtful young teenager. I remember moments of surprise dancing on afternoons with friends early in a Berlin winter or late in a Sardinian summer. I remember overcrowded places on some not-so-remote island, all aliens shaking and dancing—and I remember lonely corners, just outside a metropolis, dancing together on some lost beat with one or two or three close, very close friends. Dancing could have been a way to domesticate these places. Dancing could have been a way to generate and evoke moments in which we, the humanoids present, could dare to project our most positive expectations, our hope, our love onto each other. Dancing could have been our most adequate way to invent this social situation anew: a situational, an interpersonal transformation. *Good music: I dance. No Good music: I not dance* (the words on some T-shirt I liked marveling at).

At those moments of social *generativity*, the notion and fear concerning a potential darkness surrounding us can suddenly disappear—or is it shooed away? The distortions by sound waves propagating through the gases and objects, bodies and architectures, accessories and technical gadgetry; these distortions finally reach us. One engaged in a nexus between listening and dancing. Dancing and listening might at first seem as contrary or at least not completely identical practices. The nexus lies in the fact that either practice is neither executable nor even thinkable without a corporeal realization—in whatever material form. This following fact alone is a deep insight not really become trivial in research: Listening *is* a corporeal activity—the same way one might regard cooking, cycling, playing an instrument, or constructing a building or any machine a corporeal activity. Listening is in no way a solely passive and receptive activity, as it was regarded for centuries. Listening by humanoid aliens is not an arbitrary and neglectable non-activity; it is a constant activity of searching and being ready, of listening closer and listening from afar, as a whole. As humanoid aliens, we are in a constant state of recalibrating, of disengaging and reengaging our particular modes of sensing—and so also listening. For an anthropology of sound, there is one pivotal definition of listening by Swedish musicologist Ola Stockfelt. In 1997, he proposed the concept of an *adequate listening*:

> Adequate listening hence occurs when one listens to music according to the exigencies of a given social situation and according to the predominant sociocultural conventions of the subculture to which the music belongs. (Stockfelt 1997: 137)

This concept moves decisively away from normative, ahistoric, let alone moralist prescriptions of how to listen in an orderly, correct, or sufficiently educated and subtle manner. For some readers this might open up a Pandora's Box of radical relativism—but actually, the contrary is true: an approach of adequate listening effectively allows for focusing on specific and concrete listening situations, traditions, and habitualizations of listening as well as the idiosyncratic multiplicity of possible approaches to listening. Adequate listening following Stockfelt makes it possible to research listening as an historicized and culturalized example of a plastic, a situated, and a highly contextual and individual practice—shaped also by the intersectional specificity of one person: in my case, being a white, cis male, raised in working-class Germany in the 1970s with close Scottish-French as well as Polish-Hungarian ancestors (according to transcribed genealogies), father of three kids, and an equally strong affection of mediated sound performances as well as highly site-specific and deeply corporeal sound events, with an ongoing passion for reading and writing. In writing this book, this author includes you in a rather informal, but progressively complete contract about more sonic or more musical means of expression. Or, in Stockfelt's own words:

> Adequate listening is, like all languages, always the result of an informal (although sometimes formalized) contract between a greater or smaller group of people, an agreement about the relation of the musical means of expression to this group's picture of the world. Adequate listening is hence always in the broadest sense ideological: it relates to a set of opinions belonging to a social group about ideal relations between individuals, between individuals and cultural expression, and between the cultural expressions and the construction of society. (Stockfelt 1997: 138)

Listening *is* a social and historical convention enveloped in situative, corporeal, and technological constraints. Stockfelt's approach allows us—even in quite disturbing and irritatingly erratic listening experiences as presented at the beginning of this section—to adjust a concept of listening to its actual circumstances. Adequate listening understands any unusual or highly idiosyncratic situation of listening not as an aberration or a failure, but as maybe one new specimen of a supposedly endless series of listening situations to which humanoid aliens might be able to adapt, engage in, even to enjoy:

> The sound of big opera ensembles can be fitted onto a windsurfing board, and the sound of a nylon-stringed guitar can fill a football stadium; one can listen to march music in the bathtub and salon music in the mountains. (Stockfelt 1997: 135)

This versatile, this fluid and plastic approach to genres and to sound practices picks up the early research approaches to listening and sounding from the nineteenth and early twentieth centuries. Yet this approach to the mingledness of listening takes research one crucial step further. From the early efforts in physiology and physics to *quantify* sonic events as actually material emanations between 1850 and 1950 (discussed in the first chapter: "Quantifying Sound")—over the ongoing efforts to *materialize* listening experiences in the artistic avant-garde and its multifaceted theoretical offspring between 1914 and 1970 (discussed in the second chapter: "Materializing Listening")—sound research since the last quarter of the twentieth century entered a period of *corporealization* of sonic experiences as media apparatuses seemed to take over large portions of everyday listening experience. In these times of intense mediatization and reordering of corporeal practices, this corporeality of listening moved into the center of attention: your and my body as a whole (not solely those visible extremities to the left and right of your head) are more and more being recognized as constituting a major listening instrument. *Corporeal listening* (Schulze 2016) might sound like a pleonasm—but only if one grotesquely ignores the apparatization of sound reproduction and listening in the last two centuries. The adequacy of listening—as postulated by Ola Stockfelt—is a direct result of this focus, as corporeal listening is by definition situated, transforming, and adaptive. The times of definite, normative, ahistoric, moralist, and *absolute* definitions of listening might seem nostalgic if not idyllic to aliens preferring fixed ideological frameworks. Yet the process of research is moving further and further away from such illusionary forms of doubtlessness. *Inadequate listening*, hence, is a strongly implied and very often a necessarily required way to encounter an emerging form of *adequate listening*:

> Not that long ago . . . [v]arious musical styles were implicitly bound to specific environments and specific relationships between the performer and the listener. (Stockfelt 1997: 135)

Moving on to the next room of this building, I have no clue what sound practices could await me there. What form of *sonic dominance* (Henriques 2011) might be overpowering me as soon as I arrive? Dancing contingency, evolving generativity. Dancing is a way of hearing; singing is a way of dancing: singing is a way of hearing. Sonic corporeality, adequately transforming.

1985: Serres's *Syrrhesis*

We are not dancing. Not in this moment, at least. As you are reading these words and sentences, I might dare to assume you are probably neither in the mood nor are you physically capable of dancing right now. Or are you? How I wish you would prove me wrong. Nevertheless, it is safe to assume that reading and writing on the one side—and dancing and tasting on the other—seem to mutually exclude each other (at least in the writing, publishing, and media cultures you and I inhabit these days, in the early twenty-first century). As soon as one assumes this, it becomes almost epistemologically impossible to integrate a life of complex and plastic bodily and sensory experiences in any more fundamental anthropological reflection. Would sensory experience and any form of sign operation, any form of semiosis, be mutually exclusive? Can the age-old disease of dualism and essentialism still be harmful and lethal? A thinking thoroughly infected and rotten by this kind of dualism would definitely be doomed to be forever out of reach of any material culture, any performative acts: doomed to render these emanations of cultural practices mainly incomprehensible. *The Virus of Control* (Burroughs 1961–67). One would actually not even be able to speak about artifacts. One would never be able to speak about actions of humanoids, about sensibilities of aliens like you and me. Research on sounding and listening, as developed since the nineteenth century and as highly influential in all writing and speaking about sound till today, made strong efforts to evermore substantially analyze bodily reactions to sounds, spatial effects of sounds, and material affectations by sound. Yet, after efforts to translate sound into a new academic writing culture and to physically disassemble and reconstruct sound environments, there remains one final frontier of research in sound: to overcome the strangely installed separation between a transcendental reflection *about* and an immersive experience *in* sound. This essentialist dualism is still in full effect: speaking about sound and being in sound are considered to have next to no relation to one another. The ancient fear of falling back into quixotic ramblings and intriguing rhapsodic poetry instead of neatly laid out arithmetic equations seems to be daunting. The materiality of sound and the reflection about sound hence are taught and thought of as constituting two radically separated ontological categories. This dualism might be convincing if one postulates a separation of all humanoid thinking operations from any other sensory operations an alien might be performing. DJ, filmmaker, and music critic Kodwo Eshun confronted this in 1998:

> Instead of theory saving music from itself, from its worst, which is to say its best excesses, music is heard as the pop analysis it already is. Producers are already pop theorists. (Eshun 1998: 004)

The best accessible theory existing about an artistic artifact such as pop today—so Eshun claims here—is exactly this artifact in itself. Speaking about and being in are conjunct. The sensory body of pop and the thinking about pop cannot really be separated—no matter how skillfully. But how is this then possible? How can an artistic work be also at the same time the most thorough reflection of this very work? Are the discourses and the social fields of, say, music, sound art, and performance not distinctively separated from the social fields and discourses of research, of scholarly analysis, and of cultural critique? In pursuing a scholarly trimming of the world, such a neatly organized way of distinguishing might seem an intriguing option. And yet it is everyday life that confronts scholarly thinking with its limitations. So, a thorough answer questioning this separation might read: *Yes, and no*. The arts and their reflections are separated—and they are not. They are separated in many aspects of how they operate and how they are located and ennobled in contemporary societies focusing on economies of research and of development; but they are in many instances not at all separated in the lives of the actual authors, the *sonic personae* who are producing them—and they are even more so not separated at all in their impact, their influence, and their inspiration on other artworks. One might even dare to say: in many cases, the best critique of an artwork, or a work of music or sound, is truly a new, completely different but almost explicitly referencing artwork: a work of music or sound. These works in themselves represent a form of theory. They challenge albeit the notion of a theory that considers itself only possible in the form of a *written* argument (maybe with visual examples in the form of sketches, diagrams, statistics, or scores). This specimen of theory as part of a writing culture is still obsessively requested to be the headmaster of music:

> Like a headmaster, theory teaches today's music a thing or 2 about life. It subdues music's ambition, reins it in, restores it to its proper place, reconciles it to its naturally belated fate. (Eshun 1998: 004)

In continuing this argument, Eshun once more asserts and praises the idiosyncratic yet more detailed knowledge concerning the sounding material as well as the sensorial practices as embodied by producers, DJs, and performers:

> Far from needing theory's help, music today is already more conceptual than at any point this century, pregnant with thoughtprobes waiting to be activated, switched on, misused. (Eshun 1998: 003)

These suspected *thoughtprobes* in music: Can we really just switch them on—just like that? Activate them? Misuse them? How would we actually be able to do so? Michel Serres, the French cultural historian, mathematician, and trained seaman, has been caught experimenting with such *thoughtprobes* in musical compositions as well as in artworks, in various cultural practices as in political decisions for decades now. Book by book, essay by essay, chapter by chapter, Serres's writings unfold such an approach to theory by way of practices. With every new publication, every new lecture, he explores other forms of activating, of misusing these thoughtprobes. Serres's theoretical practice activates sensorial thinking. As in the narration of the humanoid subjectivity hidden as a *Beloved and Desired Lady* (you encountered already in the previous chapter on "Materializing Listening") in the most remote corners of a castle:

> The tower rises above the castle, the dungeon is embedded in the tower and the cell in the dungeon, a nest of structures; to reach the cell, you need to make your way through endless walls and doors, climb stairs or cross chasms via fragile aerial staircases, pass through hundreds of grilles, even a chapel. The real cell, carved out of wood, adds another box of timber framework and beams, its floor raised, within the stone walls and ceiling. No, we have not yet reached the final box in this nest of boxes: the governor has had a shutter installed in front of the window of this cubby-hole, a window through which only rats could enter; he has had every crack sealed up with oil-paper. The honoured prisoner resides behind numerous impermeable walls, thick, blind, opaque, fifteen layers of partitions. (Serres 2008: 144)

This castle is the anatomical, the logical, and the institutional castle of Western rationality: Not only is the *dispositive* a media homunculus—it surely is also a blueprint, a playground, a dramatic scheme to which the most diverse cultural practices and historical forms adhere, until today. Medieval courtship and romantic love, imperial urge and colonial raptures, experimental desires and academic explorations, technological developments as well as neurosurgical implantations and data extractions: the world as a fortified hiding place for an object of desire. *Cherchez Madame La Vérité!* Lovers and heroes, researchers and inventors, artists and performers unite in their search of excitement in adventure, in search of arousal and *catharsis*—the all too often melodramatic overcoming of one's self to become a Nietzschean *Übermensch*. This tale is one founding myth of Western subjectivity. It is not a subjectivity that rejoices in sensed matters present—but it dives, it crawls, it clutches at, and it haunts the most hidden emanations of subjectivity: The further away, the more remote, the better hidden, and closed off they are—the more rapid the desire, the urge, the greed, the will is growing to find them out, to take them out, to take them with us, to possess them. To eat them up and therefore to annihilate the desired? It is not easy to find this desired object, it might after all not even be possible to gain any access to it. It truly is an adventure—with an open ending. Serres explores this narration in order to understand what exactly is predetermining and guiding Western thinking in linear arguments, in *porphyric trees*, in *Yes/No* operations. The material side of this castle in which subjectivity is incarcerated is of major interest for Serres. The desired object that is the *sensible subject* is hidden behind walls of stone:

> The dungeon-body maintains its distance from the desired chateau-flesh. The window-eye beseeches behind the eyelid-blind and the ear hears the song of the bird-soul through its tympanum of oil-paper. Timid lovers, isolated underneath their multiple skins or rigid walls, stiff and horrified behind their battlements, whose beautiful love will be lost if ever the prisoner escaped and who will hasten to maintain their distance and throw up new obstacles, as though the only love possible were the effect of the walls surrounding lovers crashing into each other, or echoes reverberating between boxes, interferences, vibrations, harmonies, thuds; the citadel forming a giant organ. Two phantoms thrashing about inside music boxes constructed like gaols. This is the traditional notion of the body, and no doubt also that of sciences. (Serres 2008: 145)

The technological, the conceptual, and the terminological armor are what arouses the searcher and researcher: this arousal is the motor of research. A dialectic that extends to various material subtleties of this dungeon of consciousness:

> Just as the call of love circulates through the corridors, grilles and vaults of the chateau-body, haunting them, so do sense data pass through the obstacles placed into a kind of statue or automaton with twenty layers of armour, a veritable Carpathian castle, their energy purified as it makes its way through successive filters towards the central cell or instance, soul, understanding, conscience or transcendental I, to which very few gaolers hold the key. (Serres 2008: 145)

The ideal body in this tradition is built out of metals, almost impossible to transcend. It is carved out of impenetrable, indestructible granite, or even marble, as Serres describes later in *Les Cinq Sens—The Five Senses*:

> Entering the room heavily, a statue interrupts the feast, as is customary. Its marble exterior denies it the use of any of its senses. . . . Beneath the cold, smooth, untouched skin, veined like marble, the body. (Serres 2008: 188f.)

Only the rarest, most refined openings, cuts, almost wounds, and breaks in this edifice could grant possibly any access to everything around it. Sensibility and receptivity are restricted, as they seem the most noble privilege:

> Few have earned the right to penetrate the dungeon or holy of holies, the last box behind or beneath other cells: it took a priest, or a judicial figure. This is what it was to know or to love. It happened rarely. Under surveillance. Through hear-say. By twists and turns of a labyrinth. (Serres 2008: 145)

The statuary and labyrinthian dispositive of sensory perception, mediation, and cognition—as explored in the previous chapter by way of Jean-Louis Baudry—is more lasting as implemented in contemporary societies than meets the eye. It demands a surgical extraction by means of cultural history, sensory studies, and epistemology, maybe ontology:

> In my language, an organism like ours, immobile beneath a slab of marble, is called a corpse. An immaculate stone envelope covering a body, and with a statue above it, is called a tomb. An automaton, a machine equipped with an internal phantom reawakening into consciousness, is usually called a cenotaph: a black box with holes and doorways through which information can enter and exit. White marble statue or black box in the colours of mourning. Displaying a shield or coat of arms. It's hardly surprising if the experimenter who creates a window in the funeral casket should think of smell first, and toss a spray or wreath of flowers on to the stone grave or vault. The real name of the statue that arrives at the banquet—ghost, automaton, machine, hollow outline of reason bereft of sensation—is death. (Serres 2008: 190)

A humanoid alien, encapsulated in stone: This is subjectivity in Western culture according to Serres. Subjectivity needs to be isolated for these cultures, it seems—to remain this exciting goal for arousal, for penetrating, an all too obvious androcentric desire. Subjectivity is isolated in various ways: be it via isolating a *Kaspar Hauser* from all contact to any material outside world—or be it via isolating human thinking by remodeling a simulacrum of algorithms as an *Artificial Intelligence*. Both research practices assume that subjectivity would not cease to exist as soon as one would isolate it forcefully from any form of varying and of delightful material and sensory experiences. Philosophy and the sciences, technology, and cultural practices managed in these cultures to make any immediate access to thinking, to sensation, to sensibility seem as a remote and strange, a weird and arduous art no one has ever actually mastered. The process of civilization could therefore be interpreted as a process of *progressive self-alienation*. Humanoids turned to themselves, looked at themselves, listened to themselves as if they were something remote and strange and alien themselves. Whereas this operation might have provided new insights on the one hand—it provided over time a quite exotic and strange approach to the individual and its sensations. It has become almost impossible to actually sense: as sensation is conceptually only being granted via selected holes and doorways, orifices and entrance points of which the individual fearfully takes care of, fearing their penetration—and at the same time eager to pursue penetration. Western subjectivity as a concept is best represented by a shielded armor with selected and heavily controlled portals for exchange, with limited gates and lines of access, occupied by selected signals, messages, transported goods, and written propositions or graphs:

> Architecture is dead, writing has killed the building. You do not build more than screens, pages. (Serres 2014)

The underlying concepts of "separated channels of sensory perception" or of "processing sensory data" are both metaphors that went mental in Western culture and bear next to no relation to an alien's essential experience of intermodal and transmodal sensory perception in everyday life. These two metaphors of *signal processing* and of *separated channels* might be mainly following the aforementioned obsessive script of a cathartic and noble adventure to find the *Beloved Lady of Truth Inc*. Permanent and thorough self-surveillance and self-quantification seem to be the genuine target points of this obsessive script. One need actually be a statue to coherently behave according to these models. Hesitation or reflection, doubt and sensing, taking erratically more time or space for sensing—none of these idiosyncrasies would be implied in this solidified and hegemonial concept of statuarian humanoids processing sensory data in separated channels of sensory perception. The cocoon of technological dispositives in which one might find oneself confirms exactly this thinking—a prolifically materialized self-fulfilling prophecy, an autopoietic encapsulation into logocentrism: "Grammar and logic create a world in their own image" (Serres 2008: 193).

His fundamental critique of established theories of sensory perception in the Western world, in consumer media technology, in commodified psychology, market-oriented sociology, even in the commodified emanations of anatomy and medicine, this reading leads Serres to propose an alternative model. He proposes a corporeally anchored *anthropology of the senses*: "We hear through our skin and feet" (Serres 2008: 141). With Kodwo Eshun, he activates the thoughtprobes of cultural history: "We hear through our skull, abdomen and thorax. We hear through our muscles, nerves and tendons" (Serres 2008: 141). Hence, his misuse of humanoid artifacts of cultural history doesn't generate identically shaped statuarian models or closed circuits of commodified production of knowledge. His anthropological research generates something new; it is not *analyze* or *analysis*: it is *syrrhèse* or *syrrhesis* (Serres 2008: 161, Latour and Serres 1995: 122). The body, according to Michel Serres, is not only an external shell of humanoids' existence. It is very much so a genuine and crucial part of existence itself. Without our bodies there would be no existence (at least not in the way our cultures know and reflect upon it by now). Humanoids' bodies grant these aliens the sensibility and the sense for adequacy to write and to perform a culturally generative activity. The true labor in research and in the humanities, aside from all the official claims, lies according to Serres in exactly this sense: in an adequate, sensible, and fearless approach to whatever affects us—an approach that follows this guidance of affects and transforms them over time, over various situations and various forms of exchange with other humanoid aliens. But it takes time. Therefore Serres gives major advice to writers or researchers like me and probably you: We do not only need a *bouche d'or* (Serres 1985: 166), as Serres coins it, a "golden mouth" (Serres 2008: 153) that speaks eloquently; we need a *deuxième langue* (Serres 1985: 169), a "second tongue" (Serres 2008: 156) that truly and intimately tastes, silently. Sensibly. So that all these sensations could at one point (maybe at some point in the near future; but maybe also: never?) come together in a "third tongue," a "third mouth" that relies most of all on *la sapience et la sagacité* (Serres 1985: 177)—"sapience and sagacity" (Serres 2008: 163). A thorough plea for sensibility and corporeality of thinking. A plea also for a form of slow research, for a *slow scholarship* (Mountz 2015), a slow thinking. Hesitation as generative idiosyncrasy. "I am hesitant, says the third tongue" (Serres 2008: 163).

This substantial critique of a self-destructive logocentric confederation with the self-annihilating obsessions of capitalist culture, their *thanaticism* (Wark 2014), is countered by Serres's methodological approach. In his conversations with Bruno Latour—the thinker of a symmetrical anthropology of things, of networks, of a "parlement des choses"—he explicated what his main methodological intention is:

> What I seek to form, to compose, to promote—I can't quite find the right word—is a syrrhèse, a confluence not a system, a mobile confluence of fluxes. Turbulences, overlapping cyclones and anticyclones, like on the

weather map. Wisps of hay tied in knots. An assembly of relations. Clouds of angels passing. Once again, the flames' dance. The living body dances like that, and all life. Weakness and fragility mark the spot of their most precious secret. I seek to assist the birth of an infant. (Serres 1995: 122)

Serres defined his approach as a *syrrhèse* or *syrrhesis*—surely equally a slight pun on his second name, a name for the idiosyncrasies in *Serresian* writing. In *Ésprits Animaux* (*Animal Spirits*), a core chapter of *The Five Senses*, he explicates in more detail what this method entails: In syrrhesis, a usually hardly verbalized sense for something, a more bodily implicit knowledge is taking effect; a feeling, a *Gespür* (Schulze 2014), as you say in German, for the right mixture and the right proportion; for instance, when mixing physical substances in the process of creating an elaborate beverage or in the process of heating, cooling, stirring, or kneading a dish or a dough. But Serres is missing the right word for this phenomenon, this form of knowledge, this practice:

We dream indistinctly that a word capable of expressing this confluence might be acclimatized into our tongue. We cannot say concade nor syrrhesis. (Serres 2008: 161)

Missing an adequate word for this concept, he created it: *syrrhesis*. By introducing this word in the discussion of methodology, he also performs a *generative* use of language, close to the writings of Kodwo Eshun. Both authors think and argue by poetic inventions, by immersive narrations, by confluences and fictions. Both distance themselves hence distinctively from *The Adventures to Find the Mistress of Truth Inc.* Whereas Eshun never really entered this epistemological Ponzi Scheme in the first place, Serres had to make serious efforts to shake off all the learned habits, obsessions, and blackmailing of this secular, global cult. In *Animal Spirits*—obviously again a pun on pretended premodern beliefs and animisms—he willfully degrades one of the seminal texts in the history of philosophy, Plato's notorious dialogue in praise of well-educated conversation over sober binge drinking, called a *Symposium*, a feast, actually.

The guests at the Symposium hiccup, speechify or slump about, weighed down by alcohol, Plato has ensured that the banquet never takes place. They speak of love without making love, sing of this or that without actually singing, drink without tasting, speak with the first tongue—but for all the sounds they produce, do we know what wine they drank: from Chios, Corfu or Samos? (Serres 2008: 161)

And Serres asks himself, he asks us, and Plato, and he questions the whole history of philosophy: Why is this particular cultural form of thinking

(Jullien 2004) so distanced from the actions that are materially, substantially filling up the actual speakers, occupying their bodies:

> Socrates, Agathon and Alcibiades speak of love without ever making love, or sit down to eat without actually eating or drink without tasting; likewise they enter directly from the porch, over the threshold, into the dining area, without ever visiting the kitchens. Like the Gods, slaves and women stand near the stoves, where transformations occur, while the barbarians talk. (Serres 2008: 165)

In these words, Serres renders his own very noble profession, the philosophical conversation, as being irrelevant as such. Any theoretical argument one might add to this is now turned into the talk of barbarians, according to Serres—as long as it cautiously and quite ignorantly keeps the largest distance from the senses, their mingling, the bodies and their desires, appetites, their knowledge and sensibilities. Of real value could only be material processes and craftsmanship such as cooking and stirring, mixing and broiling, marinating and cutting, roasting and boiling down. All of this, yet, happens backstage in the kitchen, ensuing while the mature and male gentlemen quarrel on the main stage, pondering and politicizing, idling and babbling away. While working slaves and servile women in the kitchen are actually preparing food and drinks: in these very practices lies actual knowledge. The kitchen is the place of theory, not an office or a coffeehouse, neither a conference venue nor a TV studio. The humming production studio and the smudgy workshop, the cluttered desk in the laboratory or on the playground: this is where the sinuous dance of practice breeds new insights. While the patriarchs blather on the main stage, the women and the slaves might start a laconic dance backstage, a flirting and inventing, playing and kissing, caressing each other, tasting each other and the liquids, the fruits and the meat they indulge in—by profession and devotion. Wisdom lies in these bodies, in their dancing with a sense for the appropriate spice and stirring, cooling down and heating up. This practice *is* an epistemological one. Any chemistry of foods, therefore, needs to be regarded as inferior to the art of cooking; any analysis succumbs to syrrhesis. It is a necessary insight, a humble approval of the narrow limitations and the mostly incremental achievements even in some of the largest, most complex, thoroughly elaborated theoretical edifices—maybe, like this densely packed, perhaps overly ambitious, and at times paradoxically erratic book you are reading right now: *Every single artistic practice is superior to all art theory.*

1992: Tension in Nancy

Bodies are how humanoids exist. Sensing, smelling, touching, or listening are unimaginable without any bodily substance. Yet: could one even listen *solely* with one's body? Such a question would only be a rhetorical one, a metaphorical phrase at best, right? No.—Aside: there is probably no metaphorical phrase that is *just a phrase*. A metaphor that *means* something, to an alien like you or me, is a meaning grounded in a physical, a sensory, and a corporeal experience. The substance of a *metaphor* is its *transfer of bodies*. This *material migration*, this dynamic of humanoids, is one of the starting points for Jean-Luc Nancy's impressive corporeal phenomenology. With *Corpus*, published in 1992, he managed to teleport his readers into a thoroughly transformed and deeply globalized environment of bodies moving, living, articulating and thinking, fleeing and waiting, revolting and succumbing, overthrowing and realigning. A social and political environment under pressure of intra- and intercontinental migrations in the number of millions: a description that today, a quarter of a century later, is finally being more and more recognized as indeed factual. With Nancy, one enters a landscape of bodies, of corporeal cultures, of entities with urgent agency and erratic dynamics:

> Our billions of images show billions of bodies—as bodies have never been shown before. Crowds, piles, melees, bundles, columns, troops, swarms, armies, bands, stampedes, panics, tiers, processions, collisions, massacres, mass graves, communions, dispersions, a sur-plus, always an overflowing of bodies, all at one and the same time, compacted in masses and pulverizing dispersals, always collected (in streets, housing-projects, megapolises [sic], suburbs, points of passage, of surveillance, of commerce, care, and oblivion), always abandoned to the stochastic confusion of the same places, to the structuring agitation of their endless, generalized, *departure*. This is the world of world-wide departure: the spacing of *partes extra partes*, with nothing to oversee it or sustain it, no Subject for its destiny, taking place only as a prodigious *press* of bodies. (Nancy 2008: 39f.; emphasis in the original)

A situation of permanent migration, incessant insecurity, and scary outbreaks of mass rage and violent uprisings is being evoked in this brief narration. These situations evade the known categories and analytical distinctions on which Western philosophy and epistemology as projects of a deliberate and economically rather safe, bourgeois enlightenment rely. As soon as you might attempt to turn these situations into neatly trimmed, distanced objects of impersonal reflection, survey, evaluation, and judgment, you might either be drowning in the turbulent actions involving yourself—or be superimposing an ahistorical and roughly irrelevant structure over this heated dynamics, doomed to be falsified in no time. This is why Nancy decides to open up his writing to such a vivid description, which might seem truly scary and disturbing from the highly idealized perspective of Westernized nation states and their established cultures, economies, and everyday interactions of erudite, self-contained (and implicitly: mainly male, upper middle class, bodily not categorized as disabled) citizens. With this narration, he introduces an erratic element of guerilla dynamics into his treatise. Tumultuous fiction quite joyfully corrodes any craftily polished argument. It is an immersive and erratically moving sort of fiction that is capable of effectively introducing this for some confusingly filthy empirical world into the reduced empire of signs, propositions, and arguments that constitute an academic treatise. Such passages or fractions of empirically grounded fictions are the way empirical examples can enter theoretical writing in philosophy, cultural history, or any other field of cultural research. Yet, this is only the case as long as such a narration retains its unsettling and erratic quality—as long as it is not too hastily amalgamated, homogenized, and argumentatively eaten up by the rigid argumentative economy of a treatise. Nancy achieves this by way of returning evermore to these disturbing alien phenomena in his argument: They do not serve as neat examples—they do not even serve at all. They are not cleverly utilized and employed to serve *Truth Inc.* Not even as thoughtprobes to incite a syrrhèse. They occupy his text just because they are there. They are annoyances and disturbances: They exist.

> Strange foreign bodies, endowed with Yin and Yang, with the Third Eye, the Cinnabar Field and the Ocean of Qi, bodies incised, engraved, marked, shaped into microcosms, constellations: unacquainted with disaster. Strange foreign bodies protected from the weight of their nudity, devoted to finding their center inside, under skins saturated with signs, in effect confining their senses to a single, empty, unfeeling sense, bodies liberated-alive, pure points of light emitted entirely from within. (Nancy 2008: 7)

Nancy's body has become the humanoid alien here. His writing, hence, is—similar to Serres' and Eshun's—not only claiming an argument but also demonstrating it by transcending traditionally rigidly calculated and calibrated arguing. Nancy's narration of a continuous, postcolonial migration of bodies immerses its readers into this mutated social and political situation: this situation does not neatly present any thoughtfully defined relations between well-educated, skillfully, and rhetorically trained citizens—mostly following heteronormative principles of self-presentation, distinction by habitus, everyday practice, and adequate performative acts in an assumed public sphere. Instead it establishes a deviating concept of a humanoid's *corpus*: an area in which bodies exist, exhibit themselves, and execute their very existence. Bodies take control. A *hypercorporealism* takes place—it occupies given areas. An overwhelming impact and influx of bodies present. A mere over-presence and over-activity, an over-proximity and over-intrusion of existence. Such overwhelming bodies, bodies over bodies, exceed anything known as bodies in the established bourgeois, literary, and national cultures known from Westernized history books. The bodies Nancy is thinking about are bodies that seem in no way to be restricted, guided, or shaped by the restraints and the constraints of traditional, Occidentalized semiotics. Even more so: the whole so-called *consistent* system of interdependent and interpenetrating relations, entities, objects, actors, and their actions performed on selected objects and other actors, the whole network of actors and objects seems step-by-step to be vanishing. As Kodwo Eshun writes:

> You can't be ironic if you're being swallowed by volume, and volume is overwhelming you. (Eshun 1998: 188)

The distance between this now contemporary regime of bodies and the previous regime of bodies is introduced by Nancy with a stunning reference to and revocation of undoubtedly the one core ritual and magic trick of Catholicism:

> *Hoc est enim corpus meum*: we come from a culture where this cult phrase will have been tirelessly uttered by millions of people officiating in millions of rites.... It's our *Om mani padne* [sic] ... our *Allah ill'allah*, our *Schema Israel*. But the twist of our formula promptly defines our own most distinctive difference: we're obsessed with showing a *this*, and with showing (ourselves) that this this, here, is the thing we can't see or touch, either here or anywhere else—and that *this* is *that*, not just in any way, but *as its body*.... *Hoc est enim* ... challenges, allays all our doubts about appearances, conferring, on the real, the true final touch of its pure Idea: its reality, its existence. (Nancy 2008: 3f.; emphasis in the original)

According to Nancy and according to a science history of hermeneutics, this performative act of turning a bowl of wine into the shed blood of a martyr and founder of a religious belief, this operation enforced a deeply idiosyncratic embodiment of the very process of signifying as a cultural foundation. Contemporary cultural forms of writing, inscribing, of programming and reading, of coding and encoding, of scanning, encrypting, and decrypting, are to say the least distant offspring of this cultural obsession with turning very present material objects or artifacts essentially into representations for some absent things, ideas, concepts, inventions, imaginations. *The Son of God* as *The Beloved Ladyboy of Truth Inc.* From an alien perspective, this is truly a magic operation, a cheeky rhetoric if not demagogic trick to get one's audience to believe in a narration of thorough and universal transformation of everything around you—just by mere sign operations: The eschatology of semiosis. This eucharistic ritual as one (notably: not the only) core of Western civilization's obsession with sign operations would then necessarily be explicated by this culture's equally persistent reference to Plato's *Symposium* (as mentioned in the previous section of this chapter): the other incessantly commemorated and thus embodied situation of semiotic superiority over materialist presence and pragmatics. And yet, as Michel Serres states:

> How can it be that for the last two thousand years we have commemorated the *Last Supper*, but merely studied divine Plato's *Symposium*? . . . We have made and repeated the gesture of the Eucharist thousands of times. The Last Supper incites its own repetition through the millennia, like a star casting its light before itself; as though a particular action needed to be recorded in order not to be forgotten; as though something infinitely precious and infinitely fragile were asking us to carry it through history, passing it from one person to the next. . . . The individual representing comedy, tragedy, medicine, the media or public administration—statue, robot, apotheosis of allegory, long-dead automaton—speaks at the banquet but does not drink. Speaks of love, does not make love; speaks of wine, does not taste it. A dinner of statues, a feast of stone. Here dead words are passed about; we study them, comment on them. The allegories drink allegorical wine, allegorically; we speak about this categorically. A symposium of marbles and circuit boards. (Serres 2008: 174f.)

The weirdly idiosyncratic obsession of present hegemonic cultures with mediated and transmitted writing, with sign operations on all levels and in all areas of society, biosphere, technology, and cosmos; the predominance of turning physically present things and objects, lifeforms, and transformations obsessively and recurrently into signals and propositions: all of this could—if one dares to follow Nancy and Serres here—be traced back to a unified cultural dispositive, emerging out of the too holy complicity between the platonic banquet sans jouissance and the Christian conversion of a meal into semiosis. Again, from the perspective of an alien—not the least: alienated—anthropology, this obsession with letting *mere* sign operations, the *mere* interpretation of things, actually affect the daily life, the ongoing thinking and every single action of humanoids, this obsession is unsettling. It is an obsession of willful illusionary *doublethink*, a utopian counter-conspiracy, a craving to turn this present world into just another one—but only by the least action necessary, only by mere words and talk and imagination. Fiction replaces action. Interpretation supersedes transformation. Is interpretation then just an interpassive form of (non-)transformation? As a non-alien to this cultural practice, one might add: interpretation is—just looking into the long, theological as well as poetological and epistemological history of hermeneutics—never superficial. Just like meanings, sign operations, or metaphors are not merely added to material objects but effectively emerging out of them and transforming them at the same time, so is any meaningful interpretation equally rooted, anchored, and often actually *made* out of the material substance it refers to. It is a *grounded fiction*, a substantialized, materialized, at best a corporealized fiction or imagination. It is not just a shiny layer someone used to gloss over the raw and unpleasant world. Interpretation and resignification in this sense is more of a thorough reprogramming, a deep and almost irrevocable reordering of a humanoid's experience. Once one accepted such an interpretation as being correct, once one assimilated it into one's thinking and being, sensing and performing, once it is domesticated as a firm belief, it will not be too easy to withdraw this belief again, to *semio-surgically* extract it. From now on this belief is a fundamental condition of living and a basic semiotic operation occurring in any given moment. The life of this humanoid alien then depends on exactly this belief. The belief *is* actually the world: from now on all material samples serve mainly as convenient proof for this belief. According to Nancy, this fundamental semiosis of turning one object into an actually absent idea, this sign operation, is generating the whole canon of occidental culture: from the "*ego sum*, the nude in painting, the *Social Contract*, Nietzsche's madness, the *Essays*, the Nerve-scale, 'Madame Bovary, c'est moi,' the head of Louis XVI, engravings by Vesalius or Leonardo, the voice-of a soprano, a castrato, etc." (Nancy 2008: 5). The body of existence is hence in this cultural tradition foremost a body of interpretation—not of presence. "The *body*: that's how we invented it" (Nancy 2008: 5).

Starting with a sign operation being the foundational magic trick of Western (and now: the largely Westernized global) civilization on all levels—be it personal, cultural, artistic, scientific, or even political—starting with this operation, Nancy claims the necessity to transform exactly this pervasive approach to the body. Regardless of how complicated if not impossible such an endeavor may seem. Returning back to the overflow of bodies evoked in the author's passage cited earlier, it has become even more evident (than a quarter of a century earlier) how the long tradition of this magic trick, of evoking the invisible, the absent, the insensible, and inaudible into a semiotic presence, how all of this hermeneutic enchantment of the world is truly a fading tradition. For better or for worse. Fragments and palimpsests of various Western cultures turn into nothing more than just selected starting points for present and future cultures of an even more hybrid character, more hybrid than the excessively hybridized, bastardized, the incessantly profanizing and colonizing, joyfully usurping cultures of the West ever were. The consistency of this magic trick, a tradition between Plato and the Apostles, has already been largely decomposing for quite some time now. The remains are too often more ridiculous shreds and crumbs, weird assemblages and unsettling pastiches. Catachresis is common. In contrast to those disappearing concepts, a new notion of the body has emerged that Nancy sketches as being in a "press of bodies," "always an overflowing of bodies" (Nancy 2008: 39). It is the panopticon of a globalized world in constant and unstoppable migrating movement that Nancy sketches in his scrupulous and daring reflections with only a few sentences. This is a world in constant departure, transit and only transitory arrival—before another departure lies ahead. Such a lifeform is no longer the mere task of an intercontinental business and media class, but— much more forcibly, existential and scary, disturbing and deterritorializing— the life of humanoid aliens all over this planet. The movement of bodies in permanence is a contemporary condition of life. Kinesthetics hence might become the indispensable grounding theory for understanding culture. Humanoid aliens enter an era of spatialized thinking:

> The world is spacing, a tension of place, where bodies are not in space, but space in bodies. (Nancy 2008: 27)

The discourse of philosophy has just started a few years, maybe a decade ago, to think from a ground of spatialized existence. Thinking just begins to get its directions from the experience of entering, being, and moving in a specific location of many dimensions not too easily reducible to a zero-, one-, or maximum two-dimensional space of geometry or syllogisms. *You* enter an area that might look strange to you. In this area, an anthropology of the common alien is essential, an anthropology of unsettling habits of unknown bodies and their unforeseeable intentions. This *anthropology of the corpus*, which Nancy outlines in his small treatise, is founded on anatomical and material details of corporeal action, perception, self-perception, and experience. As such it is—as is Serres's proposal for a sensory anthropology—not a traditional philological approach to philosophy or to ontology. It is, in the end, empirical in the sense of the humanities and the arts: it is *empiricist* and *experientialist*. Both Nancy and Serres draw on the experience of everyday life and of a reflected and subtle sensibility. Both authors fervently promote this material ground as their primary source of knowledge and of insight. *Sensory tension* enters the stage of craftily performed sleights of hand, in semiotics or in logic:

> A body is therefore a tension. And the Greek origin of the word is *tonos*, "tone." A body is a tone. I don't say anything here that an anatomist couldn't agree with: a body is a tonus. When the body is no longer alive, has no more tonus, it either passes into *rigor mortis* (cadaverous rigidity), or into the inconsistency of rotting. Being a body is being a certain *tone*, a certain tension. I'd also even say that a tension is also a *tending*. Consequently, there are possibilities for ethical developments that we might perhaps not expect to find here. (Nancy 2008: 134)

As in the rest of his treatise, Nancy refers to anatomical knowledge in combination with an actually practice-based knowledge of dancers, of musicians, of cooks or of craftsmen, of practitioners of various kinds.

Similar to Serres, he draws substantial conclusions from this knowledge for the realm and the discourse of philosophy and of cultural history. Craft and performance practice hence *are* epistemologically insightful practices for both of these thinkers. They do not situate them in an ontologically detached area of existence: to the contrary, the field of practice is for them an integral *plane of immanence* (Deleuze). Practice *is* the actual area in which one is immanent—and out of which one reacts, reflects, thinks, and senses. The thinking by Nancy and Serres originates out of this immanent experience of tense practice—even more so as its further conclusions, its disconfirmations, are addressing the transcendental discourse of philosophy. This immanent experience as a firm, empirical ground to reflection qualifies this thinking as *corporeal thinking*: a sensory and a *sonic thinking* (Herzogenrath 2017).

> The world of bodies is the nonimpenetrable world, a world that is not initially subject to the compactness of space (space, as such, being only a filling-up, or at least virtually so); rather, it is a world where *bodies initially articulate space*. The world is spacing, a tension of place, where bodies are not in space, but space in bodies. (Nancy 2008: 27)

The main qualifying difference to a thinking adhering mainly to written propositions and generative sign operations is the beginning of reflecting *way before* this translation into propositional and semiotic thinking. Corporeal thinking starts with corporeal and experiential tensions, with a sense for situated, for argumentative, and for social bodies, for forms of *cohesion* (Halliday and Hasan 1976): a new style of reflection, a corporeal *Denkstil* (Fleck 1980; corporeal thinking is explored in this present book in greater detail in Chapter 6: "A Sensory Corpus"). To take *tension* as a fundamental and a legitimate starting point to thinking is to exchange the major instance of thinking: It is not anymore a thoroughly consistent, ahistorically, and often culturally and locally excessively biased established discourse network of references, discourse traditions of core propositions, and major argumentative conflicts that inhabit all the volumes of histories of Western philosophy. In contrast, these skillfully erected systems as part of historical and contemporary political power games are confronted with a substance of contemporary and reflexive tensions, in a given situation. These forms of tension are not outside any form of critique (how such a critique might be operating will be explored in Chapter 7: "The Precision of Sensibility"). Corporeal thinking might even be capable of addressing a critique not possible or even thinkable in traditional and hegemonic forms of critical thinking. This form of thinking—as proposed by Nancy—is possibly an option of sensing those blind spots that render established theoretical accounts so often rather useless, self-sustaining, and disinterested in actual experiential conflicts and entanglements. In this sense, as a discursive enrichment, an expansion of the realm of thinking into the realm of sensing and sensibility, in this strong sense, corporeal thinking truly must be regarded as a major rupture in the transculturally mutating history of humanoid thinking (of which Western philosophy must be regarded as a powerful and highly influential particular case). Corporeal thinking is transforming discourse in a way that it decisively leaves the concept of autonomous thinking behind—and reconceptualizes it as a specific form of heteronomous thinking, attached to historically and culturally specific, material, and physical environments. A materialist thinking that adheres to the sensory realities in the known and inhabited time-space continuum as experienced on this planet. What might result on the one hand in a massive restriction of thinking—as being limited to a vanishing, and possibly extremely particular case—might provide on the other hand also a massive expansion of thinking, an increase of its reference to the specific, the situated, the corporeal. This expansion must be regarded as embracing the fact of material abundance into epistemology: the abundance of things and creatures, phenomena and structures, entities and particles, gases and cultures, lifeforms and algorithms.

> Tensions, squeezings, pressures, calluses, thromboses, aneurisms, anemias, hemolyses, hemorrhages, diarrheas, drugs, deliriums, capillary invasions, infiltrations, transfusions, soilings, cloacae, wells, sewers, froth, slums, megalopolises, sheet-roofs, desiccations, deserts, crusts, trachomas, soil erosions, massacres, civil wars, deportations, wounds, rags, syringes, soilings, red crosses, red crescents, red bloods, black bloods, clotted bloods, bloods electrolyzed, perfused, infused, refused, spurted, imbibed, mired, plastified, cemented, vitrified, classified, enumerated, blood counts, blood banks, sense banks, centsbanks, traffics, networks, flowings, flash-floods, splashes. (Nancy 2008: 105f.)

To start thinking from this almost unbearable state of abundance and multiplicity—and not from a diagnosis of scarcity, to conceptualize research by assuming the supposedly endless and evermore expanding diversity and generativity of an ongoing process of entropy, is in harsh contrast to the traditional dispositive of research: a dispositive that requires to start with scarcity, with limited means and limited actors, with harshly reduced possibilities, typologies, and idealized models, with reduction of factors and massive constraints of professionally exploring the empirical world. It might be time in the twenty-first century to bring the state of epistemology on the level of contemporary and recent developments in cultural, social, historical, artistic, in scientific and engineering practices and artifacts. Writing and sign operations in general, as a major cultural technique, could hence be understood as more of a legitimizing and affirming technique for scarcity cultures. This technique that once might have been necessary as a cultural coping strategy has in recent decades turned at minimum into a rather limiting if not mischievous strategy of power and of oppression. An epistemology of abundance, a cultural technique of thinking *with*—not: against—this ongoing multiplying and regenerating of entities and emanations, of structures and phenomena; such a cultural practice might just be needed to overcome forms of hurt and rigid exploitation of all possible resources in the anthropocenic biosphere (Wark 2015a). Such a research dispositive of richness and abundance would be focusing exactly on the possible expansion, the plasticity and the materiality, the physical manifold presences of bodies, corpuses, things:

> The intimate fusion of one thing into another, of one flow into another: generalize this to as many kinds of flow as you like. (Serres 2008: 168)

This thinking would not anymore only strive for a reduction of a phenomenon to its most simple and fundamental atoms—but to observe its reactions to all the vast phenomena possibly in place very soon, today, or in the distant future. The continuous confluence of varying options and mutating entities would be the starting point of thinking: The Science of *Syrrhèse*.

> A bottle of Sauternes mimics the world, concentrates the given, delivers it suddenly: coloured, luminous, radiant, tactile, velvety, profound and caressing, suave, orchestral, a composition of brass and woodwind, spiritual. Body and world: agrarian, *floréal, prairial, vendémiaire*, wooded. Time: minutes and months, decades. Spaces: countryside and peacock's tail. Gifts or the given invade the sensorium, leaving tongues behind, travel down arteries and muscles, nerves and bones all the way to the fingernails. (Serres 2008: 182)

1998: Eshun and the senses

There is no distance with volume, you're swallowed up by sound (Eshun 1998: 188).

Possibly, this is the greatest fear of reflecting humanoids. This might be the most horrifying, negative obsession in contemporary approaches to the senses as well as to intensely immersive, physically overpowering sensory events or artifacts: to be swallowed, to be eaten up completely, to succumb to this superior and inconceivably energetic presence. The author as alien theorist and researcher meets his deepest fear. A fear out of claustrophobic, animalist, obsessive fantasies:

> There's no room, you can't be ironic if you're being swallowed by volume, and volume is overwhelming you. (Eshun 1998: 188)

This fear is not just the particular obsessive anxiety of a researching tribe of humanoids, congregating in academia. It can be found in various instances of everyday life as well as in intimate and personal relations and situations. This very fear seems actually to be a more fundamental heritage of critical thinking—not only since the last, the twentieth, but at least since the eighteenth century. In the history of science, this period stated and postulated the radical independence of research from all forces, institutions, dispositives, and narratives outside of research—and sometimes this was even tentatively realized: to be liberated from the constraints of hegemonic religious belief, of governing bodies, of a ruling ideological narration, or of institutional, even of physical limitations. This obsessive idiosyncrasy of researchers—but also of writers, artists, designers, and developers—concerning personal freedom and independence in researching, this strong hypersensitization, stems exactly from a historical moment in the eighteenth century: from a historical period when certain *weird* groups of wealthy, white, and cis-male European citizens were considering and conceptualizing themselves as being liberated from outside forces. This was a founding moment for modern research. As such, it is safe to assume that one can witness also here a kind of *invented tradition*. Yet, could it not be that this claim of independence from any affectation has become an obstacle to critical research—especially in the field of *sensory studies*? First and foremost, this strand of research requires researchers to actually be exposed to highly affective if not addictive sensory emanations—be it in fieldwork or in individual sensory practices, in listening practices:

> Not only is it the literary that's useless, all traditional theory is pointless. All that works is the sonic plus the machine that you're building. (Eshun 1998: 189)

Eshun reiterates here the diagnosis of a failing though traditional approach to theory already found in Nancy's *Corpus*. Theoretical reflection and literary interpretation, the reduction of factors and the modeling for the sake of clarification and understanding, these traditional means to achieve a sort of critical distance to highly present phenomena, they seem all in all of no help for Eshun. Instead, they seem to lock themselves out of an actually interesting, a deeply desired issue in research, in the arts, in design or composing. Distancing as strategy fails in hypercorporealized moments. Nevertheless, there might be another way to explore and to critique. This different approach though would then be in total contrast to all traditional epistemological postulates of distance and of non-involvement. It would require the exact opposite: to actually immerse oneself as a researcher even more deeply into the presence of the phenomena in question. To dive into the hot and troublesome, the scary and unsettling area of actual empiricist turmoil: This *syrrhesis* "works [as] the sonic plus the machine that you're building" (ibid.). But why should that be? Why would one as a researcher actually profit from such strategies of decreasing distance, of immersing in a research field, and of conceptualizing one's own research as a *machine to be built*? In what respect does one's research at all resemble to a machine? In what metaphorical sense is any musician, any sound artist, any media designer, even any listener, reader, viewer, or visitor of media events really building a machine these days? One would go back then to the—and it is safe to assume Eshun is alluding to this—machine theory established by Gilles Deleuze's and Félix Guattari's *machine désirante* in reference to baroque philosophies on machines by Baruch Spinoza or Gottfried Wilhelm Leibniz (Deleuze and Guattari 1972: 7). Yet, it is as well as secure to assume the general posthumanist stance Eshun tries to make. Eshun suggests leaving an exclusively intentionalist approach to humanoids' actions behind—and interpreting any alien's actions more as rather arbitrary moments of interjections in a longer sequence: a sequence resulting from vectors established by a larger and much more intertwined and heterogeneous constellation of sources, transmissions, actors, amplifiers, and emitters. The actions of one humanoid alien are never its possession alone, and never representing its intentions alone. One might as well call such constellations and their subsequent actions *a machine: an artifact with movable constituents in order to generate certain actions or certain artifacts*. One might also argue that Eshun is merely following a mechanist and signal processing mainstream as established in recent centuries of research in Western cultural history. The fact, however, that Eshun takes a humanoid actor as a mere servant of a machine, its—if you will—midwife or assistant, this fact alone clarifies: a superior category for humanoid aliens is not to be found in his non-anthropocentric anthropology. Aliens like you are nevertheless integral parts of a technocultural aggregator assembly. Nothing more, nothing less. The artifacts generated by humanoids—be they some sort of tooling equipment, certain drinks or dishes, edifices or communication devices—all these things and objects might certainly serve some purpose. Eshun, though, demands this quality also from the one category of artifacts called *theory*:

> So you can bring back any of these particular theoretical tools if you like, but they better work. (Eshun 1998: 189)

How can theory actually *work*? It is a common idiomatic phrase to state that a theoretical approach is *working*, is very *functional,* or easily *applicable*. Yet, this utilitarian understanding of theory is surely not Eshun's. How could one then put a sonic theory to the test?

> And the way you can test them out is to actually play the records. That's how you test if my book works, because I want it to be a machine. When I say works, I mean I want it to engineer a kind of sensory alteration, some kind of perceptual disturbance. I think I'd really like that very much, because even a tiny sensory disturbance is enough to send out a signal which can get transmitted. (Eshun 1998: 189)

Engineering a kind of sensory alteration, some kind of perceptual disturbance: this is the sort of reality check Eshun proposes for his theory. But his reality check is no propositional check. It does not involve the tradition of checking an argument by scrutinizing each and every assumption he makes, each and every logical (or decisively *illogical*) step he takes. This reality check is referring to an actual experience with sound: living with, dancing to sound, producing and reflecting sound—adding up to a sonic reality. Theory—according to Eshun—must be capable of being interesting and insightful, provoking and compelling, inspiring and surprising, especially in those intense moments when sound, the sound in question, is *really* present. Theory must endure the presence of its objects, even if they ridicule its impact and style—and even if this presence renders the argument meaningless or redundant. Eshun, not only a sound theorist but also a filmmaker, recognizes the artificial character of any theoretical account. Theory is dependent on its objects and subjects that cannot simply be avoided or ignored. For Eshun, maximum distance is not a convincing epistemological approach. Only if tested under the sensory pressure of the phenomenon about which it is speaking could a theory possibly be proven insightful. This test, under the most harsh and the most difficult circumstances possible for any theoretical approach, is close to the materialist critique executed by Michel Serres toward Plato's *Symposium*: Plato's theory does—by verdict of Serres—not even remotely stand the test of presence. It avoids being confronted with materialist details. Plato chickens out in front of reality.

With this proposal, Eshun leaves behind one major assumption of Western philosophy: the assumption that any theory would exist in an ontologically radically different realm than anything else in this space-time continuum. Sensory experience and everyday practices would then be irrelevant for falsifying or affirming a theory. Eshun's reality check, though, is a materialist test: to prove an argument by confronting it with the exact sensory reality it refers to. Only if it stands this test does it last. Only if his theories on Sun Ra or Funkadelic, on Kraftwerk or Drexciya, on Underground Resistance or Miles Davis stand the test in the club or while listening to those musicians, only then is it of any use. With his bold claim, Eshun proves to be one of the most radical empiricists and sensorialists of contemporary thinking: He lays the grounds for a thorough approach to a *sensory critique* (explored in greater detail in Chapter 7: "The Precision Of Sensibility"):

> You are not censors but sensors, not aesthetes but kinaesthetes. You are sensationalists. You are the newest mutants incubated in wombspeakers. (Eshun 1998: 001)

Theoretical reflections here are integral parts of a physical, intensely experienced situation: listening to a performance. Dancing to a track. Performing sound art. Being *incubated in wombspeakers*. Theory then is always a *theory out of practice*: a *theory as practice*. What the kitchen as space of practice is to Serres, the mixing desk or the sound studio is to Eshun. Sound processing software and sound generating devices of these musical practices open up a situational area in which implicit and mythic knowledge dominates and generates, resulting in new discourses, unforeseen in their logic, their thinking figures, and their ways of describing and interpreting. This theory of practice generates artifacts, tracks, that are in themselves a *syrrhesis* in Serres's sense—the same way also the writing by Eshun is a *syrrhesis*: either a sounding or a legible manifestation of a *sonic fiction*. Both design practices in sound producing and in writing about sound incorporate sensory experiences and theoretical reflections in cohesive articulations: sounds as theory and theory as sound. Theory can be a design practice—and design can be a theory practice. With this epistemology, Kodwo Eshun follows the strong lead of Jean-Luc Nancy in favor of a corporeal anthropology in combination with Michel Serres's postulate for a sensory and maximally integrating thinking. Their shared sensory anthropology demands research practices that involve an intense engagement with materials, with corporeally mixing and mingling, with sensory and immersive qualities any practitioner—be it in the studio or in the kitchen—might experience. With this step the cultural process toward a vernacular hypercorporealization has arrived safely in research: most prominent in the new research strands of *sensory anthropology* and *sensory studies* (e.g., Palasmaa 1996; Howes 2006; Pink 2009; Kalof and Bynum 2010; Classen 2012; Howes and Classen 2013). As writers, listeners, and inventors, Michel Serres, Jean-Luc Nancy, and Kodwo Eshun argue that sound is mainly to be understood as a material force that extends into the senses of humanoid and non-humanoid, of artificially and technologically generated and performing bodies. A *sensory a priori* guides and informs this thoroughly anti-structuralist, this anti-idealist and anti-essentialist, anti-hermeneutical approach to sound: an approach that serves as a guide for the non-anthropocentric and materialist anthropology of sound presented in this book.

New sensory materialism

Standing close, too close maybe, to a large, impressively dark loudspeaker. Various situations come to my mind of, well, let's say the last thirty years:

> Our body-box, strung tight, is covered head to toe with a tympanum. We live in noises and shouts, in sound waves just as much as in spaces, the organism is erected, anchors itself in space, a broad fold, a long braid, a half-full, half-empty box which echoes them. (Serres 2008: 141)

Loudspeakers are contemporary cultures' gates to sonic experience. This experience might range from early wonders of any sound reproduction in the kitchen, in the living room, or even in the office—to the many forms of audio extravaganza possible in clubs and galleries with the ambition to present sound art, experimental noise, or sonic explorations:

> Plunged, drowned, submerged, tossed about, lost in infinite repercussions and reverberations and making sense of them through the body. Sometimes dissonant, often consonant, disturbed or harmonious. Resonating within us: a column of air and water and solids, three-dimensional space, tissue and skin, long and broad walls and patches, and wiring, running through them; moorings receptive to the lower frequencies, as though our bodies were the union of ear and orchestra, transmission and reception. (Serres 2008: 141)

Technology is a means of transport by sensory experience: audio technology to travel with. Though this metaphor of travel might have started out as a merely escapist marketing claim, yet it proved quite accurately how the activity of listening forces one to relate a specific physical environment to one's own physical reality. I listen. I am a listening body. I am here, in this place. I listen to a machine listening and transmitting from another place with differing material properties:

> I am the home and hearth of sound, hearing and voice all in one, black box and echo, hammer and anvil, echo chamber, music cassette, pavilion, question mark drifting through the space of meaningful or meaningless messages, emerging from my own shell or drowning in the sound waves, I am nothing but empty space and a musical note, I am empty space and note combined. (Serres 2008: 141)

Sonic events are not a set of frequencies, of amplitudes and oscillations, of reflections and abatements in a given, arbitrary environment. In contrast, they *are* exactly this present environment in all its highly specific material aspects, its density, its dynamics, its agility and stiffness, its softness and inclination to resonance, its multitude of intertwined layers and zones, mixtures and knots that form the arena, the ground, the substance of sound. This substance of sound translates perceptually into the substance of listening, the "Substanz des Hörens" (Sowodniok 2012a). The description of this substance by models of signal transduction as well as written signal inscriptions might have been a necessary first step for research cultures of the nineteenth century. Yet in the twenty-first century, the materialist identity of a physical environment with corporeal listeners has become more and more foundational. As optics are truly different from visual aesthetics, so are acoustics truly different from auditory aesthetics: a technical model for calculating selected, idealized physical effects must not be confused with a comprehensive understanding of sonic experiences and corporeal effects in humanoid aliens in a given material environment. The analysis of sound in the framework of electroacoustic theories of communicative scarcity provides almost no feasible means for the syrrhesis of sound in a framework of technocultural abundance of sensory artifacts. The material senses are one major experiential and generative, one substantially pervasive force, according to Michel Serres. They are more massive, more powerful, more energetic, and more intrusive than all sign operations imaginable, than all hermeneutical and interpretive strata one might discover in them. It is physical evidence Serres speaks of in evidence of the culturally shaped yet anatomically manifest body. Your body and my body; both are the means by which one could possibly explore this weird space-time continuum once dared to be called "The World." From the standpoint of syrrhesis, it is hence futile and counterproductive to even try to distance yourself—as a learned habit of analysis—from any such concrete, sensory and sonic experiences.

> First, no sound event, musical or otherwise, can be isolated from the spatial and temporal conditions of its physical signal propagation. Secondly, sound is also shaped subjectively, depending on the auditory capacity, the attitude, and the psychology and culture of the listener. There is no universal approach to listening: every individual, every group, every culture listens in its own way. (Augoyard and Torgue 2005: 4)

Sound and sensory studies put a strong emphasis in the recent decade on exactly these crucial factors in sonic and sensory experience: starting from the materiality of mobilized listening (Bull 2003; Gopinath and Stanyek 2014), over the highly dynamized and physically intrusive qualities of sound in specific urban environments and its architecture (Thompson 2002; Blesser and Salter 2007), up to the "distributed subjectivities" (Kassabian 2013) attached to material streaming sound, listening devices and connected listening constituting a ubiquitous listening environment around each individual listening persona. Listening and sounding have been recognized as material in their most genuine effects and qualities. *Sonic materialism* takes this insight now as its irrefutable starting point:

> This materialist theory of sound, then, suggests a way of rethinking the arts in general. Sound is not a world apart, a unique domain of non-signification and non-representation. Rather, sound and the sonic arts are firmly rooted in the material world and the powers, forces, intensities, and becomings of which it is composed. If we proceed from sound, we will be less inclined to think in terms of representation and signification, and to draw distinctions between culture and nature, human and nonhuman, mind and matter, the symbolic and the real, the textual and the physical, the meaningful and the meaningless. Instead, we might begin to treat artistic productions not as complexes of signs or representations but complexes of forces materially inflected by other forces and force-complexes. (Cox 2011: 157)

In these foundational paragraphs by Christoph Cox, it becomes clear that sonic materialism is unthinkable as separated from complex sensory constellations. Sonic materialism necessarily implies *sensory materialism*. In the Westernized and highly networked societies of this planet, every single room of one's homes or offices, one's shopping environments or administrative, even industrial complexes, is now occupied by materially impressive, effective and impactful loudspeakers, by speaker systems and individual headphones. Electroacoustically wired membranes for recording and reproducing sounds are cohabiting with humanoid aliens in every space and every moment: in clocks and jewelry, in trousers and hats, in shoes and bicycles, in doorbells and coffee machines. The impact of sound is ubiquitous. Loudspeaker culture, as well as headphone culture, evolved massively in the last decades—alongside the epidemic expansion of computer technology into the tiniest cracks and details of everyday accessories, clothing, and furniture. This technological colonization of the material world with sound recording, transmitting, and reproduction devices is a constant reminder of the general materiality of listening and sounding—even if not mainly technologically supported. My body and your body, so one might recognize, is as much a listening device and a sounding instrument as any refined piece of commodified audio technology. Maybe even more so? New inventions of this commodified audio technology might albeit still be a very first, a very tiny step into materially colonizing the nanoscopic sensory territories of humanoid aliens (Howes 2006). The material culture of sound, hence, is as much a technological culture as it is part of body practices, of popular culture, of fashion fads, of artistic practices, and of intimately obsessive idiosyncrasies, of nauseous percepts and voluptuous affects (Biddle and Thompson 2013). The thoughtprobes have been activated. "Take time, remain silent, taste" (Serres 2008: 157).

PART TWO

The sonic persona: *An anthropology of sound*

CHAPTER FOUR

In auditory dispositives

The microphone as poem

It is an early morning. A cab brought me to a public radio station in Berlin, where a helpful assistant caught me at the main entrance, guarded by security officers and the usual technologically highly elaborated gadgetry, and some ridiculous props of the globalized security theater these days. Via elevators, long aisles, waiting rooms, and more elevators, I'm brought to a main studio where the interview will take place. After a few seconds of timid small talk to the sound engineer behind the desk, the assistant points me to the person who will interview me. As sometimes happens with radio people, the physical and the vocal appearances are maximally divergent. You can sense how vocal skills can—at least in some humanoid aliens—be a lot more trained and refined than the visual attire, habit, posture, facial expressions, looks, or clothing. A bit insecure, I take off my coat. I try to focus on what I might need as written material for this little interview to remind me of what would be important to say. The interview—as the moderator is telling me—will be not much longer than six to eight minutes—which qualifies as an extraordinarily long interview format by the standards of radio and TV in the early 2010s. Additionally, they will be playing one (or even two!) brief examples of music and sound art we will speak about. Finally, I find my seat. I put all the papers, flyers, notes, and my mobile phone on the table. An assistant brings a little bottle of still water for my voice to be sufficiently fluent in the interview. I try to find my best speaking position at the table; not a trivial task to do: In front of me is the rather large and impressive microphone being adjusted to my body size; I am seated in a quite comfortable but unfamiliar chair. In the following seconds and short minutes before the interview, I try to make eye contact with my interviewer, as well as the sound engineer behind the glass in the control room. And again: I try really hard to focus on what I am prepared to say; what issues I think could be interesting for listeners to hear about. What can I say at this time of the day—it is an early Thursday afternoon—that might effectively catch a listener's attention? I breathe in, I breathe out. I try to calm down, to relax. To feel at home in this—to say the least—thoroughly technical and not at all neutral environment. An environment made for technology.

The interview begins. Just before the start, I manage to try speaking under these very specific conditions, my head now under the heavy but very comfortable headphones so common in radio stations. By some small talk with the moderator, I try my speech and adjust how close I should be and how comfortable I can be speaking in front of this huge microphone apparatus. I do not want to appear too loud or too aggressive, but I also do not want to sound too remote, too wispy or weirdly distant. Remembering this situation now, it seems I spoke excessively distinctly and in a rather slowed down tempo—which would mark a certain contrast to my more syncopated and dynamic (at times accelerated and at others decelerated), even stuttering, colloquial way of speaking. Apparently I intended to provide the most agreeable vocal stream for any listener not familiar with my issue, my voice, my way of speaking. I adapted, hence, to the vocal, situated, and technological framework of listening, sounding, recording, and transmitting, the man-machine apparatus of radio voice-transduction established in every radio studio: *I speak now, in this few minutes, exclusively for this microphone, with this microphone—and for and with all the people connected to this.* In such a recording studio situation, a microphone implies and materially represents a large audience of many thousands or more (a humanoid alien's imagination of people in large numbers is still very fallible). Though I felt a certain urge to do so, I did *not* actually close my eyes, which I would probably have considered rude and weird toward my interviewer, a person whom I intended to approach more cordially and to engage on a personal level. Nevertheless, in my imagination, I shut out my vision, as I do while on a sound walk or while in a listening session: while my eyes are still physically open, the perceptual focus lies almost exclusively on the audible. While any visual effect is registered, it rarely induces any reaction in me. Blinded with eyes wide open. In this perceptual habit, I listen foremost to the two voices fed back into my studio headphones: the interviewer's and mine. Those two voices are the only interesting and meaningful sound sources in this radiophonic, auditorily mediated space. While speaking, I carefully try not to listen to myself too much, but to follow major ruptures and dynamic changes in my speaking, adjustments to the recording apparatus and reactions or affectations of my interviewer—considering likewise his speaking dynamics, ruptures and accelerations, allusions and references. Speaking into a microphone means to speak in an intimate, seductive, tender way, caressing the diaphragm of this machine—and at the same time knowing and respecting that this intimate way of speaking extends to possibly thousands or more listeners in a wide variety of listening situations. We are speaking *Microphone Poetry*.

The auditory dispositive of talk radio could be outlined as follows: a dispositive built around the engineering practices following physical acoustics and the signal processing artifacts of radiophonic recording, postproduction, and transmission. The rooms in which radio is performed, produced, and post-produced are clean rooms. Not in the aseptic sense of clean rooms void of bacteria, germs, liquids, or dust, but in the sense that these locations are mainly not built and not conceived for the well-being or even for the sheer joy of alien humanoids. Recording and producing studios are, obviously, built foremost for the well-being and the joy of electric currents, of electroacoustic machines, and of acoustic signals. Signal transduction is the sacred activity worshipped in these locations. All other activities and entities providing this activity—cables, wires, circuits, motherboards, disks and membranes, engineers, journalists, producers, directors, speakers, or musicians—have to be subordinated. These architectural spaces are in a radical and object-oriented sense not at all made for humanoid aliens of any sort. Any humanoid appears here to be more of a hindrance, an annoying and unnecessarily complexifying disturbance whose resistance factor by its bodily liquids, skin particles, dust, or stupidly anti-transductive behavior needs to be minimized. The microphone, as well as the whole technological apparatus built around it, might therefore be interpreted as a sort of *poem*. The mixing desk is a poem. The sound processing software is a poem. Even the hard drive on which recordings are stored is a poem. The studio is a poem (Abbate 2016).

The technology for recording, producing, and reproducing radio transmission—as well as other audio artifacts—relies on a wide variety of assumptions and laws, claims and regulations, aspirations and affordances. This complex apparatus is fed by historical studies from natural and engineering sciences as well as by ambitions for generating a maximum revenue as part of business models in the entertainment and the media industry. These studies and ambitions were carried out by a large number of humanoids on many parts of this satellite in the recent century, involuntarily even more coordinated, even more coherent and cohesive than ever before. Following research in the field of science and technology studies, it became apparent that scientific findings, together with inventions of commodities and products, with ever new strategies of marketing, propaganda, and seductive forms of storytelling, generated one of the most impressive collective artifacts in humanoids' history (Sterne 2012). Audio technology and media technology combined to provide one of the most far-reaching distributed and culturally ubiquitously implemented forms of artifacts that demand particular practices from humanoids. This cultural artifact is relying on specific capacities of technology—and therefore is foremost respecting the needs of technology. Though it gets adapted to the somewhat idiosyncratic needs of those humid, dusty, germy dirt bags, those meat sacks that tend to call themselves rather cockily "Humans" with a big H. Alas, the institutions of media and radio production make it necessary to provide at least a certain amount of agreeable amenities for those meat sacks: there are comfy chairs, and humanoids even get offered water to drink—though any liquid is really life-threatening for electromechanical or electronic lifeforms—there might be a coat hanger, and—lest we forget—the room temperature is also distinctively more adjusted to humanoid than machine requirements. Such operating environments for machined entities can be found scattered all over various territories of contemporary intensely networked societies. As a humanoid—what I allegedly am—it is necessary for me to adapt to the new and evermore rather erratically transforming environmental conditions a new machine or machined entity might need. In a certain sense, I am (moreover: *We, Humanoid Aliens,* are—as a single life form) entering, rather forcefully, this empire of machined creatures. In this technocultural sphere, humanoids might still be serving as engineers or controllers and—not least—as inventors and developers of these new, generative, and procreating entities. Yet, the ideal environment for machined operations is never the ideal environment for humanoid pleasure. It is a specific, originally man-made symbolic order of engineering, production, and operation, rooted in our nineteenth century's historical imaginary of invention. Coming from the everyday practices of a humanoid alien of the twenty-first century, such a machined environment around a microphone is truly unreal, antique, an obsessive, outdated fetish—as unreal as might humanoid practices be for machined actors. Though perhaps in a joyful way:

> The microphone sound is not realistic: microphones don't filter. We filter, we have perceptual filters—when we concentrate on something . . . we hear something. (Petzold 2010: 220)

The microphone as artifact scans the pressure waves and translates their environmental effect into signals. It is a poem in process of translating percepts. The recording diaphragm is more of a tactile sensor than an incredibly subtle and fragile ear. A microphone does not even physically *hear*: at most, it performs acts of tactile receptivity. Hearing with one's skin. Microphone recordings hence represent a historical approximation of more complex forms of corporeal listening of the twenty-second and twenty-third centuries.

Scarce signals

Transmission and signal processing are key operations in the machined dispositives of contemporary networked cultures. They are the structuring forces in the construction of microphones or video cameras, in online messaging, and in wireless devices. These machined activities provide the foundations for everyday life in the twenty-first century that have been constructed as a technological advancement in the twentieth century. The models of communication, of transmission, and of apparatuses the societies of alien humanoids run on are therefore relying on a set of theories of signal processing. Without these theories and models, contemporary societies could not operate the same way they do today. Following the ideal of careful and reflected construction inherent in the culture of engineering that provided these theories, the definitions of the informational character of signals transmitted are crucial for subsequent conclusions and developments. One of the foundational writings of information theory and of signal processing was published as *A Mathematical Theory of Communication* in 1948:

> By a communication system we will mean a system [that] consists of essentially five parts:
>
> 1   An information source which produces a message or sequence of messages to be communicated to the receiving terminal.
> 2   A transmitter which operates on the message in some way to produce a signal suitable for transmission over the channel.
> 3   The channel is merely the medium used to transmit the signal from transmitter to receiver.
> 4   The receiver ordinarily performs the inverse operation of that done by the transmitter, reconstructing the message from the signal.
> 5   The destination is the person (or thing) for whom the message is intended. (Shannon 1948: 380)

It was this concise definition from Claude Shannon's pivotal article that truly excited researchers and readers in past decades. This definition can be recognized as one of the germs that so prolifically provoked the technological imaginary and generated a vast amount of all the technological inventions cohabiting with alien humanoids. This fivefold definition triggered the networked societies of the twenty-first century. The technological imaginary of engineering culture as erected in the nineteenth century anticipated this definition quite eagerly. The definition itself is a pinnacle of minimalist and structuralist beauty: a humble hymn to concise naming, describing, and phrasing. An *information source*, a *transmitter*, a *channel*, a *receiver*, and a *destination*—"a person (or thing)"—is all you seemingly need to describe "a communication system." The beauty of this definition is as breathtakingly simple as definitions in mathematics and physics need to be. A beauty of naming, constructing, evoking, and developing that immediately inspired its readers. Engineering culture's most prolific germ occupied and populated this solar satellite with its artifacts, its apparatuses, and its products. The victory of Shannon's definition seems to be proved by the pervasive existence of consumer products and specialized tools running on its logic. Any humanoid alien living on this planet is being part of, being educated and trained in, Shannon's logic and style of thinking, its *Denkstil* (Fleck 1980). "Grammar and logic create a world in their own image" (Serres 2008: 193). The criminalist and philological precision, the cleverness of reducing necessary evidence to construct an argument, the well-trained skills in analytical philosophy, in mathematics, in physics, in natural sciences, as well as in engineering; this way of thinking has been seeded all over this planet. No humanoid alien intending to be taken seriously would willfully object to the fundamental truth phrased in *A Mathematical Theory of Communication*. This thinking style of engineering cultures as operating in the nineteenth century has become the foundational logic of everyday cultures in the twenty-first century. Its poetry of concise reduction, of idealized modeling, and of connecting distinctly defined terms can truly be considered the minimalist standard of research. Yet, almost every single detail in the definition by Claude Shannon is wrong.

Let us walk through this definition to observe the various skillful operations of idealizing, reducing, and isolating abstract concepts (Chandler 1994). First, one encounters in this definition the reduction to one singled out and uninterrupted *information source*, a *transmitter* whose only activity is operating on one—weirdly distinct—message; then there is one *channel* that has no other purpose but being a medium for transmission; then again, only one *receiver* equally exclusively occupied with the reverse operation to the transmitter; and finally, there is one distinct destination which is, a, well, "person (or thing)": truly a strange equation of person and thing that could inspire (or is inspired by?) bitter sarcasm but is essentially incorrect. This whole definition is correct only for so long if applied to its original reference field—that is, the field of militarily organized and applied information transfer. In this specific social field of organizing activities by humanoid and non-humanoid actors, it might serve as a correct way of describing and organizing collaborative actions, *only* in this culturally specific, highly refined, and almost insanely, if not obsessively idiosyncratic, field of social conduct. What makes Shannon's definition so incredibly wrong is its application to everyday circumstances with all their highly complicated and amalgamated mingledness that experientially exceeds any reduction to well-defined terms and atoms. Shannon's definition is hence wrong for one tragic fallacy: it assumes that this model is not merely a situated and relationally descriptive but a thoroughly *normative* model for all situations of humanoids interacting. The correct description of one technical process turned into a wrong model by expanding it into a general model for all communication, way beyond its original field of discovery. The promise of global truth is devastating.

As this definition of "communication system" is a theoretical concept that was developed in wartime and under the influence of a war economy and its efforts to merely survive and to use all the resources at its best, the definition, as well as the whole theoretical apparatus of information theory, has to be regarded a result of this historical era: an era of *scarcity*. Information theory is probably the most unlikely result of historical scarcity economies. But as well as signal processing, it carries the epistemological birthmarks of this historical period in which shortage was the major experience for many citizens in Europe—and it was not so remote an experience for any military personnel on duty in the United States. The ontology of the apparatus implicit in this incredibly influential theoretical outline is therefore pervasive. With *shannonist* thinking, modern cultures enter a ubiquitous imaginary of engineering, consisting of apparatuses, of command chains, of well-defined components, and of equally well-defined processes and results. This imaginary of military engineering might well be appropriate for a lifeform under a military dictatorship or a state in permanent, infinite war. But this field of military activities cannot be taken seriously as a general example of how humanoid aliens lead their lives. It can serve as an example for military organization itself, for life and culture in wartimes—but it would be arrogant, preposterous, and somewhat ignorant to assume this social field could serve as model for social interactions in almost every other field of humanoid lives (even if the *militarization* and *securitization* of everyday life in the late twentieth century seems to insinuate such a trajectory: e.g., Gillis 1989; Hogan 1998; McEnaney 2000; Roland 2001; Buzan, Wæver, and Wilde 1998; and Balzacq 2011). And yet, exactly this insane transfer happened by way of the engineering imaginary becoming the fundamental condition of life in networked societies. Idiosyncratic militarization is an underlying blueprint for activities in the areas of economy, of politics, of communication, even in design and the arts, in music, and in performance arts. Militarized reduction as a model of connecting has become hegemonic. In the early twenty-first century, it has become increasingly difficult (in some areas even impossible) to describe, to understand, and to analyze the relations and activities of humanoid aliens *without* any direct or indirect reference to military organizations. The theory of signal processing and its subsequent offspring contributed strongly to this development. Hence, consumer culture and everyday lives are militarized just by the use and application of signal processing imagery, models, terms, and concepts of actors and their activities. The dispositive of signal processing is ubiquitous—and so is the dispositive of military organization. The technological dispositives dominant in the early twenty-first century are inherently representing military organizations and relations. Thus, if one speaks of *signals* and of *processing*, of *transduction*, of *information sources*, of *transmitters*, *channels*, and *receivers*, even of *messages* and of *communication,* one is engaging in and actually affirming the historical discourse and the imagery of engineering cultures represented in the nineteenth-century military dispositive.

Moreover, this discourse of scarcity and of maximally effective exploitation of resources has economically and politically massive repercussions that will be discussed in a later section of this chapter (titled Dispositive's Capitalization). At this point of the chapter, though, it is of more interest to unfold the imaginary of historical engineering cultures implicit in the logic of signal processing. At the beginning of this chapter, the microphone and the whole circuit of signal transduction around the recording, storing, and reproduction facilities of a radio or a recording studio was described as a poem: a carefully constructed, rather fragile and subtle structure, invented for a single self-serving purpose. This fragile structure in the studio needs to be enveloped in an appropriate atmosphere and temperature; it must be secure of liquids, dust, particles, and harmful electrical currents, as well as magnetic induction. At the same time, this fragile, incredibly craftily erected web of circuits and diaphragms, of pressure waves and magnetized and demagnetized materials, is supporting the model of recording, storing, and reproducing: It is the most influential version of an *auditory dispositive* today. In this version, the dispositive promotes a thoroughly idealist concept: a concept that sound can be reduced—without any substantial losses—to electrically transduced signals; that these sound signals can subsequently be processed and surgically amputated; that they can finally be converted and transmitted—and in the end of these endless mutations, the original sound could be reproduced in a vast array of heterogeneous listening situations. The signals into which the scanned pressure waves of sound are translated are taken as the whole of sonic experience—by means of acoustics. With those signals, one is led to believe that one has full access to all possible sounds: engineering idealism, a Platonism of signal transduction, is in full bloom. This blooming of the signal, though, is not a blooming of sound: It is *a translation of sound*, a very versatile and joyful, an exciting and incredibly generative translation—but this translation of acoustics into a *poem of processing* is not a sonic experience. It constitutes a *signal experience*. If one really intends to explore and unfold the appropriation of sound happening by humanoid aliens, one needs to leave behind the notion of the *signal*—and the whole tragic, historic, and political discourse around signal processing. This discourse of scarcity and of military utilitarianism is in dire need of a hyperjump into contemporary conditions of humanoid aliens in which scarcity and military defense might represent deep annoyances and disturbing interjections—rather than major and substantial issues of everyday lives. The distance in lifeform and in concepts becomes obvious in another passage of *A Mathematical Theory of Communication* in which the definition of a "fundamental problem of communication" exposes the truly obsessive weirdness, the compulsively poetic strangeness in this concept:

> The fundamental problem of communication is that of reproducing at one point either exactly or approximately a message selected at another point. (Shannon 1948: 1)

In relation to sound, almost no humanoid alien would seriously state that it is of sole importance *to reproduce at one point either exactly or approximately a message selected at another point*. This goal might be urgent if constructing a military model for transmission of orders and signals under conditions of scarcity and warfare. But unless you and I are part of a military operation, we might at times engage in quite different, deeply joyful, or instead rather tentative experiences concerning sounds. Sonic experience—at least outside military operations—is complexly layered: it is a flux of polysensorial events, transgressing one's corporeal borders. It is possible to think about sonic processing not merely in terms of routing and splitting, addition and subtraction, but in terms of a fluidity, of a continuous and erratically changing stream and flow—a voyage of liquidity (Rodgers and Sterne 2011). This deeply visceral joy of richness, of the genuine luxury in any sonic experience, stands in harsh contrast to the feeble means used to transmit the one and only message: the distinct and differentiated signals soldiers and officers in an army might expect to receive or to transmit. Quite bluntly, Shannon constitutes in his article a thoroughly detached realm of poetic signal communication in the style of military orders—a realm that nevertheless bears next to no relation to sonic experiences in everyday lives: "These semantic aspects of communication are irrelevant to the engineering problem" (Shannon 1948: 1). The deeply colonialist and imperialist imprint of nineteenth-century research cultures, the urge to overpower the findings and to have them processed following the orders of a master of one's own kind, is inherent in Shannon's approach to the material continuum of sound that he intends to translate into signal sequences (cf. Rodgers and Sterne 2011). As soon as one would make an effort to approach sounding materiality with a *non-colonialist*, a *non-imperial* approach, signal theory and the idealist engineering ideology of signal processing are no longer options.

In the writings of Claude Shannon and subsequent research on the construction of communication and signal processing as part of an information theory, one can observe a major historical point in the anthropology of media: *the invention of transmission*. It is a truly idealist concept that translating rich and visceral materiality into scarce signals would actually be possible—as would the subsequent transmission of such signals in order to reproduce materiality in its entirety. First and foremost, this concept adheres to an underlying model of knowledge production, of commodified scientific research, and of industrial distribution and maintenance of technological inventions. The supposed supremacy of this predominant model of research—encountered recurrently in previous sections and chapters of this book—is driven by an urge to gain unhindered and utilitarian access to sound in the form of parameters that can easily be operationalized. Yet, any claim of completeness, whether in research or in other areas of humanoid culture, is foremost a symptom of unreflected incompleteness rather than anything else. Individual flaws and failures, shortcomings and limitations, exist and can never be undone completely. Nevertheless, this exact obsession with perfect, unlimited flawlessness plays a central role in the ontological realm of objectivity, by means of institutional credos, educational training, and particular illusions. The individual obsession with flawlessness that leads humanoids to engage in research—as young kids, adolescents, or adults—is but closely connected to the hope and dream of complete access to *This Whole World*. The major approach of usability, of instrumentality, and of feasibility represents the most attractive, somehow even sexually loaded, magnetism that radiates from the social field of engineering as well as from the technological sciences. It constitutes an imaginary, a desire to construct or to codevelop at least a part of *This World* anew (the social field of humanities as well as the arts engages in such desires as well—they will be explored in the third part of this book: "The Precision of Sensibility"). What exceeds this imaginary of transparent access and instrumentalization, its implied concepts, technologies, practices, situations, discourses, and habits, all of this outside the realm of operationalized sound, can rarely be articulated. More often it seems rather absurd or even insane to just desire these non-utilitarian aspects of sound. Humanoid aliens are listening to sound in the twenty-first century mainly in auditory dispositives (Kassabian 2013): under technological circumstances of signal transduction, signal processing, and transmitted and amplified sound, the sensory lives of listeners are taking place. The symbolic order of engineering culture has not only been structuring auditory media technology but predetermined auditory culture as well. What cannot be transduced is virtually nonexistent in acoustics. The auditory dispositive as an overarching *machine to hear for us* (Sterne 2003) claims precisely this form of completeness, of ultimate transparence, and, so to speak, an end of history in audio engineering. Humanoid aliens like you and me are living right now in this materialized imaginary of engineering culture.

The Apparatus Canto

The apparatus is one of the desired objects and goals of engineering culture. As soon as basic research in either research field can be transfigured into a machined representation, into a machined form of signal processing and a machine for commodified production, as soon as this transfiguration into reproducible apparatus behavior has been happening, only then is a research result considered as meaningful and impactful under the spell of engineering culture's imaginary. Building an apparatus is proof of concept, even in the sonic fiction of Kodwo Eshun: "All that works is the sonic plus the machine that you're building" (Eshun 1998: 189). The machines at the center of cultural activities, though, are not so much machines for sonic induction of corporeal experiences and enjoyments, but machines in line for a thoroughly transforming cultural process:

> Everything the military entertainment complex touches with its gold-plated output jacks turns to digits. Everything is digital and yet the digital is as nothing. No human can touch it, smell it, taste it. It just beeps and blinks and reports itself in glowing alphanumerics, spouting stock quotes on your cell phone. Sure, there may be vivid 3D graphics. There may be pie charts and bar graphs. There may be swirls and whorls of brightly colored polygons blazing from screen to screen. But these are just decoration. The jitter of your thumb on the button or the flicker of your wrist on the mouse connect directly to an invisible, intangible gamespace of pure contest, pure agon. It doesn't. (Wark 2007: 6)

Unlike the abused machines for sonic experience, these fundamentally military machines continue the project of signal transduction into the realm of humanoid experience, into everyday sign operations, into *semiosis*. In the foundational writings of information theory, however, the semantic impact of a signal transduction is recurrently denied in order to retain the idealized habit of objectivity in an untainted system, that is not contaminated with the ugly stains, jizz, and spit of humanoid aliens. From the perspective of engineering culture, as soon as machines are built on the foundations of signal processing, the semantic becomes a necessary contamination to deal with. The idealized imaginary of a neatly structured circuit of scanning, processing, and producing is still at the core of building an apparatus: it just got tragically confronted with the materiality of bacteria and ambivalence, particles and doubt, liquids and erratic behavior. Following Jean-Louis Baudry's concept of the apparatus and its transfer to the field of auditory culture by Rolf Großmann—as explicated in Chapter 2 in this book—I might now dare to outline the machined aspects of an anthropology of sound in the narrower sense. Between 1865 and 1954 the engineering sciences and researchers such as Hermann von Helmholtz, Harvey Fletcher, or Leo Beranek laid the foundation for contemporary concepts of listening: the auditory knowledge of signal transduction and auditory cognition has been established. A focus on physiological and physical aspects of sounds promoted the invention and establishment of various highly utilitarian descriptions of how sound propagates and how humanoid aliens perceive sound: Sound was to be transformed into distinct, measurable, operational units to further refinement, reflection, commodification, selling, and extraction of data. The industry of audio technology and its subsequent dispositives is virtually implied in these first research efforts by Hermann von Helmholtz. This highly utilitarian approach to sound obviously provided access to research politics and industrial production of audio technology of the period. Research today, also done in order to publish this book obviously, relies on these former efforts. The auditory dispositives of today and their implemented artifacts are on the receiving end of these pivotal research efforts. Five crucial constituents in this research since the mid-nineteenth century were needed to make this possible: First, the work of the aforementioned researchers on the quantitative, material, and corporeal properties of sounding and listening; second, their efforts to make all of this accessible to a broader interested public; third, their obsession with the strictness and the clarity of physical modeling; fourth, the translation of sonic experiences into a mathematically readable sign language; and fifth and finally, their endeavor to secure the reproducibility of their results. All these five constituents together provided the ground to establish an *auditory dispositive* of amplified, transmitted, and mediated recording, storing, and listening. An *apparatization of listening* was promoted. It was their pride, their scientific joy, their personal victories to make possible the auditory media culture of the late twentieth century. Hence, the translation of materialities and corporealities of sound is—as mentioned above—the first critical issue in constructing and operating such an apparatus. At the same time, this problematic issue represents the challenge proudly accepted by engineering culture: to be capable not only of accessing these erratic fluctuations of materiality—but also to process these and to transform them into a continuous stream of machine-readable data, an informatic string of signals and messages to operate. The apparatus, therefore, is a machine to transfigure the hard particles and things received from the environment into the soft signals and the vast potential of signal processing:

> The given I have called hard is sometimes, but not always, located on the entropic scale: it pulls your muscles, tears your skin, stings your eyes, bursts your eardrums, burns your mouth, whereas gifts of language are always soft. Softness belongs to smaller-scale energies, the energies of signs; hardness sometimes belongs to large-scale energies, the ones that knock you about, unbalance you, tear your body to pieces; our bodies live in the world of hardware, whereas the gift of language is composed of software. (Serres 2008: 113)

This confrontation between the hard, erratic materials, actions, activities, bodies and their struggles, and the seemingly stainless, idealized, lighthearted, genuinely poetic transformations of signs and signals lies at the core of the engineering sciences. Their aspired goal to construct an apparatus to perform this transformation successfully is truly a humanoid ambition and hubris at its best. This ambition to turn unforeseeable actions into foreseeable models, formulae, algorithms, and production lines gives way to an admiration of apparatuses as the most noble results of a humanoid's activity. In admiring the apparatus, in praising the engineering genius, humanoid aliens are actually praising themselves: their own genius of constructing, creating; inventing, making, producing, promoting, and selling. The cult of the apparatus at the center of engineering culture and media technology is actually a cult of self-adoration—even going one crucial step further:

> In the world of Helmholtz, Scott, and, later, Blake, Bell, Edison, and Berliner, sound's reproducibility was based on a mechanistic conception of hearing crystallized in the tympanic function. The goal was to have our ears resonating in sympathy with machines to hear for us. (Sterne 2003: 81)

An almost mystical, theosophical thinking in the field of science and technology exposes itself in this historical line. It seems that auditory research—taken as an exemplary case of engineering culture of the nineteenth century—made the basic assumption that a machine concerned with sound must necessarily resemble, both structurally and haptically, those organs that seemed to represent listening devices in a humanoid *Homunculus*. A truly unsettling and thoroughly precritical thinking style in analogies is revealed here that bears all traits of an antimodernist *Unio Mystica*-belief. Life on Earth is—in this *Denkstil*—modeled after one main superior model, the *Grand Récit*, woven around one major *Supersignifikat*, the last and ultimate point of reference: "The Lord" as ultimate reference in Christianity. Following this deeply religious and idealistically conceptual line of argument, any organ of a humanoid *must* necessarily represent the best invention for its purpose as the creation of a humanoid alien itself is a direct product of the first and last creator. *The Lord* must *naturally* be the best engineer, the best inventor, and the best researcher—be it in audio communications, information theory, or media technology. Humanoid anatomy is cherished by researchers of the nineteenth century for its very similitude to *The Lord*, or at least to a supposed godlike entity, be it in Plato's *Heaven of Ideas* or in the Renaissance-concept of an all-encompassing "Book of Knowledge." The anthropomorphized last reference and *Supersignifikat* (or supersignified) needs to provide the blueprint for all engineering, all inventing of prosthetics, and all constructing of media technologies. In video cameras and stereo hi-fi, in *Von Neumann*-architectures and in neural networks, the culture of humanoid aliens is still worshipping its very own rather arbitrary physical appearance and historically rooted cultures—and at the same time, a godlike entity is believed to have created all of this. The *anthropomorphization of technology* hence takes place by referring to a higher force—already anthropomorphized beyond belief.

Starting with such religious inspirations for research, a pervasive, truly anthropocentric *tympanum* culture materialized: an idealized idea of the tympanum in the humanoid ear basically generated all the swinging, receiving, and at the same time emitting and transmitting diaphragms of which microphones and loudspeakers are made. This membrane and its co-membranes of added and interlinked side-microphones or side-speakers, be it for deeper bass frequencies or massively higher frequencies, are the main electrified sound sources inhabiting this planet. They occupy public places, urban zones of transition, and your personal, more intimate spaces. Diaphragms are the physically dominating sonic actors in contemporary networked societies. There are almost never—or only very rarely—sound events that do *not* adhere to a throbbing membrane. Loudspeaker music is ubiquitous and dominant. In terms of a sensory and material anthropology, when you are listening to a speaker's membrane—incorporated by a net of oscillating electricity, propagating through copper and fiber threads—you are listening to electrically swinging metals, modeled to resemble selected parts of a humanoid ear. This power grid, its cables and connections, its sockets and hubs, its forks and outputs, represents the machine environment as a whole, wrapping and constricting the globalized humanoid culture on this dirtball. *The auditory dispositive is an anthropocentric excess.* As Rolf Großmann proposes in continuation of Jean-Louis Baudry, the dispositive as an analytical category makes it possible to transcend this anthropocentrically limited perspective of cultural and historical immanence. A new, non-anthropocentric perspective then provides descriptions of the apparatus that ironically reveal the facets and dependencies of this anthropocentric and deeply religious modeling. The ongoing hymnic praise of technology and of apparatuses, the worshipping of electricity and of fossil fuels, of expansive and exploitative technological inventions, becomes overly obvious: humanoid cultures might ultimately qualify primarily as a continuous *Apparatus Canto*—a poetic song of engineering culture materialized in artifacts and infrastructure: to praise the strength and the impact, the greatness and the holiness of the apparatus in its similitude to humble humanoids as children and heirs of *The Lord*.

In the earliest writings by Friedrich Kittler, this *Apparatus Canto* has been sung in a mischievous way as joyful and erratic praise of the multiplicity of premodern entities and materialities in humanoid cultures: praise of those mediating entities maliciously dancing around those poor and arrogantly self-indulgent humanoids. Take this example from the collected volume *Austreibung des Geistes aus den Geisteswissenschaften* (*The Expulsion of Spirit from the Humanities*), which he edited, introducing poststructuralist approaches to research between *Grammatologie* and *Historische Anthropologie* in 1980:

> It was the violence and oblivion of the 1770-1800 education reforms that dissolved the grand and colorful Jewish, Greek, and Roman clouds over the Occident. Countless ghost stories fell silent. History, the one and only, the "collective singular" that henceforth contains "the condition of the possibility of all individual histories," came to replace the many stories. The ghost stories that appeared to visionaries and dreamers were replaced by the singular *Spirit*, to whom all the paths and domains of knowledge are entrusted. (Kittler 1980: 8; translated and italicized by Holger Schulze and Geoffrey Winthrop-Young)[1]

A deeply ironic *syrrhesis* following Serres, aware of contingencies and unforeseeable mutations, vibrates in these lines. The author quite provocatively displays an inspiring playfulness and exciting extravaganza in deconstructing anthropocentric obsessions with "Der Geist," "The Spirit," "zwischen disziplinärem Sinn und alphabetischem Nicht-Sinn" (Kittler 1980: 13), "between disciplinary meaning and alphabetic non-meaning" (transl. HS). However, Kittler's early rather corporeal and playful sense for multiple epistemologies and varying experientialities—so boldly displayed in this very quote—almost vanished along the way and in his later works. In order to establish, by disciples and followers, a more coherent, meaningful, and thoroughly applicable method, especially interpreters and later colleagues of Kittler translated the joyful multiplicity of approaches, issues, and perspectives into an increasingly strict and restrained string of arguments. Out of a sardonically poststructuralist, anti-methodological beginning came a kind of almost neo-dogmatic set of well-defined terms and operations, figures of thought and legitimate objects of research: a progressive reduction that almost aggressively rejected all forms of reflections on class, gender, race, and abilities in humanoid aliens. The traditionally legitimate set of research objects and arguments, forms of habitus and strategies of exclusion, became more and more obsessively restricted as only epigonal branches could promote it. "Der Geist," so vigorously refuted by early Kittler, cautiously reentered his research through the backdoor of *Musik und Mathematik* (2005, 2009), of *Zeitkritische Medien* (Volmar 2009), or

---

[1] "Es war die Bildungsreform der Jahre 1770 bis 1800 in ihrer Gewalt und Vergessenheit, die die großen, bunten Wolken über das Abendland, jüdische, griechische, römische, in Luft auflöste. Zahllose Geistergeschichten sind damals verstummt. An die Stelle der vielen Geschichten ist Die Geschichte in der Einzahl getreten, jener 'Kollektivsingular,' der fortan 'die Bedingung der Möglichkeit aller Einzelgeschichten' enthält. An die Stelle der Geistergeschichten wie sie den Geistersehern und Träumen erschienen, ist *Der Geist* in der Einzahl getreten, dem fortan alle Felder und alle Wege des Wissens anbefohlen sind." (Kittler 1980: 8; italicized by HS)

of *Rumoren der Archive* (Ernst 2002). The ancient praise of poets turned in these writings into the praise of programmers. The adored poetic genius returns as worshipped engineering genius. Instead of idealizing the auratic immanence of a poem or an artwork then, now the auratic immanence of an algorithm or a transduction circuit is being idealized. In these idealizing efforts, even the angrily attacked anthropocentrism of bourgeois elitism against less noble forms of practice—such as assembling or maintaining (a possible connection to the critique of cultural studies even)—reentered the research strand, though in disguise. In the writings of media archaeology, a quite singular anthropocentrism is camouflaged by way of praising engineers, programmers, mathematicians, and their most noble yet underrated artifacts, by praising material transmission structures, pervasive algorithms, crucial calculations. Any interruption to this praise, outside of this idiosyncratic interpretation of engineering culture, is not allowed to enter the argument: be it individual affects, reflections on trajectories in social relations, or a critique toward power relations in research, not even a critique of the androcentric lifestyles between bachelorhood and monkhood dominating the work and research culture (cf. the ongoing critique of affect studies: Ahmed 2006; Stewart 2007; Gregg and Seigworth 2010). The bourgeois strategies of exclusion, of condescending and statuesque habitus, as well as the humiliation of all skeptical to this creed, are reinstalled. Multiplicity and the joy of machines and practices is lost. *The Apparatus Canto* has become sincere and chaste. Yet, this praise of artifacts, of commodified products of engineering itself, an ongoing sermon on "The Wonders of the Machine," on calculating and engineering is—as bourgeois forms of preaching traditionally are—an unadulterated praise of *The Human* (read: of the speaker and preacher HIMself). The machine itself is not praised or explored here, only the ingenuity of the preacher. The following passage makes this perfectly clear:

> The registering time does not necessarily require the narrative mode to organize the factual field in a form that we call information. (Ernst 2003: 36)

This statement apodictically rejects any *narrative mode*—though it is itself exactly presented in the very narrative mode it is neglecting: a *contradictio in adiecto*. The individual researcher's sensibilities and idiosyncrasies are neglected in this example in order to perform excessively specific forms of idiosyncrasies and sensibilities. Apparently, the more the actual substance of sensory experiences and personal affects are neglected, the more this repressed ground of any humanoid researcher is returning subversively in research practices. Repression never does erase what it represses: it more provokes evermore clever ways to articulate the repressed. Kittler's effort to leave the notorious *Machine Célibataire* Carrouges and Duchamp 1976, the *Bachelor Machine* of spiritual academia and the ideological *military-industrial-communication-entertainment complex* behind, this effort nearly turned into the opposite: the existence of academia as a bachelor machine in admiration of "Der Geist" and *The Human* is solidified as a singled-out apparatus, a machine outside any form of visceral *kinship* (Haraway 2015). A *bachelor of media* in this sense is obviously in dire need of machine artifacts to generate kinship: anthropocentric idealism revived. Operations of media research, development, and of theory outside of everyday lives, experiences, and affects constitute the *Bachelor Machine*. The actual everyday life of programming and sounding is ignored in order to praise isolated details of artistry and craftsmanship. The chocolate of which Duchamp speaks in his writings, the desired object of the bachelor, is generated by algorithms and by circuits. The results of these algorithms qualify as desire fulfilled.

Dispositive's capitalization

Walking by various urban infrastructures in different cities, I remember the city of Innsbruck under the spell of the mountains; I remember the city of Tokyo with the laughing, inviting connectedness of its inhabitants and the dynamic of bridges and skyscrapers and shrines; I remember the permanent air conditioners and electric currents as the general bass in Boston or New York, in Los Angeles, Austin, and Seattle. I lived differently under 60 Hertz in the United States than under the 50 Hertz in Berlin or Copenhagen. I remember the heated and humid presence in the delicate restaurants of Tunis and the voluptuously upsped traffic of Istanbul. All these globalized, networked cities are impressive results of a life in process and in collaboration with a vast and growing number of artifacts—implemented into a growing structure of related dispositives. Similar to the lives of humanoid aliens in former centuries and millennia, then dominated by cultures situated in other geographical areas of the planet, these artifacts are dear to their cohabitants. They form and guide their actions. They mediate their relations to other aliens and to other groups referring to other sign systems or to differing cultural codes. The dispositives providing the order for these artifacts materialize a vivid and intriguing imaginary, stemming from those humanoid aliens responsible for their installment:

> This civilization is already over, and everyone knows it. We're in a sort of terminal spiral of thanaticism. The paths to another form of life seem blocked, so it seems there's nothing for it but to double down and bet all the chips on the house that kills us. (Wark 2015b)

The artifacts still living with humanoids represent and transmit a major underlying current in cultural life. These things and machines provide connections across spatial distances, with earlier times, and with heterogeneous fields of society—fields that may actually be unknown to you or me. The artifacts of these decades, though, differing from pre-electronic ages, take on a *generative* material shape. Whereas artifacts in former periods of humanoid culture were rather materially stable und unchanging— besides their usual decay, their transformation in function, meaning, and references—the contemporary artifacts of the early twenty-first century (such as software applications, user interfaces, or communication and trade platforms) are generative on a material level: They produce and confront their consumers and visitors with an ever changing, ever updated and relaunched sequence of signals, signs, visual displays, and graphs, as well as sounds or vocal statements. Engineering culture has become mutational, disruptive, generative. The artifacts populating contemporary networked societies provide a growing structure of dispositives. This culture of inventing, promoting, selling, implementing, continuously debugging, and maintaining new technologies and their soft- and hardware apparatuses represents one of the major achievements of networked societies. However, these transformations are in a continuation of the *longue durée* to research of former centuries. Yet, these activities in the field of research are—as science and technology studies argue—not to be recognized as thoroughly essentialist insights into the structure of an object one might call "The World": To believe this would be falling for the marketing claims of the propaganda incessantly disseminated by research and development departments. Research, engineering, and inventing new commodities— activities almost inseparably intertwined—are to be recognized as major cultural forms of inventing, designing, and creating humanoid interactions by their dominant, politically prolific, and socially pervasive artifacts. These activities are foremost generative and self-sustaining: They materialize the imaginary dominant in their inventors, their propagandists, and their producers—related to their cultural and historical environment.

Engineering culture is erecting an outstretched and influential imaginary dispositive in everyday reality. It is a deep joy—and an unsettling threat. Engineering is not without agency, not driven without deeply intimate obsessions; the products of research and development do not represent an objective, naive progress toward a single desired, mysterious business lounge called "A Better Future." These activities of coherently inventing, realizing, and marketing strive to shape a material "World" according to one researcher's imaginary (and perhaps her or his peers from a particular research subculture). The book you are reading right now is surely not different in this respect. The concepts developed earlier and unfolded subsequently represent and implement yet another, hopefully more materially anchored imaginary in the symbolic representations of these narrations. You are following a *syrrhesis* unfolding right now. If my previous assumption concerning an anthropology of research might sound trivial to you, its consequences for the cultural practices and effects of academic research, and especially for the impact of engineering sciences and industrial departments of research and development, surely are not. Taken as an axiom in understanding the shape of a thoroughly technologically shaped "World" and its pervasive obsession with apparatuses and artifacts, this insight might alter the perspective of the role of artifacts in the lives and times of humanoid aliens. Technocultural dispositives and the artifacts they consist of are an emanation of a powerful imaginary taking effect. This imaginary lies at the heart of the engineering passion: a joy for bricolage and deconstruction, for reconstruction and creation. Whereas this passion has been a major cultural drive, more recently the drive might be regarded instead as a more harmful nucleus of humanoid culture. A cultural activity that generates a social order that seems to be more closely related to a form of self-annihilating deathcult, "a gleeful, overly enthusiastic will to death" (Wark 2014), than anything else. McKenzie Wark thus proposed the following description of contemporary culture:

> Thanaticism: a social order which subordinates the production of use values to the production of exchange value, to the point that the production of exchange value threatens to extinguish the conditions of existence of use value. (Wark 2014)

Social and cultural dispositives of power, of production, and of reproduction are to be questioned in a situation in which various transformations in climate, in population, and in topographies seem to pile up as a thorough threat to the future existence of all aliens of any kind on this meek satellite. In unison with working and producing culture, the engineering culture of humanoids actually generates a full take on this biosphere that would make an extra-humanoid observer wonder: Why do humanoids manically care for the production, the commerce, and the consumption of those often inorganic things, those life-threatening and dead artifacts, so often poisonous, that are so eagerly produced to mimic selected humanoid organs? Are they all really nuts, actually? Moreover: Why are so many of these activities centered around artifacts exclusively planned and executed by the *males* of this species? Why do they not prefer to engage in an interaction with their closest kin, their lovers, children, elders? Or is this machinic and openly thanatic desire really a big relief to them? A skillful flight, an evasion, an actual expansion of their limited culture beyond life? These apparatuses as simply a simulacrum of themselves—their incredibly anthropocentric procreation of technologic Homunculi to populate not only this tormented satellite but even farther territories in remote areas of space? To populate the universe with representations of themselves? Why is this rather suicidal action of relentlessly and toxically consuming the resources of this satellite, and in consequence enclosing all humanoid aliens in its technological regimes, why is this actually still going on? The concept of the *Anthropocene* recently made it possibly to describe this planetary transformation as being initialized and executed by lasting interventions from these anthropoid and humanoid aliens. Though this concept might easily be misunderstood as some fatalist acceptance of unavoidable higher forces and even a general evolutionary development that might render all actions against it quite useless, there is truly a different interpretation of the Anthropocene that even allows for a thorough political and critical approach. Is it truly a *humanoid* intervention that changed and changes the appearance, structure, and materiality of this satellite—or is it not more a specific self-sustaining entity extracted, accelerated, and shaped by humanoid aliens in a recent century: *The Capital*. This is not Anthropocene, but *Capitalocene*:

> For the explanatory challenge posed by the extraordinary biospheric changes charted by the dominant *Anthropocene* argument must engage, centrally, the relations of power and re/production that have made these environmental changes. . . . But historical change is not a long chain of social events with environmental consequences; it is a long history of co-produced ensembles of human and extrahuman nature, understood as an unbroken circle of being, knowing, and doing. (Moore 2014b: 39f.)

The cultural process of *capitalization*, of which Jason W. Moore and Achim Szepanski alike speak, ploughed through this planet and erected its cathedrals and temples (Moore 2015; Szepanski 2014a, b). Moore analyzes the process of capitalization as a major cultural force of the last five centuries that performed a transfiguration of given and not yet monetized raw materials as well as workforces (gases, soil, plants, animals, humanoids) into actors of wage-labor and resources to be turned into commodities:

> The alternative to the "Age of Man" (the Anthropocene) is the "Age of Capital" (the Capitalocene). In this, capitalism is understood as a world-ecology, joining the accumulation of capital, the pursuit of power, and the co-production of nature in dialectical unity. . . . I argue for a historical frame that takes capitalism and nature as double internalities: capitalism-in-nature/nature-in-capitalism. The generalization of the value-form (the commodity) is possible only through the expanded reproduction of value-relations that unify wage-labor with its conditions of expanded reproduction: the unpaid work of human and extra-human natures. (Moore 2014a: 1)

A magic trick is performed on the existing ontology that turned it into an engineering imaginary: a resource for invention, development, commodification, marketing, and selling. The obsessive imaginary of engineering construction lust is therefore deeply and often irrevocably—as observed in major examples in the first part of this book—connected to this process of monetization and capitalization. The concept of *subjectivity* as well as concepts such as *free trade, free speech, free research*, and *modern art* appear as similar factors serving this cultural process. The planetary metabolism called *Kapitalisierung*—following Marx (Szepanski 2014)— or *Capitalization*, is necessarily constantly expanding, it is swallowing up resources and lifeforms in a process of *objectification, fragmentation*, and *consumption* (Adams 1990: 47), and it is defecating billions of killed lifeforms, of humanoid and alien war victims, of endless acres and acres of poisoned territories in oceans, in the air and on land, and for unthinkable amounts of millennia irrevocably contaminating areas on this tiny satellite (Parikka 2015). In times of the Capitalocene, apparatuses are in a first step modeled following an idealized image of godlike humanoid physiology as a technologic Homunculus: an *idealized and thus capitalizable* sketch of the humanoid body and its mind. In a second step, exactly this sketchy apparatus—a humanoid in machined appearance—is then wired to follow sequences of highly effective purposes each related to focused and well-defined sign operations. This constellation of remodeling and repurposing to an idealized capitalization generates a vast variety of highly detached Homunculi, relying on their particular operations and purposes. The apparatus as a detached Homunculus then clearly requires an equally idealized networking and scanning structure to be able to stay in touch with other detached Homunculi (or you, or me). These activities among segregated and amputated Homunculi then enter a realm of mainly semiotic interpretations, operations, and calculations. A machined culture of interacting apparatuses is emerging, created after an idealized model of capitalizable humanoid behavior. Their idealization is tempting: Semiosis *is* highly capitalizable (Szepanski 2014b: 305–24). The screens displaying messages and visions are nothing less than crystal balls. The microphones and loudspeakers are incessantly executing a machinic *deep listening* (Oliveros 2005): machines to listen more deeply and with more focus than humanoid aliens ever could. A *semiotically* focused listening. Why would one willfully retract from exclusively listening and gazing onto them at any given moment? The machinic cocoon of dispositives is as tempting as could be: It represents the best, most exciting, most reliable, most predictable and well-arranged kinship one could ever find on this solar satellite. "A floating no-space world of personal spectation" (Wallace 1996: 813).

This process leads Donna Haraway to an admirably optimistic if not holistic and eschatological concept of *The Chthulucene*—integrating the erratic multitude of anthropoid and non-anthropoid, of non-humanoid and humanoid aliens so often referred to on these pages here:

> I am calling all this the Chthulucene—past, present, and to come. These real and possible timespaces are not named after SF writer H.P. Lovecraft's

misogynist racial-nightmare monster Cthulhu (note spelling difference), but rather after the diverse earth-wide tentacular powers and forces and collected things with names like Naga, Gaia, Tangaroa (burst from waterfull Papa), Terra, Haniyasu-hime, Spider Woman, Pachamama, Oya, Gorgo, Raven, A'akuluujjusi, and many many more. "My" Chthulucene, even burdened with its problematic Greek-ish tendrils, entangles myriad temporalities and spatialities and myriad intra-active entities-in-assemblages—including the more-than-human, other-than-human, inhuman, and human-as-humus. (Haraway 2015: 160)

This integrative approach—truly a *syrrhesis* following Serres—to contemporary and future global transformations represents a probably necessary reconceptualization of the role of humanoid, symbiont, subcellular, supermaterial, or transmaterialist aliens cohabiting with me and you on this planet. With this resignification of the alien of Cthulhu as *Chthulu* (one h shifted from the sixth to the second position), Haraway further expands her multiplication of collaborating aliens as the kinship of humanoids—and even integrates this very alien that was invented and designed by its author as a nightmarish and xenophobic pastiche of all qualities seen as erratically strange and alien and dangerous and horrifying. Cthulhu in Lovecraft's fiction is the other of its author.

Yet, if one goes beyond that and follows the *thanaticist* description of inherently misanthropic goals at the core of capitalization—as explicated by Wark, Moore, or Szepanski—then furthermore differing qualities of threatening strangeness and alienation appear in Cthulhu (which again might be the other of other writers, authors, and researchers). Under the spell of an obsessive, engineering imaginary of capitalism and its protruded dispositives, the process of metabolization and defecation on this solar satellite seems actually to call for the radically biocidal Lovecraftian *Cthulhucene: The Capital is Cthulhu*. Capitalization calls for Cthulhu to transform all known lifeforms into the most poisoned and deadly materials, a supernatural entity to—in the words of Lovecraft—"sway the minds of others, and [it] seems to be the vanguard of a horde of extraterrestrial organisms arrived on earth to subjugate and overwhelm mankind" (Lovecraft 1927: 37). The process of capitalization turned itself and all its emanations, artifacts, and entities into Cthulhu itself. Thus, connecting the concept of the *Anthropocene* with recent concepts of a *non-economy* (Szepanski 2014a,b), the apparatus-theory and the Lovecraftian motive of *Cthulhu* allow for only a superficially disturbing syrrhesis: an interpretation of the cultural process of engineering and producing culture. "Ph'nglui mglw'nafh Cthulhu R'lyeh wgah'nagl fhtagn" (Lovecraft 1928). This very *Age of Capital* encourages and promotes the imaginary of engineering and its inherent desire to procreate especially capital and money by way of producing artifacts, buildings, infrastructure, warfare, power stations, production lines, shopping malls; in brief: lasting and influential *dispositives*. Capitalization proceeds through installing and updating dispositives. It is the *Dispositive's Capitalization* that humanoid aliens experience. It is *Dispositives' Cannibalizing*: Capitalization procreates Cthulhu on earth. Capitalizing cannibalizes this planet. Aliens like you and me might in the outstretched expansion of capital only qualify as one of the various sexual organs, or just one of the various generative nuclei needed to procreate capital by annihilating this solar satellite. The planetary desire to procreate artifacts and dispositives to procreate capital ever further implies the darkest side of the Capitalocene: its pathology of depression as evoked by David Foster Wallace when he describes the characteristic anhedonic state as:

> a kind of radical abstracting of everything, a hollowing out of stuff that used to have affective content. Terms the undepressed toss around and take for granted as full and fleshy—happiness, joie de vivre, preference, love—are stripped to their skeletons and reduced to abstract ideas. They have, as it were, denotation but not connotation. . . . Everything becomes an outline of the thing. Objects become schemata. The world becomes a map of the world. An anhedonic can navigate, but has no location. I.e. the anhedonic becomes, in the lingo of Boston AA, Unable To Identify. (Wallace 1996: 903)

The infinite jest of networked artificialized engineering societies implies a state of anhedonia. *The world becomes a map of the world*. A state of incessantly evoking Cthulhu with the words "Ph'nglui mglw'nafh Cthulhu R'lyeh wgah'nagl fhtagn" (Lovecraft 1928):

> we are confronted with the challenge of reevaluating the thought-structures of modernity that continue to shape the intellectual, and therefore political, habitus of even radical critics. (Moore 2014b: 40)

Hence, a state of anhedonic depression is the signature non-move of Cthulhu's Capitalocene of Infinite Jest.

In/Resurrection

Aliens are on the streets. Suddenly, they fill the squares. It might have been announced weeks ago. But seeing and experiencing it right now, listening to it, sensing it: it envelops you in the breathtaking difference, the intensity of presence, the urgent activity, the life-threat felt by those alien humanoids like you or like me. It is terrifying. To experience yourself present. Too close. Too hot. Too unstable. A devastating chain reaction of cruel explosions might be underway. I do not want that. You will probably not want that. But a lot of humanoids are gathering. And for a cause. They are shouting aggressively, they are protesting. What happened? As soon as you go out—or even safer: as soon as you choose to follow a media outlet—you might get a shock. Something indeed has happened. Something unthinkable. An abuse of power, an abuse of the state monopoly of violence, an incident in which the law and justice were ignored. Maybe one alien humanoid put her- or himself outside the regulatory checks and balances of a more or less democratic society. An outrage occurred. This effectively assaulted quite a large group of citizens—humanoids *not* being privileged (or in the position to abuse any power) as the one person (or group of persons) in question, under accusation now. Looking down on the streets, observing the next square or crossing, I can sense the heat building up, physically: the heat of humanoid aggression, drive, anger, despair—an ever-expanding urgency, a deep and fearful desperation not to be heard, not to be recognized, not to be taken seriously as an actual, important member of this society, this contracted community. To be a worthless entity, a neglectable, minor irritation. Annoying scum. "We revolt simply because, for many reasons, we can no longer breathe" (Fanon 1967).

The struggles and protests, the uprisings and tentative insurrections, the marches and flash mobs, the temporary tent cities and rebelling citizens one could observe in recent years all around this planet in Athens, Cairo, in Montréal, in Bangkok or New York, in various European capitals, and in more and more cities and agglomerations all around the globe: occupying and representing individual urges and ignored perspectives. A struggle between various individual needs, between underprivileged precarious masses and highly particular interests of larger groups. In *Klassenkampf im Dunkeln (Class Struggle in the Dark)*, Dietmar Dath explores the qualities of these contemporary struggles and tentative insurrections. Toward the end, he comes to the following, rigid conclusion:

> As long as you do not see antimilitarist protests, which also send out a unified message in all these places, in the same clarity, as long as there is no movement that can go anywhere where Wal-Mart goes, there is hardly any resistance to the march of evil - and no thought of socialism at all. (Dath 2014: 137; transl. HS)[2]

In other words: as long as protest is not generally directed against the militarization of culture on all levels of its existence, and as long as this

---

[2] "Solange man nicht antimilitaristische Proteste sieht, die ebenfalls an all diesen Orten eine einheitliche Botschaft ausgeben, in derselben Klarheit, solange keine Bewegung existiert, die überall hinkommt, wo Wal-Mart hinkommt, ist an Widerstand gegen den Durchmarsch des Übels kaum zu denken—und an Sozialismus gar nicht." (Dath 2014: 137)

is not organized as globally as some of the most prolific supermarket-retailers like Walmart—any resistance against various hardships of our times will be futile; and any new and promising, compellingly utopian form of society, will not be established. Consequently, the rather mixed results, if not complete defeat, of the aforementioned protests and insurrections in recent years might stem from a lack of a substantial and fundamental turn toward radical and thorough demilitarization in the manifold areas of economy and commodities production, in administration, in the sciences, in culture, and in journalism. The alien humanoids on the streets, in the squares, were articulating dissent and resistance merely by their physical presence, by their noise, and by their sonic disruption. This partial and temporary *sonic dominance* (Henriques 2011) was yet ever so often mainly enjoyed in itself. The newfound confidence to perform this kind of resistance apparently seemed just to be enough for the moment. The idiosyncrasies neglected and ignored that were articulated on these places, the needs and defeats, led to these moments—but it would probably need an actually demanding statement to start an effectively disruptive conflict with contemporary political personnel. The strength and the stability, the longue durée inherently present in the apparatus and overarching dispositive of military production of exchange value, is to be addressed. A persona emerges from exactly such conflicts: it takes a process of negotiation, from a background of experienced and worked-through resistance between rather incommensurable idiosyncrasies and the apparatus as a major modus operandi of contemporary societies. One needs to seek exactly those areas of resistance, starting with the aforementioned *State of Anhedonic Depression in Cthulhu's Capitalocene of Infinite Jest*:

> The anhedonic can still speak about happiness and meaning et al., but she has become incapable of feeling anything in them, of understanding anything about them, of hoping anything about them, or of believing them to exist as anything more than concepts. . . . This is maybe because anhedonia's often associated with the crises that afflict extremely goal-oriented people who reach a certain age having achieved all or more than all than they'd hoped for. (Wallace 1996: 903)

An everyday life in unison with hegemonic cultural practices, its unfounded assumptions, conventions, and restrictions, its noble goals and values, will not provide these moments of actual conflict and actual options of shaping a persona. Yet conflict is one of the sources of an actual generativity, truly inspiring if not strongly demanding a different cultural agreement, a diverging set of practices, goals, and of techniques (selected practices and techniques will be discussed in Chapter 8 of this book: "Resistance and Resonance"): a progress from consensualism as contemporary ideology—to *agonism* (Mouffe 2013). Only then might one indeed experience what

Theodor W. Adorno described as a breaking up of a sclerotic mind, the *Starre des Geistes*:

> The rigidity which the spirit mirrors is no natural fated power to which one must humbly bow. It was made by men, it is the final result of an historical process in which men made men into appendages of an opaque machinery. To see through this machinery, to know that the appearance of the inhuman conceals human relations, and to gain control of these relations themselves are stages in a counter-process, a healing process. When social basis for this rigidity is truly exposed as appearance, then the rigidity itself may disappear. The spirit shall return to life in that moment when it no longer hardens itself in isolation but instead resists the hardness of the world. (Adorno 1971: 33; translation after: Jarvis 2007: 218f.)[3]

How could one resist this *hardship of the world*? How could one escape—no: overcome—this threatening *State of Anhedonic Depression in Cthulhu's Capitalocene of Infinite Jest*?

> The reason we feel overwhelmed is that we are overwhelmed—it isn't an individual failing of ours; it isn't because we haven't "managed our time" properly. However, we can use the scarce resources we already have more effectively if we work together to codify practices of collective re-habituation. (Fisher 2015)

---

[3]"Die Starre, die der Geist widerspiegelt, ist keine natur- und schicksalhafte Macht, der man ergeben sich zu beugen hätte. Sie ist von Menschen gemacht, der Endzustand eines geschichtlichen Prozesses, in dem Menschen Menschen zu Anhängseln der undurchsichtigen Maschinerie machten. Die Maschinerie durchschauen, wissen, daß der Schein des Unmenschlichen menschliche Verhältnisse verbirgt, und dieser Verhältnisse selbst mächtig werden, sind Stufen eines Gegenprozesses, der Heilung. Wenn wirklich der gesellschaftliche Grund der Starre als Schein enthüllt ist, dann mag auch die Starre selber vergehen. Der Geist wird lebendig sein in dem Augenblick, in dem er nicht länger sich bei sich selber verhärtet, sondern der Härte der Welt widersteht." (Adorno 1971: 33)

CHAPTER FIVE

The sonic persona

Sonic traces

I hear your footsteps. You are walking by. Then you come back, slightly slower, maybe irritated. I realize you are looking for something you seem unable to find. I can hear how you stand there, not moving. Then moving again, getting out your notebook, taking notes—maybe scribbling how to contact the person you wanted to find here originally? You pack it away, make a brief phone call, then you walk away—quite rapidly and apparently with your next meeting or task in mind. This sonic account of a brief sequence of quite ordinary activities might sound as if its author could be a creepy stalker or at least a person working for any security service surveillance department, a *Geheime Staatspolizei* or a *Staatssicherheit*. Yet, this narration is at the same time again a rather ordinary, an individual, personal, and, yes: an intimate reflection. It is intimate as it is a narration that is on the one hand very common in everyday life, common to probably everyone reading these lines—and on the other hand, such an account is not easily shared with another person, except maybe with a very close colleague, a family member, or some romantic partner. The intimacy of these situated *auscultations* is a symptom of how elementary they are in the daily life of humanoid aliens like you and me. They are anything but irregular or weird. They form a fundamental layer of humanoid sensorial experience. As a matter of fact, a humanoid's sensorium is capable of perceiving an incredibly wide range of intense and excessive as well as rather subtle and ephemeral sensory materialities. The way, the complexity, and also the mixture of how particular sensorial details are being perceived, though, can be thoroughly idiosyncratic, even irregular and surprising. The individual reach and intensity of particular perceptions is dependent on a vast array of situated, biographical, cultural, social, and historical factors. Instances concerning the individual sensorium and attacking the sensorium are not at all transitory events, momentary actions, or immaterial entities without major consequences. To the contrary, these instances are to be regarded—in accordance with sensory studies—as heavily loaded and thoroughly persistent *materialities*. The materialization of sound, as promoted since the nineteenth century by researchers like Hermann von Helmholtz, Harvey Fletcher, Leo Beranek, and many others, constitutes a core element in any humanoid's sensory experience. Sound and the senses are experienced in this material, thoroughly physical and corporeal way.

As I am writing these lines, I listen to some music. This music is streamed from some server, owned by a company with offices in London and Cambridge, as well as in New York. I am listening to a mix of recent interpretations of *Krautrock*-compositions. This listening experience is intertwined with a tactile and respiratory experience stemming from the fresher air coming in from outside, after the end of an early-July heatwave here in a Berlin summer. I can still feel the somewhat microwaving heat of the last two or three days in all my bones, on my glowing skin, my forehead, my calves, my cheekbones. Materialities of heat and activity left their traces on me. Now another track comes on in this mix; less pressing, more liquid and embracing. An urgent phone call interrupted my writing and listening activity; immediately I was teleported with my whole sensorial experience into a situation of organizing meetings, contacting various people to bring them in touch with each other and to find ways to solve a certain quite practical problem of everyday work organization at a university. An intense situation of social exchange and negotiations had entered and taken over my former rather solitary situation of traditional academic reflection. Now, I have just got back to working on this chapter. My blood pressure, my breathing cycle, the sonic traces left by music and social interaction, all adapt again to the deep, substantial, overarching, highly detailed concentration. A concentration on one single argument and issue with all its historical, experiential, and cultural ramifications, as well as its various critical and methodological if not logical counterarguments. My writing apparently seems to require this specific concentration. And here come the alpha waves. With a brief glance at a minor message box of the streaming webpage, I realize: The mix has changed.

Sensorial materialities are a crucial part of any alien's life. Material emanations from individual or collective, from creatures', climate's, or machines' actions, as well as emanations from ongoing processes and the mere presence of things around you or me, are enveloping us in every given moment, in varying intensities and transforming directionalities. The sensorial layers of existence are pervasive and prolific. Sound leaves traces. Though humanoids surely do not intend, do not work arduously to be aware of their sensorial envelopes in truly every single moment, with every single nerve of their bodies (this could possibly qualify as a certain pathology or at least a quite disturbing if not individually scary idiosyncrasy), these emanations shape individual lives. Sensorial materialities, radiating from each and every object and action, can serve as indices and hints, symptoms and signs concerning status, directions, quality, and urgency of what is actually happening right here, right now. Speaking from a strictly materialist perspective, the entities physically present in a certain situation are never radically disconnected from their environments: it might even be misleading to speak of an environment detached from actors—one might better speak of actors of various kinds constituting a continuum. With this description, one assumes a perspective of richness in perception, a luxury of materiality and physicality. Sensory activities are never scarce. The physical entities humanoid aliens like you and I actually live among are interconnected via a constant and almost unstoppable stream of particles, resonances, waves that radiate from them. Humanoids are definitely able to perceive these streams and disseminations. Maybe that ability occasionally needs some refinement, training, or even a more intense discourse on particular ephemeral perceptions, on *proprioceptions* and *enteroceptions*, *visceroceptions*: on all of these forms of everyday perception that aliens like us have—but rarely reflect upon in our culturally biased focusing on just some selected events in a larger distance outside of our bodily shapes and as part of the hegemonic dispositive. On the contrary, one might even consider this selective focus on rather distinct, easily interpretable, signifying and instrumentalizable events a very refined sort of *sensory deprivation*. It is sensorially deprived to perceive sensory activities merely as surrounding and only reduced to signals, imperatives, indices. The utilitarian perspective on sound and the senses is a perspective of scarcity, of deprivation.

In this very moment, lingering between writing and reading, listening and imagining, daydreaming and considering near future encounters and articulations, I follow some sensory traces. Sonic traces that imply an almost endless fractalization of aspects and currents. These sensory traces are far subtler and more instructive than previously thought in the cultural history of modeling the senses. Living conditions, conflicts and joyful instances, forms of habit and instantaneous practices, repeated rituals, and somewhat scary but mainly breathtaking moments of excess resound in these traces. *Sonic traces* constitute a situated and idiosyncratic anthropology of the senses. To follow these selected or combined sonic traces is, indeed, not only a research activity and a possible method of cultural research, a sensory ethnography: it is an everyday practice. An intimate and a personal necessity.

Idiosyncratic implex

In this very moment, it is a morning in early December; I am back in Berlin from my teaching and the research I do in Copenhagen. "Crow's feet.

Birthmark. Rhinoplasty that didn't take. Mole. Overbite. A bad-hair year" (Wallace 1996: 261). It is less cold than expected here in northeastern Germany, yet inside our living room and at my writing table it feels warmer than I expected. Warm and cozy. I enjoy the opportunity to write at length and to think intensely about how to develop this monograph further. "Sue (Or in a Season of Crime)" is the name of the song that plays in my room. It is sung by David Bowie, and the song is streamed from Copenhagen, from an independent radio station by the name of The Lake, conceived and run by musicians from a Danish band called Efterklang. I listen to it as I write these sentences. This soundtrack to my current working situation and writing assignment fuels my imagination and conveys a flow of sentences and phrases that apparently suit my basic idea of how this book should build its argument. The horns retract, a more ancient electronic piece comes along; Karlheinz Stockhausen's *Gesang der Jünglinge im Feuerofen* from 1955 is playing now. I smile. Home. "Carpal neuralgia, phosphenic migraine, gluteal hyperadiposity, lumbar stressae" (Wallace 1996: 91). The sensorium in a humanoid's life is never stable. It is established over time, starting before birth and intensely formed and shaped alongside early years of childhood and adolescence. "The palate-clefted. The really large-pored. The excessively but not necessarily lycanthropically hirsute. The pin-headed. The convulsively Tourettic" (Wallace 1996: 261). The contemporary, allegedly dead metaphor of *discovering one's body* is indeed a rather telling one in the case of younger humanoids. As Michel Serres points out, a body is never fixed in her or his performativity and sensitivity—it is in constant reaction and plasticity in material excess:

> We hear through our muscles, nerves and tendons. Our body-box, strung tight, is covered head to toe with a tympanum. We live in noises and shouts, in sound waves just as much as in spaces, the organism is erected, anchors itself in space, a broad fold, a long braid, a half-full, half-empty box which echoes them. Plunged, drowned, submerged, tossed about, lost in infinite repercussions and reverberations and making sense of them through the body. (Serres 2008: 141)

An alien's bodily sensorium is not a detached entity inside (or even outside) of her or his so-called "subjectivity." The mere term of subjectivity might suggest a neatly encapsulated and distinctively describable entity you or I might own, command, and call "My Subjectivity." This is not the case. "Those with saddle-noses. Those with atrophic limbs. And yes chemists and pure-math majors also those with atrophic necks" (Wallace 1996: 254). A humanoid's individual subjectivity is, in contrast, more a subtly constituted process with interwoven streams and routines, bits and pieces from a broad range of bodily aspects, performative habits and sensory inclinations one might have been accumulating over quite some time.

> Sometimes dissonant, often consonant, disturbed or harmonious. Resonating within us: a column of air and water and solids, three-dimensional space, tissue and skin, long and broad walls and patches, and wiring, running through them; moorings receptive to the lower frequencies, as though our bodies were the union of ear and orchestra, transmission and reception. (Serres 2008: 141).

The sheer and massive quantity of certain sensorial material events might engrave over time a certain sensitive inclination in a humanoid's body. This might as well generate a certain resistance, a rejection of sensorial performances too often experienced in an unwelcome way. There is no determinist line from event over experience to character, to sensorium and being. "The phrenologically malformed. The suppuratively lesioned. The endocrinologically malodorous of whatever ilk" (Wallace 1996: 257). Humanoids are no linear creatures. They might, alas, wish they would be. They might dream of stable, foreseeable, and unchangeable models, of boxes and cases they wish they would resemble. There is a longing, a desire, an urge in us aliens to turn into some machinic and static entity—nevermore to be irritated by any sensory event, by any palpable, subtle instance. Some might even assume their lives would then, being a linear process with almost geometrical successions, finally arrive at a state of blissful living, so much easier than now. "Heaven—is a place where nothing ever happens" (Talking Heads 1979).

One should doubt this assumption, this common idiosyncrasy. Nevertheless, it is a strong and accelerating motor of modernist transformation into an overall machinic existence. A desired, statuarian existence of this sort is not rarely a dialectic expression of vivid, hyperdifferentiated, and possibly overpowered sensibilities. Are such sensibilities not condescendingly regarded as personal weaknesses, annoyances, even chronic diseases? "The in any way asymmetrical. The rodential- and saurian- and equine-looking" (Wallace 1996: 261). As soon as aliens perform their sensorium in a given situation, it is not linear, it is not equivocal, and it is not identical in all its aspects. It is by definition an irritation. This irritation, this irritability, constitutes a person. As any cellular, biological being of higher complexity, intensely plastic and versatile, one's sensibility adapts in many aspects and various ways to an enveloping sensory environment. Being soft and receptive, highly malleable and responsive, is a genuine quality of humanoids. The softness, the weakness, makes one. It is a certain, maybe uncommon joy *not* being a statue, not being dead—as Michel Serres points out:

> The individual representing comedy, tragedy, medicine, the media or public administration—statue, robot, apotheosis of allegory, long-dead

> automaton—speaks at the banquet but does not drink. Speaks of love, does not make love; speaks of wine, does not taste it. A dinner of statues, a feast of stone. Here dead words are passed about; we study them, comment on them. The allegories drink allegorical wine, allegorically; we speak about this categorically. A symposium of marbles and circuit boards. (Serres 2008: 175)

> The multiple amputee. The prosthetically malmatched. The snaggletoothed, wattled, weak-chinned, and walrus-cheeked. (Wallace 1996: 261)

Whereas the words you are reading on this page are written on *circuit boards*, on a keyboard attached to a Von Neumann-machine, running text processing software and displaying my writing on a liquid crystal screen; as this technological toy is part of humanoid alien culture, it is influencing cultural practices, it contributes to reflecting listening and sounding practices—it has been domesticated into your and my daily habits, and you and I have been domesticated to act in a manner appropriate to this apparatus. This machine dispositive and my corporeal experience and sensibility have been intersected. "The hydrocephalic. The tabescent and chachetic and anorexic. The Brag's-Diseased, in their heavy red rinds of flesh. The dermally wine-stained or carbuncular or steatocryptotic" (Wallace 1996: 254). As such, it becomes part of a shared individual and idiosyncratic sensorium—though probably not contributing in the same way you as an alien humanoid would be in replying to these words written here, printed here, distributed by this publishing house. Still, it is exactly this vast amount of humanoid malleability that grants to these creatures a certain—though again: not absolute, not linear, not complete—adaptability and responsivity. This specific quality itself is yet different in differing aliens. "The morbidly diaphoretic with a hankie in every pocket. The chronically granulomatous" (Wallace 1996: 257). Dependent on biographies and on histories, on cultural experiences and on situational educations, there might evolve quite different dimensions and styles of malleability. Humanoids are erratic assemblages. "The hated and dateless and shunned, who keep to the shadows. Those who undress only in front of their pets" (Wallace 1996: 257). Assemblages that are put together in an ever new and ever surprising idiosyncratic way: with surprising new articulations, for being sensible, extremely vulnerable, aggressive, receptive, or agile in unforeseeable instances. Granted as the core of humanoid actions, behaviors, beliefs and obsessions, needs and rejections, these idiosyncrasies could serve as key to an anthropology of sound: the variety of sonic and sensory experiences, as well as the abundant amount of personae inhabiting an alien, is generated by its genuine idiosyncrasies. You are your idiosyncrasies. In respect to individual, time- and space-specific, personal, biographical, cultural, as well as historical specificities in inclinations, preferences, and tastes, a certain alien might evolve an idiosyncrasy over time. Idiosyncrasies are symptoms of existence: they are signatures of life. They constitute a specific, not reduced, not scarce, rich and complex materiality. The sonic traces of such sensory idiosyncrasies are always specific in their endless variations, their almost unforeseeable turns, detours, and erratic pirouettes: this endless multiplicity is joy. Exactly these mutations of sensory experiences are nevertheless a major annoyance for any disciplinary and methodological approach: its urge for linearity and a pointed narration could mislead one to interpretations of progress, of decomposition, of heroic search or descent into decadence. The shape and the use of one's senses is in contrast never stable, never identical, never immobile—*as long as one dares to sense* for a longer and longer time:

> Claims about the transhistorical and transcultural character of the senses often derive their support from culturally and historically specific evidence—limited evidence at that. (Sterne 2003: 18)

> The soundscape here is composed by two cockerels, a flame thrower, a kid on a trampoline, a nail gun, a muezzin, a circular saw and two wind chimes. Out there somewhere I can also hear the presence of a jackhammer and a bottled gas vendor car with an Aygaz jingle. Which I once had as a ring tone. (Kytö 2015)

A moment of an irritating yet overwhelmingly consistent confluence of divergent entities, persons, materialities. The philosopher and education studies scholar Rudolf zur Lippe introduced for such moments the term *Koinzidentalität* (Lippe 1985: 291–5) or *coincidentality*. "The psoriatic. The exzematically shunned. And the scrofulodermic. Bell-shaped steatopygiacs, in your special slacks. Afflictees of Pityriasis Rosea" (Wallace 1996: 254). Lippe arrives at this concept in his extensive study *Sinnenbewusstsein* (Sensory Awareness/Consciousness of Meaning). Aesthetics in this study are explored as foundational to anthropology; by way of historical explorations, but also in an ongoing series of experimental expeditions into phenomenological experiences, Lippe unravels a *Grundlegung einer anthropologischen Ästhetik*. According to this *Grundlegung*, aesthetic experience could represent a sensory form of reflection that grants access to idiosyncrasies of a person's sensorium. In moments of coincidentality, there can be a "Zusammentreffen von Wahrnehmendem und Wahrgenommenem als Vorgang . . . das Ereignis eines sich erfindenden Spiels" (Lippe 1985: 291): an *encounter of a perceiving and a perceived agent in the course of a playful process that is inventing itself.* Lippe's approach leads an anthropology of sound to valid erratic constellations: sonic traces—as situated in a given auditory dispositive in relation to one or more perceiving, acting, interacting, and performing humanoid aliens—are not irrelevant and arbitrary coincidences.

Such ephemeral and fragile instances represent more the actual endpoints of a sensory search, inherently corporeal and long-lasting. Coincidentality hence is not unrelated to individual bodily inclinations and excesses. The multiplicity of bodies, of sensory preferences and dislikes, of desires and repulsions shapes and characterizes *a person as an alien*. This multiplicity is never a simple and easy one. It is surgically tattooed with a multitude of diseases and formations, abilities and proclivities, rejections and desires. *Idiosyncrasies formed this beautiful body*, a T-shirt could read. "The tri-nostriled. The invaginate of mouth and eye" (Wallace 1996: 261). The multiplicity of bodily manifestations and sensorially articulated idiosyncrasies characterizes you and me as humanoid alien persons. The endless series of names and descriptions for non-standard bodily formations, diseases, deformations, constellations, and habits that entered this section by reference to David Foster Wallace permits hence a timid glimpse into this multiplicity of humanoid aliens: "Obesity with hypogonadism. Also morbid obesity. Nodular leprosy with leonine facies" (Wallace 1996: 250). The individual constellation of idiosyncrasies in listening, in sensing, in tasting and smelling, in kinesthetics or in sensibilities in general, in neuroplasticity and in the plasticity of inner organs and extremities, in arguments and in customs, in preferred pleasures and feared encounters, is forming bodily implications. These idiosyncrasies *imply* an inclination to particular activities, a preference for specific forms of further actions or demands: it is an *implex*. Taken from Paul Valéry (cf. Valéry 1957: 234ff.) and expanded to a broader concept by Dietmar Dath and Barbara Kirchner (Dath and Kirchner 2012), the ramifications of an *implex* stick with the proclivities in a given social and historical, cultural and biographical constellation—and it stresses those inherent tendencies toward an aspired differing state in the near or far future: maybe only achieved after a series of individual or collective actions, mutations, falsifications, revisions, or amplifications. Once the differing later state had been reached, it could then be called the *implex* of the earlier one. Dath and Kirchner start their broad working definition of the implex by the observation that

> Bestimmte nicht unwahrscheinliche Folgelagen seien der Implex einer spezifische Ausgangslage gewesen. (Dath and Kirchner 2012: 44)

Hence, the term *implex* describes for these authors the observation that *certain, not improbable subsequent situations are the implex to a specific starting situation*. Originally Valéry (Dath and Kirchner 2012: 340–3) tailored this concept to represent an inherent potential in an individual alien only later actualized:

> The implex ... is [our] ability to feel, react, do, understand—individual, variable, more or less perceived by us—and always imperfectly, and

indirectly (like the sensation of fatigue),—and often misleading. (Valéry 1965: 56)[1]

Dath and Kirchner now expand and apply this concept not only to formal logic, to genealogy, and to poetics (Dath and Kirchner 2012: 44)—but they mutate it even further to become a convincing Marxist political concept; with this, they go much further than Derrida in his discussion (Derrida 1985: 299–304). This political concept starts out with the intention of transforming societies and their societal strata on a political level. Transforming societal strata, though, necessarily requires and often implies—according to Dath and Kirchner—certain constellations to make way for surprising scientific discoveries: these scientific discoveries provide then in turn new inventions driving the transformations that might lead to substantial revolutions: hence, political transformations are—following Dath and Kirchner—equally implied in scientific discoveries as in social transformations (Dath and Kirchner 2012: 42). They exemplify this with the example of the industrial revolution and its inventions in the nineteenth century, which on the one hand provided the means for an accelerated capitalization yet also for other and more powerful forms of worker associations. They assume that the contemporary transformations regarding globalization and digitalization follow along a comparable dialectics. An *implex* is at play in all these cases. The implex of a situation is therefore defined as an inclination toward a certain direction of further development or action, implying if not demanding a collective or individual generativity. Cautiously, Dath and Kirchner negate all teleological or even eschatological necessity in this process: it is still required to respond to *coincidentalities* affecting it. "The Parkinsonianly tremulous. The stunted and gnarled. The teratoid of overall visage. The twisted and hunched and humped and halitotic" (Wallace 1996: 261).

> Implex, is basically what is implied in the notion of person or self, and is not of the *present* moment. It's the *potential of general and specialized sensibility*—of which the *present* is always a matter of *chance*. And this potential is conscious. (Valéry 2007: 221)

The idiosyncratic implex is hence a distinct core of a *Historische Anthropologie*, as conceptualized by Christoph Wulf, Dietmar Kamper, and others since the early 1980s (Wulf 1997, 2013): This anthropological approach does not strive—as explained already in the first section of this

---

[1] "L'Implexe ... est ... [n]otre capacité de sentir, de réagir, de faire, de comprendre,—individuelle, variable, plus ou moins perçue par nous,—et toujours imparfaitement, et sous de formes indirectes (comme la sensation de fatigue),—et souvent trompeuses." (Valéry 1957b: 234–236)

book—for a reduction to a supposed common denominator of all humanoid aliens at all times and on all areas of this planet, under all circumstances and mutations. Foundational to an anthropology of sound, this approach accentuates the fundamental malleability and the non-linear development, the cultural and sensory potential, the "potential of general and specialized sensibility" (Valéry 2007: 221) of aliens on earth. *Everyone's a different sort of alien.* I cannot know how you sense this paragraph. I cannot know how you experience a listening situation we share.

The sonic persona

This situation is occupied by sound practices, techniques of sonification, an assortment of functional sounds and heterogeneous products of and approaches to sound design and sound art. Sonic traces cohabit almost every single area of one's day. Sonic activities are overly present. Even academic writing—an activity I am performing now—the task of rethinking, reevaluating, revising, and reconceptualizing certain concepts and approaches applied herein and argued for or against, is an inherently sonic activity. One is not only enveloped but also pervaded by sounds. Being a reader, listener, and writer, I prefer now and then to listen to rather dynamic and voluminous, for some listeners even massively disturbing and annoying, sound performances or radio transmissions, while reading and writing, exploring and imagining. At some points in the course of writing, one might be listening more to typing or scribbling sounds; at other times one will be indulging in a more calm and less nervously active sound environment; at other moments, she could seek a composition or song to get her kick-started into writing and unfolding this specific aspect of interpretation much further. At first, well, *sight*, this *sonic dominance* (Henriques 2011) in research writing might seem counterintuitive. However, the moment you start to rethink the activity of writing an academic article or book, the specific events and phenomena in the everyday life of a researcher and writer from a *hearing perspective* (Auinger and Odland 2007), the whole situated constellation is in mutation. A *sonic generativity* then unfolds. There are steps from above I listen to while writing this. But this generativity is not restricted to activities only an author of a book could perform. Sonic generativity extends to almost every activity known or unknown, common or uncommon, to a humanoid alien: Sporting activities and cooking activities, activities of cleaning, maintaining, and repairing, activities of conversation and play, of physical labor and of bodily pleasure, activities concerning reflection and drafting, playtime and pastime, illness and sorrow, suffering and boredom, depression and mania. Assuming a hearing perspective excavates sonic traces in experienced situations: an empirical method of sonic and *corporeal epistemology* (this will be more extensively developed in the following chapter: "A Sensory Corpus"). Often, sonic experiences are analyzed via a detour over visual sketches, algorithmical descriptions, quantitative studies, or textual descriptions. The analytical approach in all of these cases is, to say the least, largely visually if not textually grounded: it relies mainly on static descriptions of a certain environment that seems not to change. Those approaches do not take into account the fact that any listener in a sonic environment is equally an actor, a contributor, and an immersed factor of this specific constellation of sound sources, resonances, and repercussions. Now I can hear, I can sense your insecurity might lead you to remain strangely static and unmoved in your actions. This—obviously highly problematic—bias in actual analysis stems from a complicated sensory history of Westernized cultures in the arts and in research:

> Since the Renaissance we have had an agreed visual perspective, and language to speak accurately about images. This we still lack in the world of sound, where words fail us to even describe, for instance, the complex waveforms of an urban environment, much less what those sounds do to us and how they make us feel. We are lost in a storm of noise with no language for discussion. (Auinger and Odland 2007)

Chatter and laughter in the morning in the kitchen; I feel elevated and in a mood to join in when entering. This devastating critique, originally published in 1998 by Sam Auinger and Bruce Odland, is not directed toward more exotic and advanced experiments in sound—but toward common situations in which humanoid aliens are lingering on any day. Starting with this fundamental insight, the radical difficulties of a logocentric discourse become apparent: What one sees or reads or counts in research immediately is being granted an intuitive evidence that is not granted hearing, tactile, or kinesthetic perceptions. Only recently—in the dimensions of cultural history—did researchers effectively start to focus on the historical transformations of auditory metaphors, of sonic figures of thought, and of historical discoveries of methods using acoustic equipment for measuring and acoustic forms of presentation (Sterne 2003; Erlmann 2010; Volmar 2015; Bijsterveld 2018). Following these foundational efforts, a subsequent step of research into sonic epistemologies of listening and sensing as methods themselves seems more and more thinkable. The needle is put on an older record. In the early twenty-first century, such a daring move seems at least not too easily refutable as an irrational and insane proposal. I listened to this older record a lot when I was an adolescent boy. A hearing perspective in sound studies is evolving as a transdisciplinary effort to merge the various languages and practices concerned with sounding and listening: the discourses and methods of acoustics and ethnography, of soundscape studies and musical aesthetics, of sensory anthropology and cultural history, of science and technology studies and performance studies, of media history and of popular music studies. The wind is stronger than yesterday, temperatures are falling. This ongoing merging of discourses and forms of reflection, of methods of analysis and of epistemologies in the arts and humanities, as well as in the sciences, allows for a pervasive mutation of relevant discourses. A chirping, a crouching sound. This present anthropology of sound is making an effort to contribute to this transformation: an alteration from a formulaic discourse of scarce signals and archaic notions of technological fetishization—I sense your fingers move—into a more versatile discourse of sensorial richness and the implex of a multitude of individual idiosyncrasies emerging, prevailing, returning, and transforming, incessantly dynamic, unreckoned, unsettling. Your new coat swings heavier around you, and you can hear that immediately. Such a fundamental alteration then contributes to a *corporeal science*, a *Wissenschaft des Körpers* (Sowodniok 2013), a form of research founded on corporeal practices: listening to situated, bodily articulations, to subtle resonances. An anthropology of sound enters and opens this realm of research that does *not* evade into transcendence. As a material anthropology it begins, each time anew, with indulging and immersing, with experiencing and with being affected by one actual situation of listening and sounding. Did you hear that? Outside your window? Just a second ago? A sound file playing, apparently. This listening experience is mingled and dynamic, material and situated, personal and affected, right here, right now:

> There are only relations of movement and rest, speed and slowness between unformed elements, or at least between elements that are relatively unformed, molecules, and particles of all kinds. There are only haecceities, affects, subjectless individuations that constitute collective assemblages. . . . We call this plane, which knows only longitudes and latitudes, speeds and haecceities, the plane of consistency or composition (as opposed to a plan(e) of organization or development). (Deleuze and Guattari 1987: 266)

Your mouth feels dry after a long day, and this makes it harder for you to focus on what you just read or what you originally intended to say. The imminent sensory *immanence* of a sonic experience generates this alteration. The conversion of sonic discourse hence starts with a mutation of its main perspective. A hearing perspective is an intended oxymoron: The distant and diagrammatic character of *perspectivization* is forcefully immersed into the area of the sonic—the concept of perspective is expanded. A *hearing perspective* exceeds any logic of perspective in order to disassemble and to reassemble this concept. It smells in here a wee bit too much like the room had just being cleaned. How can I assume a broader, a sensorially rich and versatile perspective, onto situated experience of sensory resonance?

A chlorine detergent? The sonic persona of an alien like me or a humanoid like you emerges from this experience of being immersed in a sensorially rich experience. As soon as one assumes a hearing perspective, the specific character of one's own persona in sound is emerging. Ephemeral and fragile sonic traces are obtruding in alien humanoids' lives: "Ces perceptions insensibles marquent encore et constituent le même individue" (Leibniz 1765: 47). A click. *These perceived marginal traces make who you are.* A sonic persona is thus one who—in the weakest definition—has at least a specific, describable, and recognizable approach to its audible, if often ephemeral and rather indiscernible, environment: a *zoon acousticon*. The heat is rising in your extremities, in your chest: you feel a bit too much on display right now. This one might be a humanoid, an alien, a non-humanoid, or a non-alien, any entity with a possible agency in sound. Any persona of this kind that is existing by and in sound can be heard, listened to, experienced, and explored; it can be unfolded in all its details, and it can be scrutinized, criticized, it can be reversed, contradicted, and affirmed, it can be amplified and diminished, alienated and reworked, transformed, mingled and rematerialized. This cracking of a stiff plastic packaging? A sonic persona is defined by this alterability, this malleability, this minglability. The sonic persona of a humanoid alien—but also of larger groups of people, of apparatuses and machines, even of organizations and institutions—this sonic persona is shaped and constituted by the sonically perceptive, performatively generated traces, the *sonic traces*, that any vibrating entity leaves in a specific culture and historical era as well as in a situated sonic environment. A microphone is being plugged in and leaves an ear-splitting thump, unbearable, every time this happens. These sonic traces materialize the situated agency as well as the individual idiosyncrasy of the entity in question in this specific context. When I enter a space, you can hear my steps, the moving of my hands, my clothes, my jewelry, my hair. If your sensory perception were largely focused on hearing, you would be able to auditorily recognize a rhythm of either more hectic or more relaxed movements that could be symptomatic for my habits right now. You would then interpret or categorize my actions and my habitus according to these sonic practices. The character of a sonic persona is mainly dependent on its particular cultural and historical significance—which is sonically embodied in one's auditory appearance: in one's sonic acts, sonic performances, sonic roles or masks (to refer only once to the common association with the πρόσωπον or *prosopon*, as used in Greek theater in ancient Athens to worship Dionysus—at least according to interpretations of the notorious *Pronomos* vase-paintings, from the fifth century BC, the only material relict). This audible embodiment stores the emanations radiating from one's highly idiosyncratic, one's individual, biographical, and instantaneous sensory constitution. Am I right now neglecting to listen to certain sounds? Am I focusing on a certain spectrum and a more specific category of ephemeral and of peripheral sounds? Are you listening mainly to spoken arguments and propositions of one especially important person, neglecting other auditory emanations? Or is he more likely to respond only from now on to dancing moves and rhythmical patterns on this dance floor right now? Is she mainly reacting to detected signals as part of an experimental setup with specifically refined, disciplinarily trained, and epistemologically insightful listening practices? A humanoid alien listens foremost to its own culture and its own historical time if listening to a sonic performance at any given moment. Your door closes smoothly. You are safe.

In the strongest definition, a sonic persona would be an alien who indeed is trained in more specific and refined ways to thoroughly approach its or her or his environment by means of a hearing perspective. A sonic persona in this meaning is capable of accessing various sensory emanations of audible, tactile, and vibratory events, radiating in a given environment. Is this strange if not distant buzzing? From a water bottle? Being a sonic persona, I do actually live in another way. Sonic materialities guide my way through the situations I am present in. The sounds from your stomach, your joints, your teeth and tongue. Hence, a hearing perspective does indeed alter the approach to one's enveloping situations and environments. Typing sounds. Scribbling sounds. Also, I smell a soup cooking on an oven, just around the corner. This reversal of perspective, from distanced and objectifying to immersed and experiential, is explicated in this fundamental distinction by Maurice Merleau-Ponty:

> Psychologists often say that the body image is dynamic. Brought down to a precise sense, this term means that my body appears to me as an attitude directed towards a certain existing or possible task. And indeed its spatiality is not, like that of external objects or like that of "spatial sensations," a spatiality of position, but a *spatiality of situation*. (Merleau-Ponty 1962: 114f.)

I like the warmth in your living room. Your favorite record and your antique cushions welcome me. There is a crucial and fundamental difference between an approach to a situation in which one refers to an exhaustive sketch of all elements at present—out of which you presumably are only aware of a tiny, almost vanishing fraction, honestly speaking. Or if one refers to his or her actual, bodily representation of this present situation manifest in actions, movements, and desires, drives and vital energies, boredom and indifference. A sonic persona assumes this hearing perspective to an experiential situation:

> It is no longer seen as the straightforward result of associations established during experience, but a total awareness of my posture in the intersensory world. (Merleau-Ponty 1962: 114)

It is the joy of offering you a warm cup of tea or coffee to welcome you. Such situated awareness is constituted mainly by a series of experiential movements and actions—never only abstractly, never verbally or propositionally only, never merely via signs and sign operations:

> The multiplicity of points or "heres" can in the nature of things be constituted only by a chain of experiences in which on each occasion one and no more of them is presented as an object, and which is itself built up in the heart of this space. And finally, far from my body's being for me no more than a fragment of space, there would be no space at all for me if I had no body. (Merleau-Ponty 1962: 117)

Your individually grown body constitutes your idiosyncratic awareness of space, your knowledge of it, your access to it. My back hurts only a bit. I need to pee. This distinction between a more propositional, an apparatic and formulaic *spatiality of position*, from an experiential and performative, a situated and visceral, a materially affective *spatiality of situation*, is the one that lies at the core of a sonic persona and its hearing perspective. The day was long, I will pick up a colleague from the airport in a minute. I have been anticipating our meeting for quite some time now, and it will probably motivate me to leave this place much too early. I will be too early. I like this. Whereas distantly objectifying processes and apparatic dispositives of contemporary societies and their administrative institutions demand an immovable and inalterable position to locate and to analyze a given situation— the individual, immersive, and personal experience of perception and affect is one that differs and moves and changes incessantly. The momentary way of experiencing and perceiving an alien is never distant. It cannot be. You need a haircut, really? Do you think? As soon as humanoid aliens *try* to imagine themselves in such a distancing and authoritarian objectifying position, they do exactly this: they *imagine*, they invent, they confabulate this seemingly objective perspective as a possibly inspiring, illustrating, surely idiosyncratic, and hopefully provoking perspective onto their actual situation. There is a smell of gastric acid in the air. This position of objectivity is a construction, maybe a very clever, technologically enhanced, and supported construction, but it remains a construction, driven by imaginary urges and confined to the realm of the symbolic. Did someone just have a smoke in here? I never really smoked, but now—I could imagine? Such a position on the radical, detached outside is in no way the actual, experiential everyday way of perceiving oneself in an actual situation you or I enter necessarily in total immersion. The window is being closed. The objectifying position is an imaginary perspective of total, omnipotent and omniscient overview. You can hear how the book is slowly being closed in the library's reading room. A phantasm, if not a rather generative one of researchers and thinkers. The electric hum around me suddenly becomes audible.

Varying experientiality

An alien's sensorium is never identical in detail. It is a plastic, an altering, a quite flexible entity. No—it is definitely *not* an *entity*: It is more a kind of resulting *quality, a tendency, an inclination or proclivity* that emerges out of the myriad of single, continuously transforming properties in any humanoid agent; it emerges out of the situations, the performative and perceptual routines one has encountered or has been establishing in the course of her or his existence. *What orbital synchronization did you arrive on?* In the various personal examples in this book, the plasticity, the erratic character, the versatility, and also the astonishment one might find in one's own auditory perception might have become obvious. But isn't this just a minor, perhaps negligible series of examples by someone with a truly deviant focus on the audible? Could such descriptions of highly idiosyncratic experiences actually be regarded as profound research approaches to an anthropology of sound? How could it ever be possible to achieve generalizable insights by such an individualizing approach? Does this endless variety of sensory idiosyncrasies not just find an end in itself? *Let me steal this moment from you now.* The examples in this book, more extensively unfolded or briefly interjected, definitely do *not* represent in themselves the whole of any anthropology of sound. These experiences of sonic traces, narrated and reflected by one sonic persona, might nevertheless serve as selected entry points into how an anthropology of sound could be operating. In contrast to approaches discussed earlier in this book, such individual descriptions, such personal narrations of listening experiences, such *sonic fictions* (Eshun 1998), do not claim to promote one listening or one sound concept that could be generalized easily. Sonic fictions claim the opposite. An erratically personal narration puts its primary emphasis on tiny fractions of an idiosyncratic listening or sensory experience. *Jouissez et répétez.* Yet: How can this impact be incorporated effectively into an epistemology for an anthropology of sound? *Transversal grief.*

In contrast to traditional, philosophical notions of an empty cosmos, a void world in which humanoids are rather helplessly navigating, struggling, in dire need of touch and contact, exchange and—not least—a stable ground, a sensory, a mental, a terminological foundation from which to depart, in contrast to that *epistemology of scarcity,* this present anthropology starts from an *epistemology of richness.* Starting from richness as a basic concept and understanding in research is hence a core issue of *sonic and sensory materialism. The heat between you and me.* Sensory materialism starts with the rather well-founded assumption that at least the known parts of what we can observe are not empty at any single point. It is actually more a densely filled, almost overloaded spatial extension into which aliens like you and me are born—and in which dense cosmos one is immediately integrated in permanent touch with another. Each material entity in this cosmos is never separated from all other material entities. *But I'm still, I'm still an animal.* This axiom of sensory materialism might sound close to paranoia, inevitably leading to sinuous conspiracy theories. This impression mirrors one's apparently contrary ontology space, being radically empty and void. Though there could be larger or smaller areas in the cosmos that fit this description, you would have a hard time finding them in any galaxy or solar system around the corner. The impact of *sonic materialism* on anthropology is profound. As a foundation it suggests an outline of a sonic persona along the following lines: humanoid aliens live through and by their senses; while they might not be actually physically nourished by sensory experiences themselves, these are nevertheless fundamental for their existence. Sensory deprivation to a larger extent might not immediately lead to actual diseases or death; yet in specific constellations and dispositives, a specific amplification of sensory deprivations will surely lead to a regression and destruction of vital character traits. A sonic persona thus deprived of sensory and sonic experiences might decompose to a mere representation of intended and required actions. Truly empty, a void, a meaningless life. Suicide then seems attractive. *Tell me we both matter, don't we?* In each individual's life, the specific signature of sensorial activity is a signature of one's social, spatial, material, and even ephemeral activities. Being a body, one senses and one lives. One smells like it, one tastes like it, one might be moving with it: one sees and hears according to these experiences, according and woven into everyday performativity. Sensory activities in this definition are actually indistinguishable from a wide variety of ways of living and behaving, of milieu and social relations, of habits and customs. Sonic performativity is a vital practice. As a consequence of this basic character of the idiosyncratic sensorium constituting humanoid performativity, behavior, and experience interwoven with various other materialities, it becomes clear that this leads to a supposedly endless possibility of *varieties of experiences.* The idiosyncrasies present in your body, in your everyday life, in your preferences, inclinations, repulsions, and aversions differ, probably at significant extent from mine. Your unavoidable rejection of certain aspects of this book is a symptom of this fundamental difference. As many aliens—as many experiential constellations: as many idiosyncratic implexes; as many sensory corpuses. *Dystopia is here to stay.*

At this point, Michel Serres's argument concerning the inherent fallacies of educated and academic eloquence touched on earlier in this book (in Chapter 2: "Corporealizing The Senses," especially in its second section: Serres's Syrrhesis) becomes vital again. As researchers and as *hommes* or *femmes or aliens de lettres,* but also merely as humanoids in writing cultures, he argues perfectly clearly that we have to be aware of one fact: what we can say and write convincingly about something, vigorously, energetically, fervently, might in the end not be true at all. Serres, a trained seaman, warns recurrently in his writings that writing actually becomes too easily sensorily detached, if not contradicted by experience. Even though it still reads and argues plausibly. The golden mouth, the *bouche d'or* (Serres 1985: 166), speaks eloquently; it has strong arguments, concise descriptions quick at hand at any given moment. Yet this might just be one of the most harmful *déformations professionelles* of academia, of research, and of a globalized and mediatized writing culture expanded to algorithmic and instantaneous writing. Rudolf zur Lippe supports this argument and expands it to a harsh social argument (Lippe 1985: 295). Lippe recognizes a strong segregation between two major classes in contemporary societies with respect to their everyday sensorial investments. He sees an interpreting, *hermeneutic class* rigidly separated with regard to occupation, wealth, habits or traditions, and access from an *exhaustion class*. By these two names, he refers to the main everyday activities by which people in these classes make their living or preserve and multiply their capital: the *hermeneutic class* makes a living by writing spreadsheets and mail, evaluations and minutes, concepts and reviews, by giving orders, sketching calculations, and implementing and instrumentalizing algorithms with a massive impact—whereas the *exhaustion class* has no other option than to exhaust themselves by way of selling all of their bodily energy, the strength of their flesh, the power in their hands, arms, legs, or lungs to a contractor in their lifetime. Whereas the latter class gets to be bodily sucked out until they are sick and ill, old and disempowered, until they die, the former class piles up, while working, even more energy, more capital, more access to new experiences and new forms of capitalization, more options for activities that take even less time and less energy. Members of the hermeneutic class accumulate wealth, whereas members of the exhaustion class can only lose the one resource they have, their bodily powers. You, the reader, and I, the writer—there can be no doubt—we both mainly or even exclusively belong to the lucky *hermeneutic class*. By reading these lines you prove this—as I do by having written them. A *semiotic capitalism* (Szepanski 2014b), redefining the frontlines and the contestants in the class struggle. The match is set before it starts.

Lippe and Serres combined now make a plea for experientiality in research—beyond the semiotically as well as hermeneutically artful constructions of empirical research in the laboratory or in digital modeling. Both authors demand an extended, intense, and also exclusive experience as foundation for actual insight. Bring, Michel Serres could be heard to say (Serres 2008: 111–17), the *hard* of physical resistance and hurt, of bumpy things and edgy creatures, of mucus and dust into the seamlessly, continuously, and malleably *soft* realm of coding and writing, calculating and imagining, phrasing and parametrizing. His emphasis on experience is an emphasis on not generalizing too quick, too hastily, to prematurely assuming one's own trivial notions are easily affirmed by anyone. A tragic assumption that will fail. To every assumption any alien could make, there are so many differing assumptions other aliens will surely be making—and maybe they will even represent a certain relevant majority. There are more sorts of aliens than even an alien itself could imagine. Serres and Lippe are making a plea for *situated empiricism and sensualism*, and consequentially for the epistemic value of intense, idiosyncratic experience full of coincidences. In their *radical empiricism*, a resonance of William James can be heard, a source from over a century ago:

> There is in general no separateness needing to be overcome by an external cement; and whatever separateness is actually experienced is not overcome, it stays and counts as separateness to the end. (James 1912: 89)

For James, experience is nothing exotic, external, undefined, or imaginary. It is a fact of existence:

> Experience itself, taken at large, can grow by its edges. That one moment of it proliferates into the next by transitions which, whether conjunctive or disjunctive, continue the experiential tissue, can not, I contend, be denied. (James 1912: 89)

The continuity of intensities, the overall presence of this vital continuation between activities and encounters, of perceptions and events, constitutes individual experience according to James. Transitions and alterations of intensities and crystallizations, periods of stagnations and ruptures of shift are characteristic of how alien humanoids experience their particular existence:

> Life is in the transitions as much as in the terms connected. . . . It is "of" the past, inasmuch as it comes expressly as the past's continuation; it is "of" the future in so far as the future, when it comes, will have continued it. (James 1912: 89)

Transitions of experience—prospectively as well as retrospectively, in remanence and in anticipation—are not usually covered by verbal arguments and conclusions, in propositions and terminological definitions. For the discourses and dispositives of the natural and the engineering sciences, it is probably necessary to assume an unaltered and stable habit of experiencing in order not to multiply the variables of experimentation beyond what can be handled. Yet, in regard to general epistemologies and as basic assumptions about the behavior and the perception of humanoid aliens, it seems necessary to reverse the established interpretations of individual experience. *I feel like I'm gonna vomit*. To call individual experiences merely *arbitrary* underestimates both the non-arbitrary quality of individual experience and of individual subjectivities. This impression of being arbitrary highlights how logocentric research and writing cultures neglect—via individual speakers as well as well-defined regulations—the fact that no humanoid alien might ever actually be able to experience this world as the well-tempered, objective, and nicely shaped model of arguments and examples, that he or she might eventually be representing in her or his verbal or written account: "Grammar and logic create a world in their own image" (Serres 2008: 193). *On the day of execution. On the day of execution.* To transcend such an abstraction-driven *scripted experience*, one could equip researchers with alternative means of articulating the *varying experiences* within a particular sonic and sensorial situation:

> Unbeknownst to many people, our emotions, cognition, behavior, and mental health are influenced by a large number of entities that reside in our bodies while pursuing their own interests, which need not coincide with ours. (Bressan and Kramer 2015: 464)

Such a genuine collectivity of aliens—consisting of aliens themselves—is better represented by a succession of incredibly tiny and particular situations and experiences, interjections and ruptures that might be erratic and scary, hasty and hectic, lame and boring, eluding and inspiring in surprising comminglings. Hence, in analyzing and tracing the activities and experiences of such a collective of aliens, a different kind of documenting, of writing, of interpreting is needed: a *third tongue*—aside from the eloquently talking tongue of the presenter and teacher—is needed, of which Michel Serres claims (as discussed in Chapter 3: "Corporealization of the Senses," section 1985: Serres's Syrrhesis) it takes its time, with "sapience and sagacity" (Serres 2008: 163). A varying selection of time and dynamics that intensely performs a *slow scholarship* (Mountz 2015). Stressing experiential moments in combination with their contextualization and historicization might provide, then, a far more adequate way to start and to guide a sensory and a sonic analysis. *Oh I'll be free.* Such an anthropological analysis, corporeal and non-logocentric, seems to be far more appropriate to the field of the sonic than one that only describes, for instance, the circuits of signal processing on the occasion of such a situation, the communication processes or the information theory behind it. *A wave of mutilation.* An experiential approach to sound and listening, to time and to space, to situation, to transitions and transformations, represents in itself an act of resistance against hegemonic dispositives of science and technology—even more so under the rigid social demands and economic requirements of accelerated trade and intensified capitalist exploitation of humanoid and non-humanoid resources. Intensely capitalized cultural practices might only rarely, in selected moments, be able to provide the time and the space for such an experiential form of activity. *I didn't know that such music existed in the World and now I know.* One would then progress only after having granted oneself the time to *actually* experience something, to deliberately scrutinize certain potential transitions, ruptures, or undertones? Experience is, for both James and Serres, a fundamental and generative force, as it contributes to the *creation of meaning* (Gendlin 1962; the approach of Gendlin will be more extensively explored in the following chapter of this book, "A Sensory Corpus"). Varying kinds of experiences of alien humanoids make it necessary to respect their genuine and generative quality: the generativity of a situated and expanded experience as well as the generativity of highly idiosyncratic preferences and rejections. Humanoids are:

> not unitary individuals in control of ourselves but rather "holobionts" or superorganisms—meant here as collections of human and nonhuman elements that are to varying degrees integrated and, in an incessant struggle, jointly define who we are. (Bressan and Kramer 2015: 464)

Taking this description—on the fringes between psychology and microbiology—as a foundation for the varying experiences of humanoid and non-humanoid actors again multiplies the possible ways of experiences. Aliens like you and me consist of aliens and contribute to aliens, mutually supporting and questioning, increasing and decreasing in impact, reflux, in circular and spiraling individual economies, interconnected and interwoven (cf. Ahmed 2006; Stewart 2007; Gregg and Seigworth 2010).

> Such selfish entities include microbes, viruses, foreign human cells, and imprinted genes regulated by viruslike elements. (Bressan and Kramer 2015: 464)

Their experience is an emergent function of agency occurring in physical and in performative materialities: a multiplicity of personae appear as articulations of *experience*. Sensory personae. Textual personae. Personae in working contexts. Personae in the context of romantic relationships. Personae in sports. Personae in sexual practices. Personae in food preferences. Personae in humor and in comic situations. Personae in sadness and grief. Personae in ambivalence. This supposedly endless multitude of sexual, bodily, habitual, or age-related experiences and appearances is therefore a mere logical necessity. "L'homme est malade parce qu'il est mal construit" (Artaud 1947): *Man is sick because he is badly constructed*. You or I and he or she and X will be an ever-changing, switching persona—drifting along material situations and interpersonal relations. Xenopersonae in flux. "Lorsque vous lui aurez fait un corps sans organes, alors vous l'aurez délivré de tous ses automatismes et rendu à sa véritable liberté" (ibid.): *When you have made him a body without organs, then you will have delivered him from all his automatisms and restored him to his true liberty* (Artaud 1992: 329). Everyone's a different alien. *I just begin.* "Alors vous lui réapprendrez à danser à l'envers comme dans le délire des bals musette et cet envers sera son véritable endroit" (Artaud 1947). *Then you will teach him again to dance inside out as in the delirium of our accordion dance halls and that inside out will be his true side out* (Artaud 1992: 329). Being an alien like you and me means your lifeform is at least as improbably deformed and alienated and transformed as mine. Humanoid aliens like us exist in this ongoing flux of becoming ever more alien, divergently experiencing. "If nature is unjust, change nature!" (Laboria Cuboniks 2015)

Anthropology of sound

I lie on the ground. There are wooden panels underneath my back. One by one adding up to a consistent and stable, a thick and sound floor. It is a house in the woods, in the southwest of Germany, the so-called *Schwarzwald*, the Black Forest. It is in the early 1990s as I lie there for some weeks, several hours every day, in a sunny square on this wooden floor, smelling the resin and the fir needles in this rather small and hunched house, built in the way they built in this area at least since the sixteenth century. Traveling back there, at this moment in my mid-20s, two decades ago, I am teleported to this situation, the smells and sensory extravaganza, to my forms of habitus, my bodily self-image then. Yet, I do not actually remember anymore *why* I really chose this place to lay on the floor, in this broad balcony for many hours every day. Maybe it was just a momentary impulse into which I then drifted further and further, indulging more and more this completely sensorial, completely reflexive practice of lying, of sensing and imagining, of remembering, connecting ideas and hunches of words or propositions—*I'm going to prove the impossible really exists*—then back to smelling and seeing under my eyelids, and for longer and longer stretches, half an hour sometimes, to selected events of the outside world, whose sonic traces led to me. I enjoyed it a lot, this is what I remember for sure, so vividly. Though, no—*enjoying* would probably be the wrong word for this activity. I found this to be, self-evidently, an adequate way of behaving and spending my days—for me, that is. In those long minutes, maybe hours every day, my body was not really a hindrance or even a main actor; I suspect, in those minutes, my body acted more as a multisensory receiver. I remember—about 20 years later, and surely deformed and reinvented by my memory—the resinous smell of the old and glazed fir wood. I remember the warm, thick, and constantly increasing heat on this wood. I engaged in being this *sensory persona*. A persona, lying on the floor. A persona in readiness.

This experience has been engraved into my corpus and idiosyncratic sensorium. The fact that such a behavior might seem strange, weird, repelling, or even sick to anyone reading these lines might be some hint that it would probably not qualify as a norm—but rather an idiosyncratic preference: where I find joy, I like to indulge in it, I draw a lot of subjectivizing and vitalizing, inspiring energy from it. Though others might also be able to find joy in this, maybe they don't incorporate this behavior into their own *sensory persona* as crucial—let alone their *professional persona*. In those moments I listened to a *Hörspiel*. I indulged being reduced to just this sensory receiver, focusing its sensing, reflecting, and thinking to all things audible. This *listening game*, this *audiogame*, received its original name, *Hörspiel*, from Friedrich Nietzsche in 1876. In his polemic analysis of Richard Wagner's aesthetics in the *Unzeitgemäße Betrachtungen* (*Untimely Meditations*), he introduced the term. From the 1920s onward, *Hörspiel* was appropriated and disseminated as the name for experimental, often not even narrative, not even scenic, *radiophonic art* on German radio:

> Then we feel certain that in Wagner all that is visible in the world wants to become more profound and more intense by becoming audible, that it seeks here its lost soul; and that all that is audible in the world likewise wants to emerge into the light and also become a phenomenon for the eye; that it wants as it were to acquire corporality. (Nietzsche 1997: 223)

Wagner's remarkable efforts to establish a theatrical apparatus for intense, totally designed, and absolutely immersive sensorial-aesthetic experiences are for Nietzsche an example of how to scrutinize listening, seeing, and corporeality in general. Everything audible—according to the interpretation by Nietzsche—becomes, in Wagner's art, an object for experience— and at the same time, this whole audible realm also becomes corporeal and visible. Sonic traces materialize in the sensory corpus of listeners, composers, performers:

> His art always conducts him along this twofold path, from a world as an audible spectacle into a world as a visible spectacle enigmatically related to it, and the reverse; he is continually compelled—and the beholder is compelled with him—to translate visible movements back into soul and primordial life, and conversely to see the most deeply concealed inner activity as a visible phenomenon and to clothe it with the appearance of a body. (Nietzsche 1997: 223)

This *implex* of Wagner's aesthetics as understood by Nietzsche actually reflects the multisensorial and the intrinsically corporeal character of sonic experiences. A *Hörspiel* in this sense retains and promotes these two potentially indistinguishable qualities: listening as a corporeal as well as a reflective, meditative activity. If sound is indeed nothing else than a "mechanical disturbance from a state of equilibrium that propagates through an elastic material medium" (Encyclopedia Britannica 2003), then a *Hörspiel* provides the adequate *auditory display* for the *hearing perspective* of *sonic epistemologies*. The lights went out. A bright lamp, as if in an interrogation chamber, was switched on. Some machinery booted up, robotic arms started to move. Soft, only slightly dissonant string sounds could be heard, distorted. The electromechanical arms seemed to prepare something in this cubic raree-show. In this cage, like nurses or assistants they moved around a dentist's chair coated with fur. Drumsticks beat on guitar strings, a metal voice gave orders and explicated the required rules of conduct. An announcer or bouncer. The music got more tense, more dissonant, the dentist's chair was lowered. Pitched sounds of hurtful drills could be heard. As if already lowered into one's dental nerves. Red lights, labyrinthine cantilène. Blue light. A sparkling mirror ball all around. The chair was raised again. Lights out. This work by artists Janet Cardiff and Georges Bures Miller is composed of different visible, invisible, tactile, and immaterial elements: the robotic arm was developed by Carlo Crovato; the drumming section was conceived and constructed by Titus Maderlechner; and the music one hears is by Freida Abtan, a piece called *Heartstrings*. Effectively, the movements of this machine are hard to predict. After experiencing this work, the allusion to one of the most disturbing dystopian texts by Franz Kafka is rather obvious: *In der Strafkolonie* (*In the Penal Colony*). Cardiff and Miller's work is a parody, if not a sarcastic rejection, of media and auditory media art decorated and made fashionable with the latest kind of automatic apparatuses: one does not see any alien humanoid at all—albeit it depicts a moment of forced treatment. A situation in which there is no subject anymore—only objects. The object of torture is not allowed to move. It must passively endure the series of kinesthetic, sonic, and visual actions occurring. The invisible alien is the target of this refined media apparatus. There is no *Hörspiel* anymore, as there is no one essentially listening. Only a dead body in rigor mortis on which soundwaves arrive. The sonic persona as actor, who decides when to sound and when to listen, is annihilated. Listening is no game here. The apparatus prevails, once again.

A sonic persona listens beyond this apparatus. Sonic personae rebel against such paralyzing machinations. Idiosyncratic sensibilities of a persona can be *heard*, but they can also be *articulated* in a fictitious, even in a legal person: following a *symmetric anthropology* (Latour 1993), institutions are to be recognized as acting, performing, and effective entities, and they do leave their own very specific sonic traces in space and time. What would be the benefit of this approach to sensory appearance and performativity? First of all, this approach allows us to analyze collective gatherings of aliens, be they institutions or vertebrae, bacteria or algorithms, toolkits or currents following the traces of their sonic persona. But secondly, as sonic personae, humanoid aliens are respected in their genuinely erratic performativity: an interpretation of rhythms and syncopations, of sounds and swings, a *rhythmanalysis* (Lefebvre 1992) is by definition inherently different than interpreting culture from its seemingly static monuments, regulations, and artifacts. Sonic analysis establishes a corporeal and ubiquitous reflexivity. As anthropology of the flesh, *un anthropologie du chair, eine Anthropologie des Leibes*, it expands reflection and critique to all things sensible—beyond propositions and equations. From playing with listening, this anthropology of sound emerges. *Hörspiel als Klanganthropologie.*

CHAPTER SIX

A sensory corpus

The material percept

With a small group of people, I wander cautiously through an area we have never been in before. With eyes closed. I can sense what is around me, though. I can sense it with my upper arms and my upper legs; with the bone structure of my upper cranium; with my buttocks and the soles of my feet, with the palms of my hands. With a multitude of active agents in, at, and around my body, sensing and probing incessantly. A *networked sensorium*, you could call a person like me, so to speak. It is sheer joy. It is an excitement of sensory excess, an excitement that is exhausting, for sure. The longer I move through this environment, the more I am surprised by how many, even miniscule, details of all the buildings, the trees and plants, of all the nearby creatures and all their actions going on, reach me in every single moment, by every particle of a fraction of a second. It seems to me that I could sense even more than I would usually, doing my errands and reading and writing in front of glowing screens of varying sizes. Am I not sensing the winds and the streams around here suddenly? Am I sensing how the colder air, as well as some warmer air, flows around me and up to me, against me? Some temperature changes, I seem to sense, with people approaching—or when I am approaching a car, a motorcycle, a bus, just parked right here or standing there for quite some time. A public display of advertisements of any kind is remarkably less warm, and any glass front of a shop or a sculpture outside a churchyard is, again, much colder. On top, I can also sense the peculiar smell of old and decayed granite and of fine-grained sandstone, the endlessly tiny particles streaming and oozing from stones—and the particles of cleaning chemicals and production processes' byproducts that surround glass fronts or displays in public. I seem to sense right now how all of this—in unforeseeable complexity, countermovements and sudden thresholds—is truly *sensible*: a series of distinct symptoms of moving objects, of things, and of creatures—of environmental, geological, of urban processes all around me. With a group of young artists, researchers, writers, and journalists, I am walking, blindly. Each one of us in separation, but together as a loosely interlinked group via our shared efforts, we are exploring how one could navigate through this space. A space that is not accessible to us any more by traditional sight via eyeballs. Can we succeed in navigating here, nevertheless? Or do I helplessly drift away in headache, in fear, or in social anomia? The tiniest indices for the materialities right here that we cherish—for some of us these are very new, and quite unusual if not uncomfortable, indices. I learn to respect these incredibly ephemeral indices more and more and to recognize them ever more easily and fully than earlier in my life. Essentially, I *train* my ability to pay attention to the subtlest details my common set of *perceptual techniques* (Jonathan Sterne) seems selectively to subordinate to other sensory events. But why should one respect *any* type of sensory event more than any other kinesthetic, olfactory, gustatory, or even auditory event, anyhow? The longer I indulge in this way of moving and sensing, reflecting and musing, this sensory practice becomes less and less weird to me; in the end, it is far less strange for me to access the events and entities around me in this particular way, encountering materialities with these practices. Could these practices become part of my sonic persona at some point? These materialities I am sensing: They are what *is* there. *The given datum.*

Some weeks later, after this extensive exercise in *human echolocation* (Daniel Kish), I am listening to a recording, late at night, at home. This recording can be found online and even written on plastic. I hear needles in my ear. I feel a buzzing, a hissing, a very deep humming. A rasping sound. The longer I listen to this recording, the more I am taken over by its dynamics and its encompassing quality. I am enveloped by—no: I am *filled* with this sound production. Its resonances are flooding my body, more and more, up to my chin, up to my cochlea, my utricle and my saccule, to my amygdala. What I am hearing is not a sort of *music*, as it has been conceptualized in premodern times. Essentially, I listen to resonances of edifices and of larger infrastructural networks, to migrating social groups, to an urban situation unfolding, snap by snap. Pinch by pinch. In the sound works by Maryanne Amacher, the artist I am listening to, such recorded vibrations and interferences, such resonances and repercussions, constitute the *perceptual material*. For decades, between 1967 until her passing away in 2009, she developed her sound artworks out of the intensely ephemeral sound events in specific listening situations. Especially in her two major workgroups, *City-Links* (1967–88) and *Intelligent Life* (1981–2009), she took the buildings she was working *with*, working *in*, and working *for* as the genuine generators of the sounds she would be working with. In two dozen sound installations in studio buildings, harbor facilities, fish markets, or insurance office buildings, she used the materiality of these situations and recorded and transmitted sounds referring to the specific history of these places and their supposed or factual usage. The parameters of her sonic artifacts hence are taken from the wall works, the reverberation times, resonating wood shields, broken up exit doors, or noise abatement measurements in windows. In listening to a piece by Maryanne Amacher, one does indeed materially listen to an actual location, an architectural building with its characteristic *aural architecture* (Blesser/ Ruth-Salter). The *material percept* stored in these recordings becomes audible. I listen to stones and steel, to glass or wood, to gum and lacquer. The material percepts of historical locations have been transmitted to me in these sonic artifacts. Amacher called her pieces *sonic choreographies.* In listening to these artifacts, my listening body is dancing and is moving, in vertigo and in joy with these sounds that are in many instances generated not by the membranes of my loudspeakers or headphones, but by the hearing nerves and hairs in my inner ear, by so-called *otoacoustic sounds*—sounds as generated by the ear in its physical appearance itself. Maryanne Amacher turned my individual ear into an instrument she is posthumously playing on: She is playing on my ears—and that is the resulting sonic artifact. *I am the percept now.*

This given environment and its specimen of sounds are present. I am immersed in this situation. I am not separated by all things happening here—be they recorded, transmitted live, delayed to a larger degree, or taking place right here—even if I digress, I fantasize, I invent or elaborate imaginary situations. I am listening, and while I am doing so, I engage in a whole variety of epistemological practices. Since the 1980s, Pauline Oliveros explored selected listening practices of an epistemological kind by the name of *deep listening.* As a refined practice, deep listening allows for a radical yet sustainable and often rather slow and unsettling new experience of the sonic. As a practice for listening research, it contributes to this anthropology of sound by providing a practice of meditation that lets one perform a *corporeal and ubiquitous reflexivity*:

> Deep listening is listening in every possible way to every thing possible to hear no matter what you are doing. Such intense listening includes the sounds of daily life, of nature, of one's own thoughts as well as musical sounds. Deep listening is my life practice. (Oliveros 1998: 3)

In a meditating immersion into the encompassing immanence of present sounds, it becomes possible to analyze this empirically given situation, right here, right now. It is an experiential approach to research—not too distant from the *acoustemology* Steven Feld proposed in the 1980s. Though decisively *not* a method focusing foremost on sonic artifacts or meditation, Feld's approach demands an equally deep immersion into specific *material percepts of a given situation*. A reflective sensibility for immanence:

> We will say of pure immanence that it is A LIFE, and nothing else. It is not immanence to life, but the immanent that is in nothing is itself a life. A life is the immanence of immanence, absolute immanence. (Deleuze 2005: 27)

Epistemological approaches to the audible and the sonic could and should thus—following Feld and Oliveros, as well as incorporating Deleuze and Guattari—open up

> the potential of acoustic knowing, of sounding as a condition of and for knowing, of sonic presence and awareness as potent shaping forces in how people make sense of experiences. (Feld 1982: 97)

Deep listening and acoustemology are inherently *sonic epistemologies* indulging in and scrutinizing the immanence of listening experiences and sounding events. As their research and listening practices operate solely by and through a listener's and researcher's body in dense empirical contact with surrounding, immersing, and altering material percepts, they even constitute *corporeal epistemologies*. In *human echolocation*, these experimental and partly artistic research practices of the corporeal are culminating and evolving. In the intensely trained and deeply epistemological listening of echolocating humanoid aliens, the experimental becomes a legitimately and practically proven method. The set of perceptual techniques that Daniel Kish, for instance, is refining and teaching takes the whole of the humanoid sensorium—smell, tactility, kinesthetics, acoustics—*except vision* to move seamlessly through an environment. All sensory abilities in aliens like us hence become capable of establishing reliable representations for a secure orientation in a given environment. This practice already existed in centuries past, called rather mystifyingly *facial sight* or *facial perception* (Supa, Cotzin Dallenbach 1944) to fulfill the urge of retaining at least a humanoid's face and skin as a responsive sensorium. The sounds genuinely emanating from any sonic agents and sonic personae and reflected, sonar-like, by target obstacles, are also actively provoked: for instance, by sound practices using the tongue for the meticulously precise *click*-sound. The research practices proposed by Pauline Oliveros, hence, follow the same path: they establish—without excluding vision—a stronger, more intense, and situated relation and exploration of sounds that can be sensed, smelled, touched, and thought about. In *deep listening*, the endless multifaceted qualities of a sonic experience are unfolded, further and further, with no end than to unfold them even more. This research practice is less applied than human echolocation, but in contrary, more focused in researcher training and in basic research: what can you sense in sounds—and what else can you open up in these sounds? How can one learn to open up even more qualities in even more situated sounds? Finally, the work by Maryanne Amacher doesn't provide a simple, applicable, or learnable method at first glance; yet, as a major artistic approach to sound art, her work radiated into manifold other sound artists who then followed—in one way or another—her example of exploring the materialities and the sonic specificities of buildings, of sites, of any location. Since then, site-specific and materially conscious forms of sound art installations are referring to the example of Maryanne Amacher; artists are following her strategies, expanding them, unfolding them, listening to spaces and physics in a given situation—materially and corporeally. This meaningful and reflected listening practice forms a sensory epistemology including, among others, selected micro-practices of deep listening, human echolocation, and others. In contrast to common misconceptions, such sensory epistemologies are *not* reducing perception to only one sense (here: the auditory)—but opening up perception to a vast multitude of a humanoid alien's sensorium (by excluding vision). Passive tactile echolocation via bodily skin perception, discerning of changes in temperature or air flow, trained kinesthetic senses, ephemeral aural perception, palatal clicks with the tongue (Kish 1982), and various individually developed practices form a corpus of sensory and sonically relevant epistemic practices. Corporeal epistemologies therefrom *exercise and expand polysensory perception* beyond the limits of culturally habitualized sensory practices. The corporeal-sensory apparatus of researchers is trained and refined here like in any other research practice operating with measuring instruments or with reproduction technology. The material percept is at the same time medium and access to research for corporeal epistemologies. Dispositives of logocentrism are mutated, reorganized, and reassigned a new and differing position.

Corpus in situ

A humanoid's body is *never without* a situation. An alien's experience is *never not* situated. At a given moment, one might decide to leave the characteristics of an actual situation aside and exchange them for other, maybe imaginary, sensorial, unconscious, abstract characteristics; then again, one finds oneself in yet another situation in an imaginary, sensorial, unconscious, abstract one. The individual body is situated and it is located. It is characterized by its temporal and environmental situation. As a humanoid alien, one is in constant unconscious relation to things, to beings, to events, to processes, and to perceptual realities and materialities around—even if imaginary. Bodies are unsurprisingly spatial reactors, situated and material.

What one might call one's body is hence not a *thing*. It is definitely not a petrified some*thing*. A body is not a thing one *has* in a transparent and fully accessible way—like you might possess your sweater, a piece of bread, or even a stretch of land. The body *you have* is essentially the body *you are*. There is no immaterial access to material entities (Miller 1998, 2008, 2010). A humanoid hence does not have a completely self-transparent access to material realities: the body that grants you or me access is at the same time the material medium that hinders, filters, alters and detours, focuses and perspectivizes your or my form of access. Access to material percepts, if possible at all, is by definition restricted and limited: it is constrained and materialized by bodies and their idiosyncratic preferences and aversions. This is the *corpus*: A materially perceiving and performing body in tension, in desire, in idiosyncrasies and individuality. This discerns a vividly living body from a dead carcass—or of rejected outcasts treated and administered as dead and rather bothersome carcasses. Aliens are corpus: the individually malformed, weirdly idiosyncratic, sensorially highly receptive if not stubborn sculptures, constituted by experiences and personal as well as cultural history and the *longue durée* of a pre-history of sensibilities—spoiled and biased, idiosyncratic and densely tattooed with desires and fears, with boredom and hectic. From an exclusively mechanistic and utilitarian approach, this fact of humanoid corpora being tainted and flawed poses a severe problem as regarded by standards of linear progression and immediate response to cause and effect. The body is a bug. Yet, from a sensory anthropology approach, exactly these deformations are the reason for corpuses to grant access to material substances: a linear body, immaterially conceptualized, is not capable of specific experiences. A linear and machinic body will represent linear and reproducible encounters with materialities: a symbolic imaginary of materials—not the material realities of a situation. Its encounters and irritations would rather be equalized, if not erased. The supposed problems of idiosyncrasy are exactly its most valid quality, providing gateways to experience. Experience as reproducible and generalizable in all its characteristics could not qualify as experience anymore. It would, in turn, qualify more as a temporary state of events with no severe consequences. Inconsequential annoyances.

The fundamental quality of situated lives of humanoid aliens might not really have changed in modern times, though the more specific material constellations and cohabitants of such situations truly have. At any given moment in the early twenty-first century, humanoids are surrounded by more devices that can emit or generate sound than ever before in cultural history: the number of loudspeakers in any location you might enter these days is at least equal to—or even larger than—the number of humanoids at this location (Herbert 2011). You might be carrying at least one mobile networked device, a cell phone, a tablet device, a portable game console. This number might multiply in the not so distant future as networked modules of active sensors, data mining, and sensory display could potentially occupy every single material object or creature around. This cultural experience of being surrounded, consulted, and supported by a vast number of machines has developed into a commonly shared reality of *distributed subjectivity* (Kassabian 2013). It is this material presence of speakers, amplifiers, and cables in every shopping mall, in every public space, in cars and public transport, in any bar or dance club, in open-air venues or intimately shared private spaces, that has paved the ground for the reflections on sonic materialism and ubiquitous listening. This relationship between corporeality and situatedness takes form in a way that is more complicated than the apparently simple notion of material presence and percepts might suggest. Strictly physically speaking, the spatial area in which anthropoid aliens exist is no void. Even with a lack of sound-emitting gadgetry, it is—again, physically speaking—densely filled with materials, gases, objects, particles, dust, air currents, and fumes: These are the material carriers of sound waves. They constitute the elastic material medium whose equilibrium is being disturbed continuously. These particles, aerosols, and things constitute the substance of the material percept. As soon as you hear anything, you listen to this distributed substance of dust and gases, cavities and matter. *Listening is an alien corpus resonating to matter.* Sensing sound is an activity realized by a medium—thus turning the listening aliens into media of resonance themselves. Multiple waves of pressure reach a humanoid's skin, bones, flesh, his or her diaphragms, eardrums, vocal chords, and cochlea constantly throughout their existence. Individually and idiosyncratically experienced corporeality is an effect of listening as situated: an effect of humanoid bodies being situated and immersed in material percepts. Perceptual activity and material presence are merely two descriptions of the encounter between a living corpus and an area of matter. This situated character of experience is the main argument in Merleau-Ponty's phenomenology of spatiality, discussed in the previous chapter of this book (especially in the section: The Sonic Persona). It is the immanence in a *spatiality of situation* that distinguishes perceptual techniques and self-perceptual practices of humanoids from spatial descriptions that represent a *spatiality of position*. As more simple machines cannot have a sense of their own corporeality, they can only note their punctual position in a geometrical space. As Merleau-Ponty writes: "there would be no space at all for me if I had no body" (Merleau-Ponty 1962: 117). Corpus generates space.

As soon as this space is generated by a corpus, yours or mine, the interpretation of such a situation, of such a scene, is a troubling issue. It is no longer accessible as an objective *datum*. It is a *generation*. This generation of space is never exclusive or restricted; it is not a lonely or solitary activity. It is taking place in the midst of other aliens, other streams of particles, in trajectories and included in the intentionality of other things, agents, processes. If one intends to analyze such a situation, a narrative approach to describe or to sketch the whole of a scene or situation is needed. The *existential analysis, Existenzialanalyse* or *Daseinsanalyse* (Heidegger) of a philosophy, even assuming solitary beings independent from others, is then to be replaced by a *coexistential analysis*—the name Jean-Luc Nancy gives his approach in *Être Singulier Pluriel* (*Being Singular Plural*): analyzing actions, agents, performative acts interlaced in coexistence. In a convincing continuation of his efforts to think corporeality under the conditions of contemporary cultures, Nancy here makes an effort to think being under contemporary conditions of copresence and coexistence. According to Nancy, *being-with-one-another* (Nancy 2000: 77) is almost unthinkable for historical approaches of subject-centered philosophy:

> In being-with and as being-with, we have always already begun to understand meaning, to understand ourselves and the world as meaning. And this understanding is always already completed, full, whole, and infinite. We understand ourselves infinitely—ourselves and the world— and nothing else. (Nancy 2000: 98)

In *being-with*, the intensely felt presence of other aliens than yourself is fundamental: *situated being*. An anthropology of sound hence needs to think listening, sounding, and resonating not in terms of linear, objectified, and neatly discerned atoms in signal processing. An anthropology of sound is necessarily an *Anthropology of With* (Schulze 2007): *resonating-with, sounding-with, listening-with*. There is no sonic performativity without sonic co-presence. Listening implies sounding, resonance; assumes listening, sounding; includes and influences listening. The confluence Nancy and also Serres (discussed earlier in Chapter 3: "Corporealizing the Senses") are conceptually aspiring to is effectively taking place as soon as one is present in a sonic environment—in *sonic flux*:

> "With" is neither mediate nor immediate. The meaning that we understand, insofar as we understand it, is not the product of a negation of Being, a negation destined to represent itself to us as meaning, nor is it the pure and simple ecstatic affirmation of its presence. "With" neither goes from the same to the other, nor from the same to the same, nor from the other to the other. In a certain sense, the "with" does not "go" anywhere; it does not constitute a process. But it is the closeness, the brushing up against or the coming across, the almost-there [la-peu-pres] of distanced proximity. (Nancy 2000: 98)

Exactly this *distanced proximity* describes an anthropology of with: it describes the cocreation, the cogeneration of a situation—a *syrrhesis* of a situated sonic scenario. This sonic scenario constitutes a *sonario* (Gampe 2014) in which the genuinely situated aspects of a sonic performance are inextricably amalgamated with the performance itself. Sonic acts by situated sensory corpora generate foremost this experiential space: *sonario*. It is this aspect of corporeality and performativity, of coexistence and cocreation, that connects the situated spatial experience in phenomenology to equally specific descriptions of situated everyday life in cultural studies. Listening and sounding in contemporary as well as in historical vernacular cultures are practices of everyday life. Listening is therefore situated as a result of everyday practices: the corporeal phenomenology of Jean-Luc Nancy is inherently (though not explicitly) interlinked with Henri Lefebvre's concept of the everyday. In following this concept, it becomes obvious that aliens like you and me experience a given sonic situation, a *sonario*, mainly as an "intersection of the sector man controls and the sector he does not control" (Lefebvre 2014: 21). This tension between controllable and uncontrollable areas of life characterizes the mingled situation of listening in an *Anthropology of Sounding With*: A sonario is, again, neither fully transparent in its dynamics, its expected environmental processes, or its specific individual influences—nor is it completely arbitrary and aleatory in what sensory events are taking place there. What a humanoid alien can encounter in such a sonically situated scenario of everyday life is open, unsure, surprising—and yet one can be very sure to experience occurrences one did not expect as well occurrences one did:

> Whereas the extant canned music companies proceed from the basis of regularizing environments by blanketing their acoustic and atmospheric idiosyncracies, Ambient Music is intended to enhance these. (Eno 1978)
>
> The concept of everyday life is therefore closely related to minor, highly personal, and mostly repetitive situations: moments of exaltation, excitement, and ecstasy also find their place here. It is this aspect of repetition in an erratic area that makes it part of the field of *ubiquitous listening*. (Kassabian 2013)
>
> Whereas conventional background music is produced by stripping away all sense of doubt and uncertainty (and thus all genuine interest) from the music, Ambient Music retains these qualities (Eno 1978)

Ubiquitous listening as everyday listening is *adequate listening* (Stockfelt 1997) in its most consistent contemporary and corporeally copresent form. It is a corporeal and mainly subconscious form of listening. It is to a certain extent opening up a situation in which one likes to immerse. It is a *listening-with*, a listening in a sonario:

> And whereas their intention is to "brighten" the environment by adding stimulus to it (thus supposedly alleviating the tedium of routine tasks and levelling out the natural ups and downs of the body rhythms) Ambient Music is intended to induce calm and a space to think. (Eno 1978)

If a piece of ambient music would meet these programmatic ambitions as stated by Brian Eno in the late 1970s, it would indeed provide a sonic artifact in resonance to a sonario: the listening corpus would then be as immersed into the sonario as in practices of human echolocation or in an infrastructural composition by Maryanne Amacher.

> Ambient Music must be able to accommodate many levels of listening attention without enforcing one in particular; it must be as ignorable as it is interesting. (Eno 1978)

Ambient Music as experienced by a *situierter Leib*, a *corpus in situ*, proceeds by *deep listening*. This corpus in situ accesses the sensorial real.

A generative sensorium

The situation of a listening experience is itself not without framing. Situatedness as a concept has been introduced into the discourse of listening and sounding in a moment when supposedly non-situated apparatuses were taking over listening practices to a large extent and transforming them into amplifying, recording, and storing practices. Since the second half of the twentieth century, this codevelopment of the technological apparatus for listening and the emphasis on the situated and personal character of listening can be observed: the hi-fi dispositive of audio culture generated a discourse of personal listening experiences and vice versa. A new focus on the listening persona's experience, her or his intimate reflections, imaginations, ruminations, and daydreams, their sensory experiences and strangely weird auscultations, could now be articulated, fearlessly. The concept of situated listening is hence related to experiences of auditory sensitivity and challenged by audio technology. One of the main issues, still not fully explicated, is the question of sonic and therefore also musical meaning: how could one humanoid alien actually generate a specific and rather stable meaning out of such a transitory and situated entity as a sonic experience? Moreover, how is it even possible at all that individual, highly idiosyncratic, and very often weirdly arbitrary experiences effectively generate meaning? Traditionally these questions have been addressed by semiotics. Yet, the strand of *cultural semiotics* (Posner 2008; Lorusso 2015) focusing on the interpretation of cultural artifacts, practices, and discourses prefers mainly stable, recurring, and less transitory things and signs, writings, and actions as objects of interpretation—be they visual or sculptural, inscribed or coated, designed, developed or tinkered. The inherently ephemeral character of sonic traces poses serious challenges for semiotics in dealing with such unseizable specimens. Ferdinand de Saussure's definition of the sign's double structure out of *signifié* and *signifiant*, and even the more complex and generative approach by Charles Sanders Pierce to define a *semiotic triangle* out of *representamen* (sign vehicle), *interpretant* (ways of sensemaking), and *object* (reference), certainly are results of a semiotic urge to secure stability in objects to be interpreted. This urge for materially stabilizing interpreted signs can result in an ontological distinction between the supposedly stable realm of practice, the corporeal, and the material on the one hand—and the supposedly ephemeral realm of theory and of thinking, of argument and discourse, on the other hand. The basic distinctions in Saussure's and Pierce's semiotics serve these days as useful and highly operational concepts for stable artifacts; albeit it appears more and more perverted if expanded to ephemeral and fragile entities and instances. The fallacy plays out as soon as the interpretation of a certain ephemeral example is generalized beyond its empirical context of discovery. Both discriminations in this case—between *signifié* and *signifiant* or *representamen, interpretant,* and *object*—permeate the age-old fallacy to claim an inherent division between "The Mind" and "The Body" as distinct and stable entities. Listening now for a second to the hard drive of the device I am working on to write this chapter, I am enveloped by the materiality of my writing environment in the most extended and non-technical sense. Enveloped by the recorded musical performance I chose to listen to a minute ago, resulting from an article on ongoing intellectual property quarrels these days, *Metall auf Metall* from Kraftwerk. *Franz Schubert*, the following piece on the record. I do not reflect the actual material and signifying properties of this environment in every single instance of my writing activity. Yet, it does have a generative effect on this activity—constituting the erratically idiosyncratic continuum of thinking, deconstructing, questioning, and reinscribing this *Anthropology of Sound*. It effects thinking, it alters operating with meaning. Framing, fueling, and fostering my sensorium.

Materiality and non-materiality, action and non-action, language and non-language, humanoid and non-humanoid are historically dichotomous categories—founded more on each other than on any empirical evidence. To dismantle this imminent threat, writings in semiotics by Charles Sanders Peirce, by Ferdinand Saussure, by Max Bense, or by Umberto Eco insisted on returning especially to the *material percept* of significant objects, inscriptions, gestures, or situations. An immaterial and historical dichotomy is often resolvable by inciting the explosives of materiality. Peirce and Bense, for instance, are thus unsurprisingly *monist* thinkers. They worked on transcending and annihilating distinctions between materiality and meaning. It is a truly ironic fact that later applications of semiotics in various fields so often lost this monist impetus. It seemed apparently all too tempting to bypass the inherently material and erratic appearance of signs and focus mainly on linear sign operations in themselves; here, monism is interpreted as reduction, not as expansion: the idealist *déformation professionelle* of academia prevails. Essentially, it qualifies as an abuse, if not a methodological fallacy, when semiotics are reduced to sign operations: propagandists of this reading of semiotics turn themselves into mere *code engineers* with next to no inclusion of cultural practices or material percepts into their analysis. *Semiosis*, after all, the process of generating—hence using, appropriating, and understanding signs—is defined as a process operating in *material* substances of media:

> Signs are always anchored in a medium. Signs may be more or less dependent upon the characteristics of one medium—they may transfer more or less well to other media—but there is no such thing as a sign without a medium. (Bolter 1991: 195f.)

There is *no immaterial, no immediate* way of transmitting meaning—just as there might not be any meaningless use of material substances. Semiotics converge with a monist and a sensory materialism. The sensorium is made out of material percepts indistinguishably amalgamated in materials with meaning. The semantic category of *coherence* thus has been expanded and explicated in linguistics by the non-semantic category of *cohesion* (Halliday and Hasan 1976; Schulze 2000). Cohesion, the inherent tension of materials, can hence be a useful category in understanding how material qualities, ties, contrasts, connections, and breaks, flows in an artifact or a performative act, constitute meaning. Cohesion is real in a humanoid alien's experience of its environment. Material percepts have a certain cohesion, a texture, a structure, a feel, and a specific shape, a pattern, and a material consistency that can be physically described, scrutinized, criticized, neglected, praised, enjoyed, or even dismissed. Cohesion represents the real in material percepts. It is sensorially active and efficacious. This excitingly presentist and materialist quality is at the same time a major quality of a humanoid alien's corporeality. In describing the material cohesion of a material percept in relation to your body, you approach these material realities as being part of your corporeal dispositive. This connection between the cohesion of material percepts and the cohesion of a sensing body becomes apparent in Nancy's definition of *Corpus* cited earlier (in Chapter 3: "Corporealization of the Senses"):

> A body is therefore a tension. And the Greek origin of the word is tonos, "tone." A body is a tone. I don't say anything here that an anatomist couldn't agree with: a body is a tonus. (Nancy 2008: 134)

This very tension constitutes a fundamental trait in an alien's corporeality. One might perceive some surroundings as of a certain cohesion in relation to oneself—yet exactly this ability of being able to perceive an apparent cohesion manifests unmistakably one's own tension and one's sense of tensions. It is my individual corporeal tension that enables me to perceive and recognize the cohesion in material percepts. This stunningly reciprocal effect is at the core of a humanoid alien's highly generative sensorium. Rooted in monist materialism, it becomes possible to explore a generative theory of the corpus and the signs, of materials and meanings: a theory that might lead semiotics back to concepts of unstable and plastic signs in motion, in mimesis, in resonance—a monism of malleable and mutual meaning and materialities:

> suppose you were at a party and felt you were bored and needed to go home. But suppose that instead of going home, you opened up the boredom and found anger. And suppose that in finding the anger you found also that you needed to stay and say something directly about the anger to someone. In a similar way as we pursue a goal, the goal seems to change. But later we say the new goal is the one we really wanted all along but we didn't know it. (Gendlin 1992: 203)

Eugene T. Gendlin has for several decades now explored the generative character in semiotics. As early as 1962, he wrote on *Experience and the Creation of Meaning* (Gendlin 1962, reprinted 1997), leading him—thirty years later—to a concept for this relation between experience and meaning. In his article "The Wider Role of Bodily Sense in Thought and Language" (Gendlin 1992), Gendlin lays out extensively how processes of semiosis as language operations are interdependent on processes taking place in corporeal experiences. To anchor sign operations in a corpus of humanoid aliens, Gendlin hence introduces the concept of the *bodily felt sense*. Such a *felt sense* preceding any actual articulation of meaning—be it mimic, gestural, verbal, or visual—is rooted in proprioceptive sensory events humanoids incessantly perceive. As a humanoid alien, one feels one's corpus, the given situation, the relation to other aliens, and present constellations of expectations, obsessions, desires, and fears. This mixture of materialities and affects is present. Proprioceptive events are thus not mere interpretations of material percepts: they are the corporeally sensed, material percepts as such. As in the example by Eugene Gendlin cited above—boredom at a party, anger and the need to talk—a certain bodily felt state of affectivity leads the way into articulating the personal interpretation of a given situation, artifact, or character string. For some readers from the academic profession, this surely comes as a surprise: the impetus for articulation must not be another verbal articulation—but a bodily occurrence. Any proprioceptive event can guide one by means of its affective tension to translate this perception into the cohesion and coherence of a significant gesture, a telling facial expression, a disruptive action, or a tentative, perhaps insecure statement. The articulation of meaning—verbally, performatively, sonically—emerges out of these states of tension that radiate cohesion. This process of generating meaning out of a situated bodily sense for idiosyncratic urges and corporeal events characterizes the corporeal anthropology of humanoid aliens. It constitutes a corporeal generativity, an intrinsic effect of affective tension and temptation, of almost irrefutable necessity to follow this *implex* (Dath), this implied direction of action:

> This coming is characteristic of the body. What else comes like that? Sleep comes like that, and appetites. If they don't come, you just have to wait. We all know that. Tears come like that, and orgasm. Emotions come like that, and so also this felt sense, which is wider and at first not clear, comes like that. (Gendlin 1992: 194)

Semiosis is therefore, following Gendlin, an initially corporeal activity. Generating meaning relies on and is advanced by an anthropoid alien's sensorium. What you can sense will affect your actions and your interpretations of a given environment: sensorial monism in a nutshell. The situation and its material percepts, as well as your corporeal sense in it, generate meaning:

> You can feign joy or anger but to have them, they must come. So also does the muse come, when she is willing and not otherwise. And new ideas, the lines of a new design, and steps of therapy come this way. (Gendlin 1992: 202)

The ground for meaning to be found is thus not a scrutinizing of concepts or arguments, but a basic affect. Such an affect, realized as a bodily felt sense, can subsequently open one up for the intrinsic and specific properties of a situation and the practices around it. Quite laconically, Gendlin writes:

> Any situation, any bit of practice, implies much more than has ever been said. (Gendlin 1992: 201)

These actual situations, these actual practices of listening, of sounding, of manifold sensory activities, generate a flow of cohesion, material tensions, perceptual strings in which an alien operates on a daily basis. Gendlin made various efforts to explicate the reach and the impact of this corporeal generativity in a humanoid's corporeal sensorium. Yet, the generativity of one's sensorium and its intricate implications are under various circumstances of dispositives, economies, and routines actively neglected and repressed. The traditional, mainly propositionally operating philosophical and scientific argument represses these massively generative qualities of loosened and corporeal intentionality as well. It is therefore important to grant the present situation of an activity—*right here, right now*—enough space, and time, to unfold its generativity.

The common rejection of this concept can thus be explicated by two descriptions in Gendlin's list of explications of the bodily felt sense. In a strictly logocentric interpretation, hooked on nominalist concepts of consistency, these descriptions read as a contradiction: if it is true that "(b) The body has intentionality, that is to say, it has (feels, knows, is, implies . . .) situations" (Gendlin 1992: 202), then this must necessarily contradict with "(e) The body can imply something quite new which has never as yet actually occurred" (Gendlin 1992: 202). How can any entity in the known space-time continuum be at the same time defined by a given situation and its parameters (b)—and at the same time direct its actions into an area not yet known (e)? How can a new activity merely be possible if its agent is deeply embedded in its situated context? Corporeal ties seem to contradict pragmatic untying.

If one assumes that contexts are finite and deterministic, then, indeed, no action transcending these limits would be imaginable. Yet, it might be that this definition of a situation needs to be transcended. The concept of context as *propositional* accounts of intentions, limitations, and meanings is effectively prohibiting any generativity beyond this account. As soon, though, as one understands the given situation as corporeal and sensorial, it becomes obvious how new articulations and activities can result from a limited situation: language *is* then nothing external to the corpus. A verbal or a non-verbal articulation can be implied in the corporeal sensorium. Corporeal generativity radiates new articulations: "(c) The body has language implicit in it. (Situation and language are furthermore implicit in each other.)" (Gendlin 1992: 202). From the perspective of anthropology, this is a pivotal step toward a non-anthropocentric anthropology. This phenomenon of a less intentional but highly responsive proprioceptivity realizes an often neglected potential of semiosis: this potential lies in the situation—and the corporeal sensibility for a situation. New articulations and actions emerge from the situation of being entangled in specific affective tensions, leading to cohesions in direction of an articulation, resulting in surprising new signifying gestures, statements, propositions. New meaning emerges from an arbitrary situation. Meaning is resulting from material percepts and their tensions—not alone from sign operations and verbal arguments in some immaterial "Heaven of Ideas." A generative sensorium is the agent and the arena in which this emergence takes place. *Generativity* is therefore the name for an embodied appearance of a not yet explicated meaning in *statu nascendi*. The material sensorium is a heuristic catalyst.

Corporeal epistemologies

The corporeal sensorium is present. As long as it is present, it is in tension. As long as it is in tension, it is receptive to material cohesions of the space-time continuum you and I inhabit. A humanoid's body is thus also an exploratory and an epistemological device: just by being alive, we are this device. One is a corpus as a primary and continuously reflexive instrument to access material percepts as well as the interpersonal and cultural sphere. In this very moment, you, the reader of this section, are enveloped in a variety of sonic events. You might be sitting at your desk, in a library or on a train, or in your own living room. In any of these cases, you may sense some sounds coming from other humanoid aliens around you, other adults or children, even animals or machines; you may hear remote whispers and discussions, movements of bodies and textiles; maybe you hear them using a tablet, a smartphone, or even some kind of ancient desktop computer. Besides all of that, you are also involuntarily hearing the sounds of the infrastructure around you: the whirring of the air conditioner, the humming of old electric cables or noisy neon lights, the opening and closing of doors, the creaking of wooden floors, of old chairs and tables. All these sounds are present, and they are contributing to an individual and situated sensibility and performativity—before one even starts to engage in human echolocation or site-specific sound art. But is there actually a specific knowledge extracted from these sounds? And how can it actually be acquired? Could sonic experiences provide access to genuine forms of knowledge? What are the limitations in acquiring such a knowledge of sound? A prospective epistemology of sound begins necessarily with an account of actual epistemic practices concerning sound. There are two major approaches to fuse epistemology with sound: (a) *auditory and apparatus-based epistemologies* and (b) *sonic and corporeal epistemologies*. Sonic and corporeal epistemologies are the focus of this anthropology of sound; yet, in order to do so it seems necessary to clarify the difference between both specimens of epistemology. *Auditory epistemologies* are foremost using, refining, and exploiting technological possibilities of apparatuses. As part of research in science and technology studies, they constitute a truly well-researched and thoroughly defined field. It encompasses a whole range of publications, studies, and research projects that explore the historical development of specific research approaches, technological innovations, and commodified apparatuses. Being attached to and constructed around the ear as the one and only listening organ, these apparatuses intend mainly to evaluate appropriately certain research findings by hearing: from the stethoscope to the headphone, from auditory car analytics to technologies of sonifying scientific data, between *audile techniques* (Sterne 2003) and *sonic skills* (Bijsterveld 2018). A whole range of researchers, investigative projects, and methodological studies (e.g., Sterne 2003; Bijsterveld 2018; Kursell 2006; Volmar 2015) have hitherto explored the manifold specific methods and technologies by which technologically refined and culturally implemented techniques of listening have been developed and introduced into the canon of recognized research practices and apparatuses of a globalized science culture. *Sonic epistemologies*, in contrast, are training, refining, operating, and expanding particular forms of corporeal skills and a craftsmanship of the body. Until recently, they have rarely been researched. Inspired by *sonic materialism* (Cox 2011; Cobussen, Meelberg, and Schulze 2013; Schulze 2016), more and more researchers focused on epistemic qualities in listening and sounding—often inspired by or even oriented toward artistic practices. Knowledge *about* sound and *about* listening is still predominant in the scholarly discussion: knowledge *by* sound and *by* listening, in contrast, seems to be devalued quite lightheartedly as merely a form of artistic esoterics and amateur enthusiasm. The *apparatus canto*—as explained earlier in Chapter 4: "In Auditory Dispositives," in the section The Apparatus Canto—prevails on the expense of corporeal epistemologies. Historical studies on listening are therefore still more widely accepted than sound studies effectively *using* listening as an epistemic practice in research. Quite a paradox. The observations of the first part of this book are apparently still correct: the foundational logocentrism of academic research—its original sin—still promotes its obsession with idealist concepts of apparatus culture, willfully neglecting the erratic everyday practices of humanoid alien culture. To transcend this form of *logocentric angst*, one could ask therapeutic questions: What would the research questions of a *sonic* approach to research be? Who could be relevant experts to evaluate such corporeal approaches? And finally: How could an epistemology actually operate *in the realm* and *by the means* of sound?

Sonic epistemologies can be found in many fields. Fields in which everyday practices dominate that have just not (yet) been established and ennobled as epistemic practices. For the most part, these practices lack the quality of reproducibility, as well as documentable exactitude and distinctiveness, and as such they fall short of the academic standard that is expected from research practices. They are often seen as unintelligible, subjective, even esoteric practices that simply do not justify any further research or theoretical reflection. They may at most be considered a form of skillful craftsmanship, maybe a form of *embodied knowledge* (Gallagher 2005), which could in turn be granted the honor of constituting a form of *tacit knowledge* (Polanyi 1966). But, in doing so—even in the more symbolic honoring of craftsmanship—the logocentric concept of epistemology still prevails. If sonic epistemologies hence are to be taken seriously, it is necessary to ascribe to those alternate, thoroughly sonic forms of knowledge the same dignity as forms of knowledge that are more easily transferable to discrete and reproducible, semiotic and alphanumeric codes: a translation into code that contemporary consumer culture can instrumentalize so perfectly in industrialized research. Coming from a *new sensory materialist* perspective in anthropology, however, assuming a *generative sensorium* in humanoid aliens with an *idiosyncratic implex*, all possible sensory and sonic forms of knowledge can provide options to acquire knowledge. Not only the culturally and historically arbitrary and mainly idiosyncratic obsessions with logocentric and visualizing representations can provide sensory representations of physical emanations: but all imaginable representations in smell, touch, sound, movement, taste, or dynamics can lead a way into insightful representations. The whole of sensory percepts is potentially of an epistemic quality. *The materialization of the senses*—as being initiated by Hermann von Helmholtz for instance—is yet to be completed in actual research practices, publications, discourses, and critique operating in these areas of the sensory: in dynamics and taste, movement and sound, touch and smell. From the scarcity economy of meek characters and signals, it is time to move on to an *economy of plenty* and multiplying diversity of the senses, of experience and performativity, of all materialities accessible and not accessible to humanoid aliens. From identity to generativity: let the corporeal sensorium unravel.

One example, maybe best known in the field of sound studies, is the approach of *acoustemology* as proposed and exercised by Steven Feld. In the field of cultural research, this approach allows for scholars to open up the social, cultural, and communication practices of a specific culture via the *listening* researcher. An acoustemological analysis is hence

> an exploration of sonic sensibilities, specifically of ways in which sound is central to making sense, to knowing, to experiential truth. This seems particularly relevant to understanding the interplay of sound and felt balance in the sense and sensuality of emplacement, of making place. (Feld 1982: 97)

Acoustemological research incorporates methodological elements like corporeal, deep, or reduced listening. The listening body of the individual researcher is thus pivotal in acoustemology, as well as in other sonic epistemologies. In contrast to claims of an anonymously executed and ubiquitously, ahistorically reproducible research, this approach introduces one major new fact that is well known to actual researchers, though it is too often regarded as a taboo better not spoken of: to apply a certain research method successfully relies on the individually refined skills and practices of the individual researcher—and hence on her or his personal traits in gender, body, age, cultural, and social backgrounds, as well as various mostly non-institutional forms of autodidactic education and training. Research findings can *never* be reproducible *in all details*. In acoustemology—and similarly in *any* academic education—the set of personal proclivities and idiosyncratic obsessions is effectively guiding research and securing its quality. For humanities this is a trivial fact, as no one would seriously claim she or he could also have written, let's say, *Contingency, Irony or Solidarity*; *Grammophon, Film, Typewriter*; *The Audible Past*, or *L'Anti-Œdipe*. From this perspective on the individual researcher in her or his historical, institutional, personal, and spatial situation, the assumption of general reproducibility becomes even more inappropriate for the sciences: *In principle*, anyone could apply and combine existing methods of analysis with existing methods for gathering empirical data. Yet again, it requires a quite personal set of interests and skills, of knowledge *outside* the research field, and a truly idiosyncratic obsession leading one to do research on— for instance—specific constants concerning reverberation times, on spatial representations of sound in speaking or orienting, or on bodily reactions to sonic experiences. *Corporeal epistemologies* make this impact of embodied idiosyncrasies on methods in research their starting ground. Without idiosyncratic knowledge and skills, passions and revulsions, obsessions and fears, any substantial research would essentially not be possible. The idiosyncratic listening body of a researcher is thus a major instrument in research, even more so concerning methods like *acoustemology* or *human echolocation*. A researcher's participation and her or his intricacy of awareness and reflection in an empirical field situation provides the main access to empirical phenomena. Auditory sensibilities are factual prerequisites for sonic research. Until recently, such practices could not be learned in academia but either at an art school, maybe a conservatoire, and at best in autodidactic training. This seems to change in the twenty-first century in the same way as coding software, developing automata, or even surgical operations have not been part of academic training for centuries. Refined sensibilities and idiosyncratic skills are truly crucial to such contemporary research practices. If research would actually be as arbitrary and impersonal as often stated, no colleague would then ever be able to reasonably evaluate the work of another colleague in peer review. It would in turn not even be necessary, as a mere *Calculemus!* would be sufficient. Corporeal and sonic epistemologies require as research practices the same self-reflective rigidity, embodied knowledge, and refined skills one might demand of any other method in the sciences; these individual epistemologies necessarily undertake an even more intense reflection on the role of the individual researcher as the impact on predetermining, framing, and shaping a research outcome is so obvious. This personal bias can be hidden much more easily if referring to an impersonal apparatus or method just operating and producing results. *The machine did it—I was just the operator!* Yeah, sure.

Similarly, such deep listening practices of acoustemology return in a specific focused and instrumental version in the practices of human echolocation. Both practices, acoustemology and human echolocation, expand regular scholarly practices of cultural field research into a heightened attention to audible phenomena. Hitherto, this method was mainly explored by practitioners who themselves were sight-impaired or blind, such as Juan Antonio Martínez, Lawrence Scadden, Ben Underwood, and Tom De Witte, and they developed the sensory apparatus of tactile and corporeal listening. Daniel Kish, one of the leading inventors and developers of human echolocation practices, effectively designs and implements new *perceptual techniques* (Sterne). These practices do not rely on physical listening devices as "machines to hear for us" (Sterne 2003: 81), but they train, refine, and reframe the auditory sensibility of its protagonists (Kish 1982). Like acoustemology, human echolocation incorporates and embodies practices of reduced, corporeal, or deep listening. Epistemic practices are here equally exercised by a researcher and her or his own corporeal-sensory apparatus. Research on human echolocation refines these skills in introducing the entirety of senses of humanoid aliens as an empirical basis and a sensible approach to the world. The ostensibly reduced approach of an established academic logocentrism—restricted to visual icons and discursive, textual representations as arguments—and the as well logocentric cultural forms of academic administration are being drastically opened up. Corporeal epistemologies introduce a more realistic, materially factual, and polysensory perception. This expansion to the polysensory richness of humanoid perception in experimental and artistic studies, in historical critique and theoretical explorations, in field research and listening practices, can be regarded as a main characteristic of research in sound studies: merging existing research practices in the sciences and humanities with newer ones in the arts and design to establish a truly polysensory epistemological set of post-logocentric methods. One of the most impressive outlines in sound studies can thus be found in the works of Bruce Odland and Sam Auinger:

> Odland and Auinger are learning to make sense of the sound environment we live in by listening with attention, hearing, exploring, and attempting to understand the cultural waveform as a language. (Auinger and Odland 2007)

By means of ongoing listening practices in everyday life—relying on corporeal epistemologies—and by extending them into specific sound performances and installations, both artists articulate *sonic syrrhesis*. Articles, books, or lectures are not their main instruments of presentation; the installation of actual sonic environments they are continuously transforming, enhancing, stressing, and shaping are. A *hearing perspective* (Auinger and Odland 2007; more extensively discussed in Chapter 5: "The Sonic Persona") is their guiding principle and at the same time one of their major concepts. As sonic personae, they perform corporeal epistemologies as intricate sensory aesthetics:

> O+A collect, filter, and expand resonances found in nature and cities and try to unlock their meaning. These sounds are often shut out of our mental picture of a space as "noise." By listening to and studying these noises, they become useful sound sources. (Auinger and Odland 2007)

With this truly empiricist method, they

> do not import exotic sounds to their installation sites. Instead they distill a musical information from the ambient city noise. (Auinger and Odland 2007)

In entering one of their works, be it a site-specific installation like *Sonic Vista* (2011) in Frankfurt am Main, or a recorded sonic artifact like the piece *Innsbruck 6020* (2006), the listening alien enters a deep and subtly refined environment extending into various forms of knowledge and traditions of research:

> When we make large scale sound installations in public spaces, our starting point is the basic environmental soundscape of the site. Architecture, history, acoustics, and social dynamics of a given space are taken into account. (Auinger and Odland 2007)

Corporeal epistemologies are put in practice: They allow for a generative experience of the material substance of sound. In entering a sound installation by Sam Auinger and Bruce Odland, or in listening to a recorded sound performance, one is guided into an experience of *thick listening*: a form of listening immersed in the substance and the historical as well as sensational, fictional, and obsessive layers coating and entwining any sonic experience. *Sensory critique in actu.*

The listening body

One's body is a device for listening. Unsurprisingly, it is home and arena to a vast multitude of desires, duties, processes, obsessions, fears, scars, cramps, and knots, to lingering and idle states of experience—to enjoy and to suffer from time to time. This troubled material assemblage of a humanoid alien avatar becomes in the course of its more conscious existence, in the course of various movements, repercussions, experiences, and traces, a certain sensory persona: a *kinesthetic persona*, a *vocal persona*, a *mimic persona*, a *gustatory persona*, an *olfactory persona*. A *textile persona* and a *laughing persona*, a *conflict persona*, and—obviously—a certain *visual persona*. A *sonic persona*. This multitude of personae is never finite. It evolves and it transforms in the course of further experiences, duties, conflicts, and unforeseen forms of pleasure. A humanoid alien's body, then, as a viscerally living corpus, is the material substance, the founding ground from which an individual existence emerges, draws its distinctions from, and undergoes various experiences. An idiosyncratic corpus under pressure from various technological dispositives requires these varying personae to emerge. A sonic persona is made out of a *sensory corpus* struggling with changing auditory dispositives. In these struggles, one negotiates a viable persona. The listening body of a researcher is hence an example of this sensory corpus under pressure. Yet, it is an indispensable ground for sonic research. Corporeal epistemologies rely on the researcher's corpus. This listening body was probably most strikingly explored by the artistic research practice of soundwalking following sonic traces. As Hildegard Westerkamp proposes:

> Start by listening to the sounds of your body while moving. They are closest to you and establish the first dialogue between you and the environment. (Westerkamp 1974)

If you never went on a soundwalk, this might seem to you - from just reding these assignments - the most unsurprising experience ever. But if you actually go on a soundwalk, you experience and you realize: Indeed you leave sonic traces. You proceed in the material substance of resonance all around you. You wander around, you focus on your instantaneous listening experiences. To do so was my personal custom since, well, maybe since I was a kid or a teenager. The listening body is my device.

> What else do you hear?
> Other people
> Nature sounds
> Mechanical sounds. (Westerkamp 1974)

You perform an auscultation of your surroundings, your vicinities, your nearby friends or colleagues. The more you indulge actually *being* in this moving situation on a soundwalk, the more you will sense how this very corporeal and very epistemological kind of walk will affect you: how you will think through sound (as one would think through images, through propositions, through historical documents or theory models, through graphs or equations). Corporeally, you appropriate a sonic area in continuous immanence. You *become* these sounds. *You are this Hörspiel.*

> Do you like what you hear? Pick out the sounds you like the most and create the ideal soundscape in the context of your present surroundings. What would be its main characteristics? Is it just an idealistic dream or could it be made a reality? (Westerkamp 1974)

Small, incredibly tiny, are these sonic percepts. Inaudible to some. Yet they are *not* irrelevant. Sonic percepts envelop the actions of aliens. You are constantly in corporeal sympathy, in antipathy, in indolence with material percepts. They are present—and all too present. The materiality of this soundscape could be transformed. Your idiosyncrasies become responsive. Especially when one is *nervous* or *bored,* if I am *anxious*, or you are in a *tense* or *uptight* mood. Sonically shaping existence, subjectivity, performativity, reflexivity. Your personal sonic fiction is the sensory real. Gottfried Wilhelm Leibniz wrote more than two centuries ago:

> Ces petites perceptions sont donc de plus grande efficace par leurs suites qu'on pense. Ce sont elles qui forment ce je ne sais quoi, ces goûts, ces images des qualités des sens. (Leibniz 1765: 47)

The most miniscule percepts can determine a sonic persona. They constitute one's taste and sensibility. They relate to a monist and materially encompassing continuum: "cette liaison que chaque être a avec tout le reste de l'univers." (Leibniz 1765: 47)

The listening body relates to the real. Close and sensible. A humanoid alien can relate materially to various differing aliens. This corporeal *physics of existence*—as Austrian philosopher and Michel Foucault scholar Walter Seitter proposed it (Seitter 1997)—grants the actual access to things and materialities. The materiality of *this* given moment in all its sinuous complexity and its manifold, infinite aspects; this materiality is physical: it requires the most radically non-transcendentalist, radically immanent concentration to grasp it in at least a majority of its details. A detailed narration of all particles audible is hence not an arbitrary exercise. It unravels the actual substance of hearing and sensing in this very instant and corpus: the sonic *plane of immanence* (Deleuze 2005; Deleuze and Guattari 1991; Thompson and Biddle 2013; Lavender 2015; Szepanski 2015; Macarthur, Lochhead, and Shaw 2016; Moisala et al. 2017; Schrimshaw 2017). The empirical enters the conceptual: the percepts occupy the space of words and propositions. The realm of the senses expands into the realm of the argument. Matter forms existence. The corpus experiences and records sounds, in every cell and nerve being worn out or anticipating specific sonic experiences:

> The muscle apparatus registers auditory desires (and fears). Sounds trigger physical repercussions. . . . certain parts of the cell structure of my body have changed after absorbing certain musics. I reacted then differently; not only to different musics; but also differently to certain people, and to the states of reality with which I had to deal. (Theweleit 2007: 30; transl. HS)[1]

---

[1] "[D]ie Muskulatur ist eine Registratur auditiver Lüste (und Schrecken). Die Töne haben ihren körperlichen Niederschlag. . . . bestimmte Teile der Zellstruktur meines Körpers haben sich verändert nach der Aufnahme bestimmter Musiken. Ich reagiere anders; nicht nur anders

Pleasures are stored on your corpus. "My headphones, they saved my life" (Björk 1995). A highly malleable and responsive alien anthropoid will be thoroughly and materially transformed, she or he or it will be percolated through and kneaded by sonic pressure waves in specific rhythms, textures, forms of cohesion. Thus one is able to record certain affects and thought-feelings, *Gedankengefühle*, a bodily *felt sense* (Gendlin) while listening to a sonic or musical performance—maybe stored on vinyl discs, on magnetic tape, on polycarbonate discs, or on the discs or microchips of solid state storage devices:

> On some Mingus records, from Coltrane or Billie Holiday, on Sun Ra's *Heliocentric Worlds*, in some of Mozart's piano concerts, in many rock pieces, on Dylan records, on many others, certain emotions I had while listening *to them* are so precisely stored *on them*, that I am not content to just call them "memories." Also not a remedy for revitalization. These records have actually recorded something while they were running; they have not just played back. (Theweleit 2007: 30; transl. HS)[2]

Founded on the listening body, this *sensory corpus*, the research process is thoroughly reconceptualized as an experiential, situated, and openly idiosyncratic process. A *hypercorporealization* touches all things research. Idealist notions of an abstract and anonymous researcher lose the attraction of the trickster-shaman. The listening body emphasizes the *Sinnenbewusstsein* (Lippe 1985), the sensory consciousness as sensory awareness in research: a training in ephemeral sensibilities, in refined listening and hearing in the most polysensory way. The leaves on the birch tree, rustling outside; a high and distant squeaking of cars; people running to the door in the apartment above me. I can hear some focused and dampened conversation on the playground around the corner.

---

auf bestimmte Musiken; auch anders auf bestimmte Leute und anders auf die Zustände des Wirklichen überhaupt, mit denen ich zu tun habe." (Theweleit 2007: 30)

[2] "Auf manchen Mingus-Platten, bei Coltrane oder Billie Holiday, in Sun Ra's *Heliocentric Worlds*, in einigen Klavierkonzerten Mozarts, in vielen Rockstücken, auf Dylan-Platten, auf vielen anderen, sind bestimmte Gefuhle, die ich beim Horen hatte, derart genau gespeichert, dass ich nicht zufrieden bin, das einfach nur, Erinnerungen' zu nennen. Auch nicht ein Hilfsmittel zur Wiederbelebung. Die Platten haben etwas aufgezeichnet, wahrend sie liefen; nicht nur etwas abgespielt." (Theweleit 2007: 30)

PART THREE
The precision of sensibility: *A political critique*

CHAPTER SEVEN

The precision of sensibility

Nanopolitics

Do the things that people say you can not do the things that people say you can not do the things that people say you can not do the things that people say you can not do the things that people say you can not. (Calix 1996)

Incredibly tiny, almost imperceptible fractures of moments. Moments in my days in which suddenly I can sense a certain—*glimpse*? *Glitch*? *Anticipation* would be far too big a term for such ephemeral, well, *inklings* of an experience. It might not even be an experience at all—just the wish of it, perhaps? In these unimaginably tiny fractures of some moments, politics not only enter but they expand and territorialize and usurp. Politics, in this sense, are neither party politics nor politics of communal or social relations. They are *nanopolitics*: neither present in the foreground nor intensely discussed. They enter everyday lives by way of all the micro-decisions one makes, by way of sensory preferences and routines, by way of inclinations and aversions you and I might tend to follow. In his treatise, *W.A.N.T.: Weaponized Adorables Negotiation Tactics* (Law and Wark 2014), McKenzie Wark sketches a convincing outline for the functioning and the impact of nanopolitics:

> *Touch me*, says the haptic interface smiling through its App-rounded eyes. *Play me*, says the swirling cream icon on the glassy screen. *Love me*, says [sic] them all. They look so familiar somehow, so human with their comfortable shapes, caring feedback loops and happy colors. They are an everyday domestic occurrence, as they sit by our bedsides or keep our pockets warm. . . . The propensity to affect and in turn, feign affection, is exactly what is weaponized. (Law and Wark 2014: 1f.)

So, how can *nanopolitics* be defined? Whereas macropolitics are the well-established forms of national governance through party politics, national institutions, and corporations ("politics"), and the concept of micropolitics has been introduced in recent decades to describe the politics of local or communal organizations, companies, and associations (Burns 1961/62; Mintzberg 1983; Neuberger 1995), the area of nanopolitics is situated below this: Nanopolitics govern and predetermine all the individual, sensory, and corporeal constellations, situations, and practices ("body politics," "perceptual politics," "pragmatics")—or, in brief: "How to think politics with and through the body" (Hansen, Plotegher and Zechner 2013)? Examples for nanopolitics are the tiny, quirky, *zany, cute*, and *interesting* (Ngai 2012) gadgets and tools, games and applications, their audiovisual effects and narrative particles, that execute an everyday seduction: on one's skin, in your nerve net, and on my practices of listening, seeing, touching, moving in everyday life. Drawing its players, its consumers, its users, readers, viewers into their outstretched system of tracking and surveillance, of data mining, of profiling by purchase, of labor and a new phase of somewhat *ursprüngliche Akkumulation, original accumulation* (Marx and Engels 1867/1968: 741). A camouflaged colonization of the intimate and personal, not an im- but an *experialism* (Wallace 1996) of our individual bodies and perceptual techniques, takes place. *Experialist movements* of these kinds take over your sensing body and mine. They are the actual *body snatchers*—originally invented in a sort of *Angstlust*, a deeply ambivalent thrill, by Jack Finney and Philip Kaufman in the postwar United States of the twentieth century. Experialist takeovers occupy any perceptual technique one could imagine, any actually practiced sensory habit.

> Reading Horkheimer and Adorno against a background of Partridge Family slowed down to a narcotized slur. (Wallace 1996: 597)

Days, weeks, months, seasons, and years in these heavily networked societies of the northern—and increasingly in the southern—hemisphere are intensely filled with product presentations of the latest adorables, with advertisements and extended entertainment formats actually making propaganda mainly for these new gadgets. Recurrent gatherings and global live transmissions are staged around the unveiling of a new telephone turned universal machine. One of the most intrusive and aggressively attacking special forces of these gadgets is obviously the user interface itself. This particular contact zone between player and game, consumer and media corporation, is the expanding battlefield of *experialist nanopolitics*: politics at your fingertip, your swoosh and swipe, your obedient listening or indulging praise.

> Our attachments are our temple, what we worship, no? What we give ourselves to, what we invest with faith. (Wallace 1996: 150)

Recently, since the late 2000s, a new gem of everyday weaponry was introduced into the shared mediaspace of humanoid aliens. By the time you read these lines, this material user interface might well have vanished into history—or at least it could have become just some minor tool of everyday life. The *touchscreen*, in all its more or less refined variations and mutations, has entered a wide variety of situations in life in heavily mediated and networked societies. It is a joyful and seductively simple interface: it reactivates gleefully to any humanoid's fundamental tactility. I like to touch. My skin, the skin on my fingertips, suddenly becomes—with the proliferation of touchscreens in all areas of life—even more important in all sorts of activities one can imagine, be it in the field of labor, of leisure, of computation and planning activities. The so-called *intuitive* access so often stressed with the introduction of tactile interfaces makes bold use of a humanoid's *Sinnenbewußtsein* (Lippe 1985): Their skin, their flesh, their corpus—it likes, it craves, it desires to be touched and to touch, to interact physically, to move and to contact, to get a corporeal sense of an environment, of a thing one encounters, of any person or creature or plant. The *nanopolitics* of the touchscreen is an experialist invasion of one's skin and dexterity—as already was the introduction of the typewriter, the computer keyboard, or the computer mouse. Nanopolitics are kneading and revolving the sensory corpus. The skills of appropriating and domesticating (Berker, Hartmann, Punie, and Ward 2006; Hartmann 2013) the ubiquitously dominant apparatuses, connected and streaming incessantly, might come at a point where the sensory volume, their overwhelmingly massive impact on individual corpuses and sensibilities, is a major, mainly physical function. Pervasively transforming the sensory body of any humanoid playing with, using, consuming them:

> There is no distance with volume, you're swallowed up by sound. There's no room, you can't be ironic if you're being swallowed by volume, and volume is overwhelming you. . . . Not only is it the literary that's useless, all traditional theory is pointless. All that works is the sonic plus the machine that you're building. (Eshun 1998: 188f.)

But no: *you* are not building the machine. Someone else has built this thing enveloping your life and intruding into your most intimate space of sensory contact. Developed by some research and development teams, scattered over the planet, remotely contacting each other on the various milestones of their development projects, an occasional chat or video-conversation thrown in; guided, redirected, misdirected, and in the end corrected and reassigned to a new team by commissions and project directors often only remotely accessible and only slightly aware of the actual work their teams are doing; corrected incessantly by their superior authorities, using focus groups, external studies, and secret information about their competitors. Out of this distributed and bumpy process of designing and developing a new artifact around the interventions of commissions and vision papers and a vast amount of ongoing mail-conversations and online- as well as kitchen-chats, an artifact evolves in the end: you receive this fine artifact of programming and designing craftsmanship—ready to seduce you, to take command, to install itself as your new major incentive of desire. Nanopolitics of bricolage and persuasion.

Intensely designed sensory events of visually, haptically, kinesthetically, and sonically calculated applications are encouraging humanoids, coercing aliens to interact, to engage, to spend their time and a large load of their capital on exactly these *weaponized adorables*: designed to accumulate the most of any capital around. As *sonic nanopolitics* songs and tracks, sound logos and sonic environments, inject themselves into *your* sensory corpus and inhabit your sensual life, all too often *your* sex life as well as your urge to accumulate, to purchase, and to spend capital. As in the episode "Fifteen Million Merits" in the series *Black Mirror* by Charlie Brooker, you and I, we both struggle every day, cycling and cycling without end, without perspective (besides a badly generated, fictional image of the road you and I are cycling on). Yet even if one would actually achieve enough credits, enough *merits*, one would spend them exclusively on badly designed and highly superfluous gadgetry, on gems and shiny rubbish, useless digital shit (Brooker 2011). "This is the whirlpool, a friend" (Wallace 1996: 237). Humanoid aliens are the noble savages, objects of prey to the experialism of the military-industrial-communication-entertainment complex. The piezobeeps of ubiquitous surveillance, *beep! beep!*, are pinching your days. Sonic warfare for the next intercontinental civil war. Every beep represents large sets of data gathered. *Beep!* Your existence being tracked and incorporated into this experialist nanopolitics. *Plonk*.

Do the things that people say you can not. (Calix 1996)

Sensory critique

Critique of a cultural artifact—be it written, designed, cooked or painted, composed or directed, coded, performed, or articulated—requires, foremost, a focus on the artifact itself. What might sound trivial as can be, actually is not. More often in cases of sensory or sonic artifacts—tools in the stream of nanopolitics—it might not be too easy to draw a strict distinction between the artifact one encounters and one's individual affective, habitual, or reflected reaction to this artifact. The usual blurring of the lines between assumed object and subject, between assumed artifact and perceiving entity, becomes crucial as soon as one focuses on sensory artifacts that turn the sensory corpus of you or me into the actual arena of their performative acts: olfactory, gustatory, kinesthetic, and also sonic artifacts. Distance from the events happening is not easy to maintain here. They do not only affect you: you actually turn into them—and your transformation is part of what this artifact achieves. No form of distancing reflection here can provide basic requirements for critique, as an intensely experiential immersion is required as the first step. Kantian categories of distancing, objectifying, and conceptualizing seem impossible to apply. You need to eat a dish, you need to smell a perfume, you need to listen to sound art merely to be able to say anything about these artifacts. "This immersion will compromise you," or so the Kantian suspicion whispers in academics' ears. Actually, how could one really refer to such a supposedly unstable, excessively relational, contextual and situational, even individually generated, not to forget biographically as well as historically grounded, experience as an artifact? Is there, in the end, anything one could speak and write about in the mode of *critique*? Must such an *affective* enrichment—if not transformation—of the academic discourse not necessarily lead to the abolition of any meaningful evidence?

Turning for once to more traditional objects of critique might provide a certain hunch about how to approach these newer and immersive non-objects of critique. The following list contains maybe outdated artifacts, even anachronistic for some readers of this section, that are objects to critique on a daily basis: a selected newspaper article, a series of TV shows, the newest novel of a literary author, a recent sculpture or installation in the fine arts, an opera staging, a concert performance, a pop record or a blockbuster movie, even a philosophical treatise, a computer game, selected media gadgets, a party program, architectural or urbanist sketches, a mobile phone, or an eagerly anticipated fashion item. This list represents a quite exhaustive collection of what effectively served as objects of critique. In all of these cases, the person articulating a form of critique obviously *never* was an anonymous and representative non-being. Critics are and were humanoid aliens—educated in and emerging out of a course of idiosyncratic biography, articulating their critique at a certain age, arguing with a selective bricolage of references, drawing from few areas of profound knowledge; overloaded with—and skillfully working against—their individual biases stemming from those very idiosyncrasies acquired in the course of their lives. Yet, *exactly these idiosyncrasies* make a biographically and individually shaped alien humanoid worthwhile to follow as a critic. How would she or he approach some of these newly released artifacts with an intention to scrutinize them in the form of critique? With what take will this very alien surprise, enlighten, and convince us now? This form of critique is definitely *not* a formulaically presented and peer review–proof specimen of writing.

Nevertheless, this critique is highly influential, convincing, understandable, and—most of all—a major audience can relate to it. In this case, an embodied and incorporated knowledge is applied to an urgent example and convincingly described, evaluated, compared explicitly or implicitly, and finally concluded with a judgment that allows for a decision as to whether or not one should be interested in this artifact. Critique in all the earlier examples is concrete, material, and rich with examples; it is sensible and relatable. Such a *corporeal sensibility* also constitutes the research strategy of a *sensory critique* (already alluded to at the end of Chapter 2: "Materializing Listening"). It expands a merely logocentric argument consisting of set propositions and normatively restricted forms of logical operations in the realm of language and signs to far broader forms of articulation encompassing all sensory capabilities of humanoid aliens. By this method, the actual, material situation of listening is being scrutinized—not only an idealized and restricted concept of it. The inherent and endlessly folded complexity of a sensory experience can thus be unfolded, selectively at least. In contrast to most modernist assumptions concerning rationality and reason, it is safe to say: the individual, idiosyncratic persona, the sensorily educated person, might actually be the only entity in the known world of aliens and robots that could imagine being capable of efficaciously criticizing an artifact. That is a bold claim, to be sure. Couldn't a non-humanoid alien with a non-persona be able to undertake a far more complexly layered and less individually limited, less idiosyncratic review of an artifact? One can be very sure that such a means for review is currently in development and—maybe when you are reading these lines—will be a crucial part of your life. The pivotal difference in impact of critique, though, does not rely on some exhaustiveness or completeness of analysis. The exact contrary is true—especially as the first truly successful efforts for mechanized reviews point out. Incompleteness, disequilibrium, and a certain idiosyncratic focus of analysis are criteria that make an impressive critique worthwhile. Here lies the main difference between *critique* and *analysis*: *analysis* claims and performs a rationalist completeness to test the incompleteness, flaws, the inconsistencies and contradictions in an artifact; *critique,* though, transcends these basic tasks of pattern recognition by addressing underlying tendencies and obsessions, compulsive simplicities and culturally hegemonic though misleading concepts. Analysis hence remains focused on the artifact in a kind of limited immanence assuming that any artifact would have been rationally conceived; critique, though, starts at the artifact and expands its scrutiny to areas maybe no one before and surely not the inventor, developer, or author ever had in mind. This is the educational, the provocative, the generative potential in critique.

A *sonic and sensory persona*, educated, trained, and sufficiently inspiring in its critical practices, actually integrates perspectives of non-personae in their approach. The sensorially critical writings of David Toop, Brandon LaBelle, Steve Goodman, or Salomé Voegelin are vivid examples of this kind of critique. Their approach to an artifact—be it a design product, a sonic environment, a performance, or a sound art installation—is departing from their particular experience and sensibility as a listening body and sonic persona. The conclusions by Toop hence must necessarily differ from those by Voegelin—and this is exactly their genuine quality and the foremost reason for their impact. The personal and idiosyncratic as an agency in sensory critique is *not* excluding other forms of idiosyncrasies and personalities; rather, it is actively assimilating, involving, and considering them as necessarily relevant perspectives concerning the artifact in question. An impressive critique metabolizes all possible forms of critique one could think of, all *possible sonic worlds* (Voegelin 2012). A convincing critique in this sense is a synthesis of potential approaches to critique: a *syrrhesis* in actu. It is generated by this *Möglichkeitssinn* (Musil 1930) of a humanoid alien: a *sense of possibility*, a potential to be activated—the capability to imagine and to sense intensely even the most unimaginable reflections and aspects concerning an artifact or an event. Substantial critique in this sense requires the ability to imagine alternate realities, divergent lifeforms, and deviant ways of thinking and sensing. It is a deeply *anti-ideological* and *anti-habitualized* practice. In traditional accounts of critique—mostly in the tradition of Marxist sociological and philosophical research—this practice has been focusing on a critique of *written* or at least *verbally* articulated forms of ideology. Even the well-founded efforts to criticize the *Californian Ideology* (Barbrook and Cameron 1996) since the 1990s, as proposed by Richard Barbrook and Andy Cameron, again mainly seem to focus on verbal accounts or verbally explicated practices. How could it then be possible to perform a critique concerning *sensory* events and forms of experience, as well as highly individual ways of feeling, of desires and urges related to *sonic* and sensory artifacts? How could a sensory critique not merely be possible but be profoundly justified and well-grounded?

In the early twenty-first century, major ideological practices and beliefs are no longer distributed by writing them down and publishing them in large volumes—as they were in the nineteenth and still in the twentieth centuries. In those ancient, prehistoric times, you could (and you still can) refer to author names and *grand récits* that stand for a specific worldview, for political forms of shaping everyday life, and even for a distinct political agenda. Yet, this seems less and less possible in recent decades. To what major author or theoretical strand would I refer to describe this narrow historical period of the current years and their political, technological, cultural, as well as scientific developments? Or would I possibly prefer to speak of certain brand new digital gadgetry, of styles of eating and leisure practices, of online video clips, cat videos, as well as weirdly atavistic propaganda videos, visual hymns to current warfare technology? Mario Perniola, Italian philosopher, apparently got a similar feeling as early as the 1990s. For these less verbally, less propositional, but more experiential, more sensorily presented forms of ideology, he proposed a term and developed its theoretical foundations of *sensology*. With this term, Perniola refers to the quite new phenomena of an intensely globalized, capitalized, mediatized, and heavily networked form of governing; transcending historical borders as well as the common checks and balances between businesses, police, and entertainment, between legislature, executive, and jurisdiction. His writings on this matter recurrently refer—more often implicitly—to his experience and his earlier premonition in the dawn of Italian *Berlusconismo*. The regime of Silvio Berlusconi in Italy in 1994/95 and between 2001 and 2011 (with only tiny interruptions) serves as one of the first and most impactful examples of a post-democratic and sensological form of government. For Perniola, the future and contemporary form of politics resides and operates decisively and consistently *outside* of any actual political discourse. Political decisions are thus withdrawn from any area of responsibility and of accountability by any actually responsible protagonist. Berlusconi—and similarly a wide set of successors like Vladimir Putin, Viktor Orbán, Donald Trump, or Recep Erdoğan—introduced and refined the tricks and gimmicks to control a post-democratic public sphere by the means of sensology: in Berlusconi's case, focused on a TV network like Mediaset, on various torrents of gossip, and a *medial persona* (Schulze 2014) of Berlusconi as *Il Cavaliere*.

The main modus operandi of Berlusconismo and of similar post-democratic rackets is an articulated and quite aggressive form of smirkingly displayed anti-ideological posture and rhetoric: the actual camouflage of the underlying sensology. It rejects the common discourse to search in politics for the best decision for a given problem, a discourse that allows for politicians to be held accountable; an anti-ideological and sensological posture, though, swaps this with a ridiculing and entertaining joke or a comic gesture, a mimic tick or another performative act presenting the performer as an unquestionable, eloquent, and charming strongman, left-handedly in charge. The main issue here is *not* actually to resolve any of the urgent social, economic, environmental, or merely administrative issues; but to retain the posture of a potent, well-groomed, versatile, wise, and quick-witted persona. This is the main goal, and to achieve this, any malevolent trick can be handy. In doing so, the *medial persona* activates the latent proclivities in an audience to react in a joyful, agreeable, and relieving way. The performing politician jumps out of the actually entangling discourse and reaches a state of performative playfulness. He (still rather seldomly: *she*) leaves the discourse and enters the circus. With this trick—as Mario Perniola explains—prefabricated sensations are evoked in a media audience. These *Ready-Felt*s, as Perniola calls them, are deeply implemented in highly networked and mediatized societies; their constellation shapes an ideological framework that does not operate with propositions, but with affects: a *sensology*. Whereas the *ideologies* of the nineteenth century implemented a set of *Ready-Thoughts* in their followers, the *sensologies* of late twentieth and early twenty-first centuries manage to implement a set of *Ready-Felts* as an even more strategically destructive virus in a humanoid alien's subjectivity. Individual ready-felts exceed one's reflexivity. You *might* feel a certain urge, a specific wish, a strong desire—*before* you are even capable of reflecting on its particular historical, ideological, and cultural ramifications and repercussions. You are *overpowered* by strategically abused affects. This is not only *falsches Bewußtsein* (Adorno), a wrong consciousness that one could deconstruct with an arduous effort; it is an almost inextricably *falsches Empfinden,* a substantially implemented and malformed sensibility. Sensory critique represents the only means to operate in this realm of surgically destroyed sensibilities. With Perniola's theory of sensologies, the nanopolitics and sensory regimes of present, historical, and future times finally turn into an object of political critique. Sensologies of present times try fervently to evade any propositional position open to critique. They even aggressively prevent any expansion of the realm of the propositional into the corporeal: they flee the propositional and exchange it with a conceptually designed, easy to abuse model of emotional reaction. These ready-felts then operate in this destructive

> circulation of Sensologies . . . both the realization and the abolition of the metaphysical project; on the one hand, the externalization of feeling actually suppresses all autonomous impulses of the body and its affects, but on the other hand every primary intellectual effort is thwarted. (Perniola 1991: 134; transl. by HS)

Sensibilities are turned into feeling as prefabricated. This new ready-felt can then hinder both any individual affect and bodily felt sense on the one hand—and any logical and propositional critique on the other hand. The whole nexus of sensing and reflecting is corroded. Both have become impossible. What remains is a discombobulated mash of instrumentalized emotion-particles of buzz, outrage, a spiteful roar of laughter. Sensibility is externalized and objectified as an emotion: Emotion in these cases is no more than degenerated sensibility. It is *the sensorial processed*. Ready-felts of this kind are not anymore grounded in the individual sensory corpus of an alien like you or me; they are grounded foremost in controlled dispositives. The idiosyncratic sensibility is turned into a normalized, cleansed set of ready-felts as open ports for hegemonic sensology to plug in and play you. Signal processing becomes recognizable as ideology. Sensologies turn you and me into a commodified arsenal of neatly crafted emotions ready to be exploited. These sensorial techniques are then in turn becoming major issues for cultural research. *Sensological* or briefly *sensory critique* is thus required to question established forms of performing sensibilities, emotions, and feelings. How does a given sensology of a historical or contemporary sensory culture transform, expand, focus, or shape the sensory persona? How are affects, and feelings, and sensibilities reduced to specific ready-felts—and at the same time reorganized, refined, and trained? The sensory corpus of a humanoid can then be analyzed as an extension of a certain technological dispositive, a user interface, a situation of performance, an architectural and urban framework, a technological infrastructure. Your ready-felts are your uplinks to the apparatus.

Apparatuses naturalized

Apparatuses are never only apparatuses. Dispositives are never only dispositives. They melt, they merge, they tend to disappear. A progressive naturalization of dispositives and their constituting apparatuses takes place. What once was regarded as being thoroughly artificial, weird, *non-humanoid*, even *anti-humanoid*, and supposedly never an integral part of an alien's sensibility and experience, soon will become a quite intrinsically cherished, admired, even nostalgically remembered and loved form of experiencing. Going to a cinema where they might still show movies on celluloid; writing on an ancient standing desk like a financial accountant from a nineteenth-century trade company; engaging in religious rituals and committing oneself to any of the historical forms of devotion and abstinence that one of the well-known Buddhist, Christian, Muslim, Jewish, or other more sectarian belief demands. All these dispositives seemingly had almost vanished in recent years and decades—and yet, the joy of re-enacting them, in a half-nostalgic, half-blood curdling way, encouraged various actors in the relevant fields to support a comeback of these practices and their related artifacts. Humanoids are enjoying forgotten restrictions. The return to historically lost or abolished regulations in the form of materially distinct dispositives (like a cinema, like a standing desk, or like religious rituals) is apparently fulfilling a certain desire. A desire to return to a neatly ordered past—however illusionary and *invented* this past might actually be. Régis Debray, French cultural historian and devoted Marxist, describes this phenomenon as an *effet jogging*, a jogging effect (Debray 2006). This term derives from the observation that in contrast to cultural pessimists of early automobilization in the mid-twentieth century, the development to a total and self-destructive automobilization never actually lead to the predicted atrophy of extremities and muscles, a loss of the ability to walk or run. In contrary, the self-reflexivity of culture translated automobilization into a culture of working out, doing sports, training muscles more intensely than ever before in modern history: "depuis que les citadins ne marchent plus, ils courent. Fanatiquement" (Debray 2006: 1). *Since the urban population does not walk anymore, it runs—fanatically.* Debray concludes that cultural practices and techniques are never lost—they simply return as soon as new cultural practices, considered advanced now, have become the new normal. Since supermarkets have become ubiquitous and lost their originally distinctive value, people go shopping in farmer's markets; since status updates in social media became a standard for everyday writing, the paper notebook and the fountain pen returned; since sounds are mainly stored as digital data, analog storage media return, such as the vinyl record, the cassette tape, or even reel-to-reel tape recordings. Humanoid cultures progress in dialectic countermovements, not as an unhindered rise forward and upward:

> In short: progress is retrograde, and if it were *not* in one way or another, it would be existentially fatal to us. As if history would give us with one hand what it takes with the other: what is unlocked by the tools and objects, is closed again by our works and our memories. (Debray 2006: 4; transl. HS)[1]

This dialectic of cultural developments and the tension between artifacts and practices, all of this constitutes a cultural archive stored in billions of humanoid and non-humanoid aliens and robots. Yet not all of the practices or dispositives one might dare to return to have even been abolished.
Some of them to which contemporary, modern, and alert aliens like you or me might want to return never actually did vanish. Too often, they merely stopped being considered the pinnacle of progress and contemporary culture. They have become too common, outworn, just plain boring. Their return is hence more a return of one's attention to them. They return into the spotlight of a culture where they again obtain the glorious shine of excitement, contemporaneity, and the future. The reason for this dialectic of vanishing and returning, of becoming outworn and refurbished, lies in the rather laconic character of everyday usage. Most of the apparatuses one might be using on any given day are neither reflected in our usage, nor did they vanish. They became *naturalized*. This means that dispositives that were established in earlier decades of our individual lives—or even before you or I were born—get to be experienced as an integral, natural, and unquestioned item of our lives and basically the order of things. Or

---

[1] "En clair: le progrès est rétrograde, et s'il ne l'était pas d'une façon ou d'une autre, il nous serait existentiellement fatal. Comme si l'Histoire nous accordait d'une main ce qu'elle nous reprend par l'autre: ce qu'outils et objets déverrouillent, nos œuvres et nos mémoires le referment." (Debray 2006: 4)

as Douglas Adams wrote so fabulously on humanoids' perspective on the history of technology and new media:

> I've come up with a set of rules that describe our reactions to technologies: Anything that is in the world when you're born is normal and ordinary and is just a natural part of the way the world works. Anything that's invented between when you're fifteen and thirty-five is new and exciting and revolutionary and you can probably get a career in it. Anything invented after you're thirty-five is against the natural order of things. (Adams 2002: 111)

It might be hard to affirm distinct ages as transitioning humanoids from one era into the next, albeit Adam's outline is strikingly convincing in its implicit biographical narration of opinions, resentments, and unfounded assumptions: The older some (never all) humanoid aliens are, the less some of them seem willing to integrate new apparatuses into their everyday lives—and the more some of the aliens tend to essentialize and nostalgically overrate these apparatuses they grew up with. This *essentialization of the all too well-known* is, again, a major problem in any individual researcher's biography. Though rigid research ethics demand scrutinizing any minor bit of knowledge relevant for a research project, it is quite clear that it is exactly the unscrutinized and unquestioned assumptions that constitute the actual axioms, the foundations of research. There simply is no research project that is not based on claims considered to be proven sufficiently by earlier researchers: traditional bits of knowledge. This naturalization of inventions and insights becomes a troubling problem as soon as the dynamics of research are increasingly tied to the process of globalization in a transcultural trajectory, integrating evermore diverse, maybe even contradicting everyday practices, mutually exclusive usages of media and technology as well as propositions concerning the standardization of interpersonal communication, of local and intercontinental traffic, of urban or rural behavior. The sensory experiences and the individual evaluation of these practices might then be forced to change, to adapt and adjust rapidly. Perspectives on life, on the everyday, the personal, and the intimate might undergo vast transformations. This poses no problem as long as one believes that personal experiences are largely irrelevant for an anonymous epistemological subject as introduced to modern philosophy in the course of enlightenment. In the field of sound and sensory studies, though, this exploration of specific experiences in all their subtle, kaleidoscopic, and erratic formations demands exactly this reflection on the process of naturalization, of habitualization, of the non-reflected and the normalized.

The process of *essentialization* as a form of *normalization* is countering and expanding the known processes of crafty inventions and developments, of global expansion and scientific curiosity, of capitalization and mediatization. In the form of *normalization*, the essentialist urge has been explored recently in sociology. Jürgen Link explored the history and the characteristics of this strange idiosyncrasy in an effort to understand this *normalist desire* (Link 1997). According to Link, *normalism* is being defined as a person's pursuit of social participation realized by affiliation to the median and the majority of people in a statistically rendered *Gaussian bell curve*. This process of normalization is hard to swallow for researchers concerned with the cultural history of science and technology. At least selectively, it falsifies a supposed urge to innovation, modernization, and progress as crucial motivations of inventors and scientists. Actually, it is probably not. Normalization, the urge to still belong to a supposed majority, seems to counter any progressivist ambition. In the process of modernist normalization, a more homeostatic idea of society takes place (Link 1997: 358): the idea of unhindered progress is replaced by the idea of a sustainable and well-functioning circuit. The predominance of closed circuit models in the *Bachelor Machine of Research* (discussed earlier, in Chapter 4: "In Auditory Dispositives") and its obsession with self-sustaining systems of production and consumption with the maximum insolation from external systems is returning in this highly idiosyncratic proclivity to homeostasis. Link states that, in their major administrative and infrastructural models, modern societies implement a so-called "Signal-, Orientierungs- und Kontrollebene" (Link 1997: 360), *a layer for signalizing, for orienting and controlling*. In the process of modernization and mediatization, this layer turns more and more into the only valid reference for the *normalist desire*. Only the advent of modern techniques of data gathering, data storing, data mining, and comparing of datasets, as well as concepts of the normal distribution and the Gaussian bell curve, made it possible—according to Link—to pursue the goal of normalization. Only the modernist functionalization of social interactions and various processes in a particular culture made it possible to establish a moralist discourse on the normalist character of certain ways of life, professions, obsessions, and individual desires. In the words of Jürgen Link:

> In ständigem Kreislauf werden also Verhaltensweisen zu "Fakten," "Fakten" zu "Signalen," "Signale" zu Verhaltensweisen usw. Die Transformation von Verhaltensweisen in "Fakten" und "Signale" tendiert zur Funktionalisierung aller mit den Verhaltensweisen womöglich verbundenen Intensitäten auf den Signal Charakter hin. (Link 1997: 362)

This translation of particular acts of behavior into "Facts" and then into "Signals" and then again into recommended forms of behavior establishes quite openly a functionalizing of all possible lifeforms for their signalizing quality. A critique of signal processing (proposed earlier, in Chapter 4: "In Auditory Dispositives") becomes truly vital here: the shannonist concepts of *signals* and of *processing*, of *transduction*, of *information source*, of *transmitters*, *channels*, and *receivers* in the normalist society shape this pervasive functionalization. Functionalization roots the modern society in the historical discourse and the imagery of engineering cultures of the nineteenth century and its military dispositive. Data mining in this sense reproduces excessively militarized social relations on all levels of contemporary and future societies. You are part of the *military-industrial-communication-entertainment complex*—if you agree or not (the same way you and I still are part of a globally hegemonic Christian or monotheistic belief system—even if we were atheists). The history of acoustics, of audio technology, and of sound performances and music production is an inherent part of this development. In the process of cultural appropriation, of domestication of formerly new technologies and media, the only slightly elderly media gadgets get sedimented as essential items in a humanoid's life. According to Adams, the mere age to be counted by years and decades—surely next to nothing in the scale of cultural history and tectonic plate movements—is the measure after which a culture and a generation seems to evaluate the items in their technosphere as familiar and comforting, as an appreciated disruption or as perverted and alienating. From a radically relativist position, the endless progress would then result in an eternal shift that would never find an end but would turn any new technology "against the natural order of things" (Adams 2002: 111) finally to a "normal and ordinary" (ibid.) constituent of a humanoid alien's life. The comedic trick in Adams's argument is apparently that the shift in evaluation seems to take place almost automatically, without any willful intervention. Yet, obviously, as recurrently proven by science and technology studies, this shift in evaluations is a historical process negotiated by the various agents in it: inventors, industries, competitors, the press, consumers, even ignorant and hostile non-users. In the course of this social negotiation, the technological invention *itself* does not remain untainted: sonically speaking, loudness and volume is regulated, emissions are reduced, standards for transmission are codified, user interfaces are adapted, and the acoustics of new concert halls—originally blamed as alien and inhuman—are taken to be the absolute norm shortly thereafter (Thompson 2002; Bijsterveld/Cleophas/Krebs/Mom 2013). The process of *domestication* therefore extends not only to the individual and personal appropriation of a new technology, but also to the response by the producing industry and the inventors to complaints and wishes by consumers and critics. Still, in the end, the market domination might be achieved and the new, finalized technology can provide a standardized testing method for behavior adapted to a normalized median: for instance, I, as a listener, adapted my listening in the late 1970s and early 1980s to the *stereo dispositive*—introduced ten years before I was born—and I almost necessarily regarded this listening experience consequentially as far more natural and immediate than surround sound or wave field synthesis. To a large extent, one's sensorial evaluation represents foremost one's individual *éducation sensorielle*. Each new sound reproduction technology and its underlying discoveries were once regarded as deeply disturbing and provocative for listeners who were trained in even earlier perceptual and audile techniques. Naturalization inevitably occurs, and it drags normalization along: it takes a humanoid with major self-confidence, rebelliousness, and an uncommon desire to stand out and disapprove of previous technologies as inappropriate and poor.

From the position of a sensory critique, this progressive naturalization and essentialization of technologies is at the same time a process of expansion, deprivation, and transformation of the individual sensory corpus. It represents the appearance and the expansion of a new sensology and its rise to dominance. The naturalization of compression algorithms and of sensory representations in various formats is a vivid example of this: any MP3 audio file relying on the listening models established by Harvey Fletcher (cf. Chapter 1: "Quantifying Sound") resembles a gramophone more than anything else. The listening practice of a humanoid alien is deformed and prefabricated by such a model. One's sensibility is by far not as stable individually or collectively as is likely to be assumed. In contrast, it is highly responsive and malleable, it is soft and vulnerable, it is in tension and adhering to cohesions and repercussions. Thus it is a very likely victim and object to ongoing cultural and sensorial transformations. New technologies and their practices, new dispositives and their particularly required forms of habitus, are not entering a humanoid culture without consequences: You and I, we are no insensible statues—even if one likes to perform a pose of being untouchable, impermeable, immovable, and firm. *Wir sind keine Roboter* (at least not in this statuarian and servant sense of the original word *рабoтнūк*). More recent sensologies are driven by concepts of rather linear and punctual signal transmission—though experts are very much aware of the actually major issues of even constituting, sending, and fetching simply a clear signal:

> Sense data pass through the obstacles placed into a kind of statue or automaton with twenty layers of armour, a veritable Carpathian castle, their energy purified as it makes its way through successive filters towards the central cell or instance, soul, understanding, conscience or transcendental I. (Serres 2008: 145)

This mechanist, reductivist, and clearly *shannonist* concept of instrumentalizing and exploiting the sensory (as discussed in Chapter 4: "In Auditory Dispositives") degrades anthropoid aliens openly to the earlier mentioned statuarian *homunculi*: as if contemporary knowledge on information technology, on network architecture or data mining would be the end of science history and as such the final metaphor to guide contemporary research questions: "a black box with holes and doorways through which information can enter and exit" (Serres 2008: 190). These concepts of *The Human* again will go down in history to be replaced by then-contemporary models of the late twenty-first, the mid-twenty-third, or the early twenty-fifth century. Its denaturalization is any naturalized apparatus' future fate.

The precision of sensibility

The sensorial apparatus of humanoid aliens is plastic. It is (as discussed in Chapter 6: "A Sensory Corpus") quite substantially vulnerable and highly volatile to being numbed in selected areas or to being oversensitive in others, to being shockingly responsive in some situations and rather immovable in others. This sensorium is, obviously, by no means infallible: it is *as* fallible, flawed, and inherently broken as any other material or immaterial entity yet encountered. An anthropology of sound heuristically needs to assume this fundamental *im*perfection in order not to superimpose a humanoid imaginary of absolute perfection to actual samples of real things and processes. Yet this potential to fail corresponds to a potential to generate. This sensibility, this non-statuarian, this genuinely unstable character is its most critical trait— and its most generative as well. Sensibility in aliens like you or me might not be stable over longer periods of time, but the senses also do not *have* to be stable to that extent. Humanoids can be highly adaptable to an incessantly transforming environment and to particular situations they are subjected to. In this very moment as a writer, I doubt if I am truly capable of focusing my attention on this section of the chapter right now. After a long weekend of family visits and necessary errands and pressing deadlines, it feels alien to sit in front of the glowing screen again and just move along. Still, in recent years, I acquired a certain confident habitus that can help me bridge these truly unsettling seconds of fundamental insecurity, doubt, and feeling that get lost in writing. As soon as I start reading the first words and sentences of a section, as soon as their rhythm and sound, the relevant issues and arguments, examples and references, are again present in my mind, I get into this regular, familiar writing flow. The initial instability and insecurity of writing has vanished; I contributed to this vanishing personally by simply moving along, in an acquired habitus. This externalized stabilization is probably the most important function of a habitus.

Hence the sensibility you or I might think of as appropriate in a given situation is not necessarily at hand and accessible in precisely these situations. An alien is not transparent and not easily on hand to itself nor to others. A genuine opaqueness qualifies one as a humanoid alien in contrast to a dependent servomechanism. This dark situatedness, this instability and irritability of a *bodily felt sense* (cf. Chapter 6: "A Sensory Corpus," section A Generative Sensorium), is the root for its strengths, its impact, its radiation.

This situated responsiveness is the reason for its plasticity. Any intense and daring activity in the arts, in performing and composing, in the humanities or in design, but also in the natural, the technical, and the engineering sciences, requires a fundamental potential to be irritated by the tiniest details and insecurities—in order to return with more intensity to work on exactly those irritating details:

> The distance between the latest trash movie on cable television and *Eyes Wide Shut* is in the details, and only in detail, though in a mass of details. Roughly estimated, there are about 125 billion details of which we are talking here. (Goetz 2000: 61; transl. HS)[2]

This distance between rather uninspired business as usual in the arts or the media and a shockingly ingenious work (like the last Stanley Kubrick film, *Eyes Wide Shut*) lies exactly in those details. It needs a fundamental sensibility and a readiness of the author, the producer, the whole production team to be irritated by the slightest detail to complete this almost inconceivable task. Working with physical objects and materials, with corporeally accessible situations and their conceptual framing, is one of the main activities in the arts and in design: these fields are, contrary to popular belief, not at all restricted to a verbal, interpretative, hermeneutic and logical, or even arithmetically and algorithmically plausible argument. This form of activity, though, shapes most of contemporary research in the humanities, the technical and natural sciences. The distance between an argument in words, signs, or numbers and an argument in a specific situation, its experiential and bodily character, its sonic, kinesthetic, haptic, and sensory details could not be any larger. It is a distance not only between two cultures or subcultures, but also between two tribes or ethnic groups in the professional field: a distance between a fully transparent and explicit analysis in all steps on the one side—and on the other side a critique that operates for the most part implicitly and rich with premises. In public discourse this fact is easily ignored, as one might be tempted to assume that the explicit and transparent analysis is the main foundation for contemporary scientist societies: societies that actually rely predominantly on algorithmic codifications in law, administration, and infrastructure and verbal articulations in politics, culture, and education—seemingly more than on individual and situational sensibilities in all their idiosyncrasies and specificities. Yet, as soon as a *sensory critique* is needed, as soon as a need for overcoming disturbingly *naturalized apparatuses* is

---

[2] "Die Distanz zwischen dem letzten Sat-1-Trash.-Film und *Eyes Wide Shut* liegt im Detail, und zwar nur im Detail, allerdings in einer Unmasse von Details. Grob geschätzt handelt es sich um zirka 125 Milliarden Details, von denen wir hier reden." (Goetz 2000: 61)

stated—a situated and corporeal sensibility is the source for critique and a substantial scrutinizing.

The precision of measuring and of argument is not the only form of precision humanoid aliens are capable of. Precision can also be strived for in the realm of the senses, in *proprio-*, *entero-*, and *exteroceptive* activities. Sensing and perceiving are not operating in an imaginary, fictional, or poetical realm. The precision of sensing and of perception is material. The precision of sensibility can be in many cases more accurate in certain situations than an instrumental precision using an apparatus and its mediating concepts constituted by symbolic as well as imaginary orders—unless it enters realms that are rather inaccessible for any regular humanoid alien. Sensibility's precision is operating therefore in the realm of the real and its expanded materiality.

The precision of sensibility relies on a bodily felt sense. These days, it is easily dismissed as *only* idiosyncratic in a bad sense, as relying on *mere* introspection, as an example for bad psychologizing; it is often supposed to be *exclusively* an expression of some meaningless introversion, an excess of *squeamishness*, of detested *sensitivities*. Though in everyday life it becomes quite obvious how a humanoid alien like you and me is relying in almost every single action and activity on a felt sense—and rather not on an explicit account of verbally phrased possibilities to select from with a sober and rational mindset. Humanoid aliens are entangled in situations of practices and crafts, navigating them more by a bodily sense than by deliberate decision making. The knowledge present in corporeally guided decisions is not only a silent or *tacit* knowledge (Polanyi 1966)—it is even more a form of knowledge that enables and inspires us to make a move, to perform, to take action, to speak. This felt, sensory knowledge is an individually realized ground for an alien's action in specific situations, concerning specific persons and their actions, an appropriate and desired acting in a social situation. This sense, though, is not hardwired, and it is also not preinstalled in humanoid aliens: they need to acquire it in the course of their lives. They learn and they fail; they might get better at it; they might acquire flawed routines of behavior; they learn again. The bodily felt sense is the background from which you or I evaluate a sensory experience, we find our stance concerning a certain taste, for conflicts in life, for professional activities, for future friends or colleagues. It is a sense promoting a certain trajectory for a decision: "Bodily implying is a value-direction" (Gendlin 1992: 203). This value-direction guides any sensible, subtle, situated, tactical, and artistic performativity of humanoid aliens.

The physiological fundament for this precision of sensibility lies in a major physiological activity of humanoid aliens, the *proprioceptive perception*. For cultural research, it might seem rather strange and unsettling to focus on such a supposedly marginal sensory activity. Yet it is anything but marginal: whereas traditional aesthetic and sensory studies prefer to focus mainly on *exteroception* of objects, processes, and activities outside a humanoid's body, an immense amount of sensory activity is directed inwards, toward myriads of single percepts: from one's *enteroception*, the perception of one's various inner organs and their position and state, to one's *visceroception*, the healthy functioning of organs, tissues, and corporeal areas. All these sensory activities by far exceed everything that has so far been the object of any major theory of perception. It is necessary to reverse this traditional order of the senses. The *perception of surfaces*—mostly visual, sometimes tactile or haptic, rarely auditory, kinesthetic, or even gustatory or olfactory—still seems to dominate the discourse of perception with a strong focus on *exteroception*, the perception of anything outside of the body. Compared to the intricate and subtle complexity of the *perception of the corpus*, all these layers and folded percepts in one's body, this outside perception looks rather dwarfed—a banal, if not simplistic, special case of perception. Proprioception, after all, enables one to access material things and activities. To put it bluntly: a comprehensive, intensive, internalized bodily and highly sensible perception of matter is only possible by including a complex, deep-reaching, and widely radiating proprioception—even extending to one's physical environment in the broadest sense. Proprioception integrates and reacts to exteroception—whereas exteroception is likely to nourish the illusion to encounter "The World" without any perceptual bias. An overly strong focus on exteroception stabilizes the objectivity delusion.

Sensibility hence involves an alien's perception of itself—not ending with internal and physiological activities. Proprioception as this core of sensibility incorporates thinking, feeling, consciousness: sensibly perceiving oneself as living and performing agent. This conception of oneself is significantly different than the one presented in older, utilitarian models of anatomy that tend to explain one's body as an industrial production line. The knowledge of medicine and biology, of the neurosciences, is far subtler than its derived and popularized models. Yet, the process of producing, of transmitting, of distinctly transporting a transparent object on a calculated trajectory to a given target apparently remains a secure and comforting model—from signal processing over media design to efficacious remedies, exercising one's body, collaborating on an artifact, contemporary warfare, and international politics. Transmission trumps receiving:

> L'emission l'emporte sur l'écoute, nous savons comment lancer un son et comment il se propage, nous pouvons le relayer, nous savons mal recevoir. (Serres 1985: 147)

We know how to project a sound and how it propagates: we are bad at receiving. An anthropology of sound is founded on this fundamental insight of sensory anthropology. A *sonic persona* is a humanoid alien reversing this archaic order of sensory modalities. A sonic persona leaves sonic traces and crosses sensory constellations. A sonic persona exercises an *Art of*

Receiving: a *Craft of Conceiving*. The technologies and apparatuses, though, for transmission are in dire need of this complementary expansion. How could it be possible to keep oneself ready enough, alert enough, attentive enough—in a multitude of everyday moments and instants—to recognize and to incorporate the most unexpected *petit perceptions* (Leibniz 1765)? The sense for a musical instrument or a tool kit, the right location for a microphone or a loudspeaker to be situated, the appropriate words in an uncommon encounter: aside from all the learned and materially present knowledge, one decides in fractures of seconds from the ground of one's felt sense. What moment is this? How could I use this tool right now? What action should you take right now? The *precision of measuring*, securely established as one exteroceptive form of exactitude, needs the complementary form of *precision of sensibility*. This sensibility has always been a crucial sense in the crafts and the sciences, in the fine arts as well as in performance. But it has been neglected in the status of being a central function in any research activity. Even in the work of the analysts—in chemistry or physics, in cooking or in engineering:

> When scholarship or knowledge is reduced to analysis, the guests at the banquet lie down in distaste on their cushions, in a different order and language, keeping their distance from the hearth where some crafty genius combines, composes, blends, creates a new order, a different scale of sapidity: a slave or woman with dirty hands, pouring incompatible liquids into a single crater, as though into a stomach. The analyst gags in disgust at these messy characters, in revulsion at the bubbling broth; he prefers to vomit. Thus emptying his stomach of the mixture and confusion to which he is addicted. (Serres 2008: 166)

With precision of sensibility, *a slave or woman* works with dirty hands at a cluttered workbench: "Prenez ceci, dosez, puis cela, mêlez" (Serres 1985: 181). *More of this, a pinch of that, stir it, knead it, let the dough go*. A bodily felt sense is guiding these actions with its tension pulling toward the appropriate, the *aptum*—trained in the skills to compound and to blend; and trained in standing the often detested heat, the volume, and the radiating aggression of merging and coalescing:

> Fire fuses many things together. The raw gives us tender simplicities, elementary freshness, the cooked invents coalescences. Conversely, analysis slices and dices raw; synthesis requires flame. As a result, the latter tends towards knowledge and culture; the former remains unrefined. What if the philosophy of knowledge had not yet begun? (Serres 2008: 167)

An anthropology of the senses implies this *anthropology of knowledge*: The grand philosophy of science being historicized and culturalized.

Being materialized. In *syrrhesis*, the responsivity and sensibility of the alien cooking and mashing, extracting and reducing, kneading and layering, fusing and chilling, provides an alternate epistemology: a series of efficacious performative acts generates hitherto unknown material constellations, consistencies, substances, and relations. An anthropology of the senses operates exactly in the midst of these materialities, these actions and interactions. Its major method is the immersion of the researcher into a specific situation, its practices and sensible events in order to explore, to criticize, and to unfold its anthropological potential:

> All of our body cells constantly receive not only food, but light and waves, media stimuli and stimuli from the air, including a tremendous amount of stimuli emanating from other bodies, from other persons. (Theweleit 2007: 26; transl. HS)

An anthropology of the senses, hence, is a materialist and sensory anthropology. *Figures of light and water.* A researcher's generative sensorium is her or his main analytical and syrrhetic instrument: "We immediately perceive the 'whim' of persons when they enter the room; especially from people we know well." (Theweleit 2007: 26; transl. HS)

The syrrhesis of an anthropology of the senses relies on sensibility and on its precision in a given moment. It generates a confluence of practices and skills, of various forms of knowledge, and divergent discursive, cultural, and historical traditions. It expands its contemporary inspirations into future and past and possible worlds. This precision of sensibility radiates *sensory fictions*. It evokes and it traces. How does a humanoid alien appropriate the sensory and sonic? Sonic receptivity and sonic generativity in the making. Or, as philosopher Wolfgang Hogrebe wrote in 1996: "Ahnungen 'tunneln' Propositionen" (Hogrebe 1996: 26): *Hunches "tunnel" propositions.*

Idioplex

This space of a certain height, a certain dimension, a certain volume of oxygen, of other gases and particles, a heated room, with a certain lighting, with a certain arrangement of chairs, of mechanical, electrical, and electronic objects and connections, this space here is occupied in this very moment by a certain number of humanoid aliens. In this very moment I imagine you seated in a library, at home or in public transport. You are probably—hopefully—curious to experience what will be the next step in this book you may have read so far; or did you just open this page by chance? My situation as a writer differs from your situation as a reader or listener. Though it is not so different, as we both are engaging in focused attention on an evolving or finalized text. It is a rather exotic and idiosyncratic listening situation—that nevertheless represents a major activity, for instance, of recent centuries in humanities, politics, and the sciences. And yet, it still represents a major reality of everyday, solitary activity in networked societies. It might be enhanced by an audio stream on the side, by interjected chats, status updates, an occasional online search, or even a phone call; still, this rather exhaustive and stressful bodily situation—in historical comparison, sitting at a desk is a trained and tense, thoroughly stressing activity (Eickhoff 1903, 1997)—is considered a regular and normal one. I notice that the music being rehearsed on the floor below me just stopped. I liked its swing and somehow amateurish progress, evermore failing and stumbling, stopping and restarting. I am writing this book in various situations, on various writing devices, and in a multiplicity of moods and atmospheres, daytimes and locations. The research for this book was made in various situations of my life as well, in highly differing working and family environments. Actually, I tend to think, a lot of individual traits and biases, obsessions and repulsions, affects and disinterests, have shaped the outline of this book, its book proposal, and its current form that you are holding in your hands and reading. This book as a whole is obviously not merely written by myself. Any humanoid's actions and artifacts are emerging out of a network of other connected humanoids and non-humanoids, encouraged or discouraged by different interpretations of lifestyles and ever-changing and transforming goals in an individual life. Lest we forget all the friends and colleagues, lovers and partners, momentary encounters and longtime teachers, collaborators and assistants. Does it seem to you strangely inappropriate to speak about such generic characteristics of an academic publication at this point of my argument? Are you irritated, maybe aggressively annoyed by this turn of the written flow on these pages? If you are, you are rightfully so. You are reacting to an individual idiosyncrasy that the author of this book just performed. Annoying, appalling, tiresome, repetitive for sure. This conflict between my certain urge and inclination to continue writing this book in this way and your certainly being surprised or angry by me doing so represents a genuine difference between our two sensory corpuses. You and I apparently—and not much to anyone's surprise—differ in our biographical, cultural, and maybe even historical traits of a specifically focused and defocused sensory awareness, a *Sinnenbewusstsein* (Lippe 1985). You, being a rather humanoid alien, probably, cultivated a certain sensory and sonic persona over time as well as a textual, a writing and a reading persona; me, equally being a rather alien humanoid, cultivated yet another, largely differing sonic and sensory persona over time as yet another textual, a writing and a reading persona. The idiosyncrasies in both our individual varying experiences necessarily clash on these pages. The idiosyncratic implex of the sonic persona I am is unraveling on these pages:

It stands, apparently, in a certain contrast to your idiosyncratic implex of a sensory and sonic persona. It is a common encounter. In case you follow this book consistently and thoroughly agreeing with all my arguments and interpretations, it would surely qualify as a rather unexpectedly harmonious encounter. I, for one, would be very surprised by this; but maybe you are not. Such coincidences occur.

The *sonic fictions* (Eshun 1998) a persona lays underneath and weaves around her or his listening experiences are manifold. They are embedded into larger sensory fictions, and they are highly differentiated according to the various sensory personae, situated personae, and contextual, pragmatist personae one might have cultivated over time. To think about the variety in sonic experiences and the consequential variety in sonic personae is one of the main starting points for this sonic anthropology—a sonic theory of an emerging and developing multitude in all its glorious idiosyncrasies:

> Unsaid, I hope that philosophy opens up perspectives for me in my relation to the world, to others, and to myself, which I have not yet seen, instead of normalizing in a process of universal agreement my theoretical and perceptive view of things. (Pothast 1988: 19; transl. HS)[3]

In 1988 the philosopher Ulricht Pothast published a unique book he described as an example of "ungehorsame Forschung" (Pothast 1988: 16), *disobedient research*. His book had the title: *Philosophisches Buch: Schrift unter der aus der Entfernung leitenden Frage, was es heißt, auf menschliche Weise lebendig zu sein* (Pothast 1988): "Philosophical book: Writings as guided from a distance by the question of what it means to be alive in a human way." His writings on an anthropology of sensing in everyday life combine fundamental philosophical reflections with situated and often largely personal narrations of the situation and the contextual prerequisites for these reflections: idiosyncratic sensory fictions. The narrated *context of discovery* of this study generated a sort of *Erkenntnisroman*, an *epistemological novel*. Like Eugene T. Gendlin, Pothast also tries arduously to find the ground for largely rationalist and verbal accounts, decisions, articulations in a corporeal sensitivity. Pothast argues that for an appropriate and seemingly generative activity among other humanoid aliens, one needs to get in "touch," in *Berührung* (Pothast 1988: 124–61), with the *Innengrund*, the "inner ground" of one's sensory corpus as guiding environment. Equally to Gendlin—but from a thoroughly different philosophical tradition—he

---

[3] "Ich hoffe unausgesprochen, daß Philosophie mir in meinem Verhältnis zur Welt, zu anderen, zu mir selbst Perspektiven öffnet, die ich noch nicht gesehen habe, statt meine gedankliche und wahrnehmende Sicht der Dinge in einem Prozeß allgemeiner Einigung zu normieren." (Pothast 1988: 19)

argues that it is necessary to cultivate this corporeal and sensory relation to oneself in order to get a sense for one's own decisions, articulations, and performative acts.

In an article 20 years later, Pothast explicitly relates his concept of *Innengrund* or "inner ground" and identifies it with Gendlin's concept of the *bodily felt sense* (Pothast 2009: 83). He agrees with Gendlin that foremost a persistent return to one's own bodily felt sense or Innengrund can provide criteria and strategies to dismantle the clichés, archaic patterns, and dispositives in one's own everyday actions: a self-reflection in sensorial terms. Both Gendlin and Pothast propose and perform this sensory critique as a form of resistance: a resistance starting from the very idiosyncrasies of one sensory persona—in order to achieve an individual "Entblindung" (Pothast 1988: 105–23), a *deblinding* from all the sensologic dispositives and obstacles. Critique starts here with a personal self-critique of actions, sensologies, and habitualized patterns and pathologies. And from this reflection and disassembling of individual routines, a revolutionary impact emerges: The precision of sensibility turns into political critique.

CHAPTER EIGHT

Resistance and resonance

zeige deine Wunde

Then something got plugged in. The higher bands were suddenly blocked out, even the middle frequencies were lost. As if I were a bottle and my own cork was suddenly applied to my earlobes. I was deeply scared, no doubt. Someone so wholeheartedly attached to listening, to hearing, and to speaking, to auditory cognition and to sonic experiences of the most extremist kinds as I considered myself at that time, someone like that being partially deafened—without any warning? Maybe not without *any* warning, as I realized a few weeks later. I was being warned. Such a hearing loss—which the German language names rather suggestively *Hörsturz, a downfall of hearing*—I had to endure three times in the last decades. This might seem a lot to you if listening is not pivotal in your professional or intimate life; but it might seem not too much to you if your life is also one of a sonic aficionado. In any instance, as my *hearing was falling down*, I only realized later that there were quite explicit warning signs in advance. Most of these accidents occurred after a longer time of intense sonic focusing, of being overly bodily attentive, and maybe even excessively present, alert, responsive, and communicative on all levels of my public persona—way beyond any physical limits familiar to me. Each time, there were minor moments, right before the actual hearing loss set in, that I experienced one particular sensation: I felt that my blood pressure seemed to be quite high, also the pulse of my heart had been incredibly accelerated so I could even sense the tender veins in my ears pumping with blood. I felt my blood. The intensity of a strongly experienced auditory permeability was translated into an actual physiological intensity of intravenous activity. I could sense this activity under my skin, around my muscles, at my fascia, my nerves. I sensed a high tone of buzzing in the upper and frontal area of my brain mass; this intense traffic, the contacts and energetic arches, was translated into a strong headache. As if I were belted with massive pressure around my upper skull. The sensological processes circulating around me, partly planned and executed by me, and surely affirmed and fueled by me—this I felt intensely—now extended deep into my sensory corpus. The sensory dispositive present and installed in this location and actively taking effect included myself. I was made part, constituent, and generator of this technological artifact. In no respect was I now considering myself alien outside of this historico-techno-social apparatus that this specific dispositive represented: as a malleable humanoid corpus, I needed to be considered an integral and major supportive constructive component of this dispositive of listening and sensing, speaking and reacting, recording and documenting, staging, presenting, and resonating. Meatsacks are useful building blocks for "The Technium" (Kelly 2010).

Being useful for a dispositive is anything but agreeable and joyful. It might by enjoyable and comfortable to make use of a dispositive or even to conceive, establish, and maintain, even to historicize and analyze a dispositive. Yet, being effectively assimilated and utilized *by* a dispositive is deeply painful. It is disturbing, and it kicks you into an abyss of profound, existential doubt—even on the occasion of a rather minor instance of only a temporary form of hearing loss. For humanoid aliens, the hurting body is no accident. It is their substantial existence as such: *vital materiality.* The pathological symptoms, wounds, or scars showing on a humanoid's corpus are manifold. Cultural origins for each of those pathologies are never easy to diagnose or to trace—yet neither are they easy to dismiss at all, taking into account complex interdependencies as well as surprising chain reactions, transfers, and ramifications in the body and the person. As soon as a dispositive has been installed, you are dependent on it, very quickly. It then extends into your and my, into her and his, very corporeal intricacies. Just now, you entered a public transport system, in Shanghai or in Copenhagen, in Tokyo or in Tunis. In order to enter this system, you are required to log in. As soon as you log in, you hear an affirmative sound. A pinchy, needle-like, tiny hurt—or is it a much deeper, quite satisfying, fatherly bell? Now you are allowed to enter this closed system, you are admitted to take the next subway arriving in this station or to ride on this bus. The system has agreed. The system took you on. You are affirmed, your whole existence, being, acting. The system loves you, and you are so thankful to your mother, "The System." It acts upon you and me as if it would be connected and working, rather stable and uninterruptable, infallible. You rely on it. In leaving your home, you did not only enter *this* system; during the hours before you entered various systems earlier this day, as you perhaps turned on your computer, turned to your tablet, your smartphone or watch, you immediately had to listen to disjointed system sounds, alert noises, and auditory warning signals, startup chimes, perhaps accompanied by your favorite music in the background or on your headphones. You have been logged in then—with audible feedback sounds—to a series of partially independent, partially interdependent systems. In case you did not actually use public transport but your individual car, this machine would also grant you access to its system, these days preferably by a series of auditory signals. These sounds constitute a continuous sequence of vibrations and resonances out of which your personality is made: a sequence of tones that turned into your persona, your *sonic persona*: "Ces perceptions insensibles marquent encore et constituent le même individue" (Leibniz 1765, S. 47). Being rejected from "The System" affects you sonically in one way—but being admitted actually substantiates your very existence even more: You are shaped as a persona by affirming tones. They heal, they secure you, they ground your next steps. Societies of control extend their reach into your very sensory confidence: sensological control turns citizens into trained meat. The personal sonic corpus is normalized toward the triggers of an auditory dispositive. Idiosyncrasies need to be erased, all erratic properties of a sonic persona, let alone its vulnerabilities, its sorrows and anxieties, its doubts and ambivalences, need to be ignored and in the end deleted. These sounds of control, admittance, or rejection are weaponized sounds one adores:

> Where do weaponized adorables come from and what do they want? . . . For half the battle is won when a want is adequately recognized. (Law and Wark 2014: 4)

These adorable sounds eradicate any major impulse to criticize or to question them. This auditory dispositive seemingly renders any resistance against it not only impossible but also unthinkable: who would even dare to take system sounds seriously that only last microseconds? That would be ridiculous, right? Sensology successfully installed. Control mechanisms remain unquestioned. Vulnerabilities hidden and repressed. Situations of therapy are direly needed, *zeige deine Wunde:* an almost transcendental healing can be experienced in an installation by Joseph Beuys of the same name: *zeige deine Wunde* (1976). Rather uncommonly, only the word *Wunde,* the "wound," is written with a capital letter—whereas the first letter of the title is significantly not: it sets in with a typographical wound. Only one single wound is mentioned in this title, yet an anthropology of the senses goes beyond an almost eschatological idea of the one if not original sin or wound; being wounded is contrarily a foundational and complex condition for humanoid aliens: manifold and mingled are these wounds, prolific and continuously healing, reopening and closing—wounds that resulted not infrequently out of desires, needs, wants, adorable wants:

> Counter their wants with your own! Or if not with your own, at least with wants that aren't wanted, or aren't expected. (Law and Wark 2014: 4)

Showing one's wounds equals exhibiting idiosyncrasies; awkward, embarrassing, and potentially pathetic: being an alien, one's most alienating trait of character materializes in these wounds. Being a vulnerable humanoid serves as a starting point to refine one's sensibility, one's precision of sensibility—a source of resistance:

> Learn the signs of a want, wear the right one: one can only fight wants with other wants. (Law and Wark 2014: 4)

No response

Good morning, dear reader. They stand around you and they do not reply. They do not even show the slightest mimicry or gestural symptom of having understood what you just addressed as your urgent issue right now. *I'm afraid I can't do that, dear reader.* Have they really heard what you just said? Are they not only deaf on a scarily fundamental and habitual level, but are they also essentially disconnected to any common forms of response, request, or reply a humanoid alien like you would be performing right now? Why don't they respond to your actions and requests, for Christ's sake? What hinders them from just resonating, moving, and swinging with those pressing and obvious tendencies and waves, all those overwhelming intensities of movements, of warmth and of close encounter: why don't they just follow and let themselves be guided by these trajectories? Just go with the flow? *Good night, dear reader. Conversation terminated. You are welcome.* Now and then one might—albeit unwillingly—enter an environment of estranging unresponsiveness. You enter an environment in which anthropoid aliens and their habits, rituals, and discursive regulations seem to be rather restricted, formalized, and fixed—in comparison to the one familiar to you. Probably this impression is a result of the usual conflict between the familiar and the surprising, but still you are estranged. It seems to you that, as an outsider, you might not even be able to address this group of people at all with your individual interests and thoughts, inclinations and doubts. It seems to me that merely entering this unresponsive environment is perceived as a thoroughly freaky act—turning you into a dropout even more alien than all the other aliens present here. Why are all these humanoids who seem completely alien to me acting in this environment as if they would be almost non-alien? They perform a drag as if they could claim to be *national*? *Indigenous*? *Linear*? Could it be possible that this specific alien environment is defined by *non-responsiveness* as a core attitude? Could one imagine a social subculture demanding a thoroughly homogeneous and non-responsive behavior from all its constituent humanoids? Or is being non-responsive more of a (hopefully) undesired side effect of some intense tuning and deeply coherent and mutual exchange among those alien humanoids? A closure toward other aliens that effectively represents a strict if not scary consistency to the indigenous?

Such impressions and ruminations might only represent a momentary impulse, just an arbitrary account of individual fears and obsessions, complexes and unfounded assumptions; maybe out of a general mood of self-pity. But even if the person indulging in such reflections would be in a situation of self-pity, the actual sensation of being overlooked, ignored, and fundamentally not respected in a given situation might as well be happening. It is a genuine part of life as a humanoid among other humanoids to experience this kind of detachment and alienation. Still, the particular situation of being detached and excluded in such a deeply fundamental way is a situation of torture and of cruelty, for some even of joy in the face of another's suffering. More a scene in a gory horror movie than a desired encounter in everyday lives. These days, such moments and affects are more consistently framed by societies that claim to exchange former hierarchies of aristocratic and social status for hierarchies of literacy, education, and capital providing profitable access to a broad variety of means of distribution and production; and yet there exist now for quite some time more and more approaches to society that try to transcend any dys-/utopia of crystallized beneficial institutions (Berardi 2009; Hardt Negri 2009; Caffentzis 2013). Could it not be that recent developments in the political structure of global democracies that have been coined *post-democratic*, *neo-despotic*, even *neo-authoritarian* and *neo-reactionary* actually paved the way toward a genuine non-responsiveness in politics, in administration, even in relationships, in friendships—modeled after the blueprint of *customer relations*? It might be the case that especially contemporary rhetorics of *transparency*, of *flat hierarchies*, and of *customization* and interest in customers' appropriation of products and services might just be a means of concealing a fundamental non-responsiveness on all levels. Following a basic rule in psychodynamics, exactly those qualities or goals or traits a person, a group, or an institution recurrently claims to have, it usually does not have at all, does not seek for, and will never achieve at all. What one claims to have, one every so often only has in claims.

For an *anthropology of sound*, these aspects of a fundamental non-responsiveness are crucial, disturbing, and provoking. If resonance is denied, if it is damped and abated, then the conceptual and generative nucleus of any research on sound is meaningless and annihilated. If resonance is regarded as an effectively irrelevant category for interpersonal exchange, then a major impact that sound studies could have on research, politics, and culture is negated. How could research in sound studies operate at all in societies that tend to operate more and more in a closed and self-sustaining way; excluding any external and substantial critique of their ways of operating and opening more and more controlled gateways into a monetarily filtered community of varying forms of capital? Or, even worse: am I not writing these words in exactly the situation of a world that has already turned into a sequence of gated communities capitalizing all areas of existence? Or are these thoughts just outpourings of an obsessive and frighteningly dystopic *social fiction* one might indulge in now and then? With affects and fears that are not unfounded—albeit not really suffocating societies like I just horrifyingly declared? In societies relying to a large extent on administrative regulations and depersonalized operations and processes—preferably in the form of algorithmic interfaces and equally algorithmically structured guidelines for customers' or citizens' complaints, requests, or inquiries—such situations of non-responsiveness are a common and frightening experience *in der verwalteten Welt* (Adorno 1956). How could alien anthropoids *ever* deal largely unimpressed, almost businesslike, with such encounters of denial by non-responsiveness? Reversing the perspective: what could be the personal gain in approaching aliens apparently in need of support and of trust by essentially not responding to their needs? Could it actually be a form of self-defense and a result of anxieties to lose one's carefully maintained public persona? Could there ever be a way for all participants to break out of such a menacing situation, pathways for resonance evermore narrowing if not closing down?

The *sound of responsiveness*, in contrast, is a familiar one: It is trembling and reacting, versatile, maybe all too sensitive in following any movements and oscillations occurring. It is a sound that radiates in consequence and close to any event or disruption, any continuous or discontinued activity around. Responsiveness resonates with qualities. Or, as Austrian philosopher Fritz Heider defined it, resonance is characterized by the fact,

> daß Dinge Eigenschwingungen ausführen und Medien aufgezwungene Schwingungen. (Heider 1926: 135)

Responsiveness as resonance hence relies, following Heider, on *things* being able to perform oscillations out of their own right—whereas *media* perform forced oscillations. Media would then be genuinely responsive, whereas non-mediating things—if they exist at all—would mainly rely on performing their own articulations. Frankly, at this point of this book, I doubt if such non-mediating entities can be found anywhere on the globe or our time-space continuum: maybe they constitute more of a helpful, extremist counterexample with factually no existence in reality? *Non-responsiveness* can, one might then conclude, be understood as a willful and material denial of any mediating and reacting function. This description alone is proof of the intrinsically incommensurable and truly hermetic character of non-responsive behavior: as there is simply no material motion at all that could be observed, described, or traced, *non-responsiveness* is hardly even accessible to terms of the sonic. The sound of non-responsiveness is not even silence. It is the radical and continuous absence of even the slightest perceivable distinction between silence and sound. *Non-responsive non-sound* is *aesthetically* a rather inspiring if not tempting concept. It extends to a sensory corpus that is basically not radiating and emitting any, not even the most fragile, tender, and miniscule motion or activity in any perceivable respect whatsoever. It might seek tricky ways to radiate a motion by other senses, but this would have to be considered cheating and bypassing non-responsivity in being responsive just in another area. Radical non-responsive behavior is essentially close to a steady state of complete entropy: a concept that is as tempting for humanoid aliens as it is inconceivable and unbearable on the fundamental biological level for any humanoid. There is a strong death wish realized in it. Non-responsiveness is voluptuously flirting with *Thanatos*. Probably the most intriguing and recurrently discussed examples of silence and unresponsiveness are, of course, the *camera silens*; or, to be more precise in terms of acoustics, the *anechoic chamber*, a room that was primarily designed to absorb a vast amount of reflections a sound event might otherwise generate. Non-responsiveness is the more exotic, the thoroughly weird behavior in things, media, and creatures. The mere complications in describing its non-effect reflect quite nicely the complications of actually crafting such a thing or chamber to be non-responsive. Responsiveness is a given property; non-responsiveness requires a costly effort to maintain excessively artificial measures. Non-responsiveness needs arduous and ongoing exercise, discipline, and strictness, whereas responsiveness needs more a form of courage for excess and the capability of dealing with the consequences of a strong and multiplying desire. The anechoic chamber is a perfect example of this: whereas a concert or lecture hall, a club or a cultural institution, needs an aural architecture capable of securing a certain clarity and relatability of articulations of various kinds, in different areas of a building, for highly differing purposes between eminent performance and resonance and intimate conversation and reflection—the purpose for an anechoic chamber lies in the opposite direction: the *camera silens* has only one purpose that is to be executed in the most extremist and total way, without any exceptions and with no audible remains, no sonic traces staining the sensory experience of this chamber. The best technical solution to provide such a totally non-responsive character of a room seems still to be—as of today—to build a totally new room in an existing room: a new room that has none or very few, mainly absorbing connections to the encapsulating edifice, to the outside world. Disconnection is key. Key for the sole and radical purpose of an uninhibited and non-distorted recording of one elaborated sonic performance for one particular technologically and culturally highly advanced and specified apparatus of recording, storing, and reproducing sound. The contemporary culture of sound reproduction is thus manifested in reverse in an anechoic chamber—in its inherent ideas, concepts, and desires of a good recording being a perfectly clean recording by given standards. This concept of a radical cleansing of sonic traces reproduces the *shannonist* concept of signal processing as a neat organizing of a distinct sequence of scarce signals (as discussed earlier in Chapter 4: "In Auditory Dispositives," in the section Scarce Signals). As a shannonist and an audiophile, one listens to a world of cleansed signals, in a quarantine with next to no contaminating noise. Non-responsiveness is a major desire of the phonophobic shannonist.

A recording is an artifact. A microphone is a poem. Both do not nearly serve the perfect representation of an audible sonic experience you or I could make in a given environment. They serve—at the end of several decades of technological and cultural transformations—more to contribute to an existing assemblage of connected media technologies and now established practices of listening that emanate fitting discourses and generate even concise and again fitting concepts of listening. This assemblage, alas, demands a vast reduction and repression of any sound events that might hinder, distort, diffuse, or even blur this desired and actually phonophobic ideal of a clean and transparent transmission or recording. The concept of technological sound reproduction as it has been established in recent decades effectively implies and requires a highly selective, shannonist construction of a so-called *sound source*. The textile hiss of my pants is definitely not a sound source. Your sighing and mumbling while working, highly focused, on a visual or sonic artifact on your laptop, escorted by various minor sounds of your hard drive or your keyboard, is also not a valid sound source. It only can become one as soon as we focus *solely* on these exact noises as the main content of our recording or transmission; yet then all the other noises so important to you and me before are being rendered to *noise*. In the conceptual framework of signal processing and its preference for distinct but scarce signals, you never escape the existence of noise: essentially, you even multiply all the sounds considered as noise:

> Saying this is bad is like saying traffic is bad, or health-care surtaxes, or the hazards of annular fusion: nobody but Ludditic granola-crunching freaks would call bad what no one can imagine being without. (Wallace 1996: 813)

A multiple, parallel, a mingled and dynamic perceptual situation is almost the given norm in any listening situation you or I might be experiencing. It is a highly artificial and somewhat weird concept to assume this, given an ordinary listening constellation, would serve as a strange and extravagant special case to be avoided or normalized. It is definitely not. Yet it has turned into an annoying freaking out situation in acoustics by the technological developments since the nineteenth century and their thoroughly phonophobic struggle to extract distinct and isolated signals out of a rich and dynamic sonic experience: from these prerequisites of research and engineering at the time, Hermann von Helmholtz or Wallace Sabine started laying out (cf. Chapter 1 "Quantifying Sound") the foundations for acoustics, and the construction of few and distinct sound sources was mandatory: modeled as highly recognizable signals in an almost autonomously conceptualized process of transmission. Non-responsiveness became hence implicitly a major goal of acoustics; technology thereafter provided the means to readjust a noisy environment by selection of a microphone, selection of thresholds and of noise reduction to focus on selected sound events as sound sources. This focusing, though, is not necessary to this extent in the audible realm—and it is neither in the realm of the visual where the term of *focus* comes from: to focus does not mean an erasure of all disturbing noises besides the focus point—but a stronger stressing and concentration of attention on a specific area blurred at its fringes. The fact that focusing in acoustics translated to an actual *excluding and deleting of distortion and noise* is a highly consequential misunderstanding. The following concept of *noise abatement* (Bijsterveld 2008, 2018) is probably the best example of how the idea of completely excluding any disturbing sounds had replaced the original concept of stressing some and weakening other areas of perception. No response became the best response, in technical terms. A truly strange reversal of priorities, and yet another example of the freaked out performativity of *weird* and WEIRD research cultures, research protagonists, and research issues: "Western, Educated, Industrialized, Rich, and Democratic (WEIRD)" (Henrich/Heine/Norenzayan 2010). The artificial construct of non-responsivity must be recognized as a necessary starting ground for any acoustics—and yet effectively it constitutes a radically exotic freak of physics.

In the course of this book, you and the author now seem to have entered a technologically *negative anthropology*. Is this the *Black Iron Prison*?— as joyfully explicated in the highly ironic and willfully inconsistent mock-conspiracy theory of the *Principia Discordia* (1965), a highly influential subculture book? Did the *Black Box* of technology grow into everyone's personally horrifying and desperate Black Iron Prison? Have alien anthropoids, the actual engineers of this prison, turned themselves into the dullest and most obedient servomechanisms of a sealed technological capsule? One's own sensologies holding each and every one in bondage? Institutionally, as well as procedurally and technologically, it might seem too easy and too obvious to describe today's world as dominated by despotic superstructures and all their more or less administrative threads intending and successfully managing to subject individual humanoids, me, you, him, and her to their own procedures, technologies, and institutions. Still, such totalizing conspiracy theories more often crash and crumble very fast, as soon as a coherent and linear description of their functioning, their effects, and their intentions are tested against the miniscule and detailed activities of specific actors in concrete situations, buildings, projects: the everyday life in all its sinuous sleaziness rapidly falsifies most conspiracy phantasms. As soon as particular elements of such a phantasmic "Theory" might be proven right, though, they also morph as rapidly from a dystopic fiction to a horrific, boring, and sad reality: a crude fantasy novel becomes a neorealist short story. What happens thus to this *theory fiction* of a closed and omnipotent dispositive in the early twenty-first century? Could resistance still be possible? *Sleep tight, dear reader.*

Erratic heuristics

"*Dachau Blues! Dachau Blues!*" (Captain Beefheart 1969: track 3). The erratic hits you —and it does not miss a beat: "*BONKERS!*" (Razcal 2009: track 1). It hits you, and this hit is unmistakably a statement: a political demand, an existential claim, a universal want. Erratic actions take no prisoners. You do *not* encounter them—yet *they* attack you from behind, in unsuspected moments. Usually you are attacked, seduced, and abused on a daily basis by the common claims of an established dispositive that is never questioned in its demands and impact. What happens if one counters this truly disturbing ground of idiosyncratic and erratic normalization against one's intentions with yet another idiosyncratic and erratic normalization? An *Aesthetic Of The Erratic*, or more, a *Kinesthetic* or a *Heuristic of The Erratic*, would not exist as an orderly treatise—unfolding step by step on secure grounds of well-founded research. Rather, it would exist by means of an erratic hit. Which surely would be followed by another erratic hit. On which follows yet the next erratic hit. All of which lead—consequentially, but surely not finally—to even another erratic hit itself. *A heavy bass line is my kind of silence.* It is a cut, a dissection, an incessant revocation of common sense: Your sense and my sense—they are not common for sure. They are alien to each other. They are *xenocommon*. They are being articulated in forms of language not even remotely comparable on any level. Maybe both forms of articulation—yours and mine—are not even reasonably to be called *a language* at all. At least not a form of language most people could recognize as such. *Everybody says that I gotta get a grip / But I let sanity give me the slip.* Praising discontinuity, the hurtful jump, the unexpected violently hitting you; a surprising dynamics. *Some people think I'm bonkers / But I just think I'm free.* Dynamics that follow irregular, maybe many irresponsible obsessions, aversions, affects, and idiosyncrasies, all too vague ideas and wishes, sudden mannerisms and embodied affinities. *Could I myself decipher a strict logic in here?*, you might say to yourself. Yet exactly *this* indecipherability is surely one of the most powerful instruments, tools, plugins: to open up, to crack up, to dismantle a thoroughly non-responsive, consistently and seamlessly closed and continuously welded cocoon.

This truly is one of the most noble artistic techniques of modernism and the avant-garde in the fine arts and in music: in its efforts to crack up any existing regime of non-responsiveness, any Black Iron Prison of unquestionable structures, laws, and operational routines: DETOUR. DISRUPT. DESTROY. *Man, I'm just livin' my life / There's nothin' crazy about me.* No orderly, neatly organized development anywhere; nowhere do you find the least thread of explanation or of thankfully received introduction. Is this the meaning of it all? *Some people pay for thrills / But I get mine for free.* Or is there a highly consistent and logical order hidden somewhere underneath, underground? Just not yet unearthed? A deep and subtle structure that drives and generates secretly this quite blunt surface structure? A secret *Illuminati* code behind these erratic movements and articulations? Do we, you and I, just need to read more, to explore and to analyze more, to understand more, bit by bit, to become polyhistorians and polyglots in order to finally, at some point, understand with great relief this weird order of strange and erratic cultural artifacts right here? *Man, I'm just livin' my life / There's nothin' crazy about me.* Or, maybe (actually, I fear even to just write it down)—is there not the least of a meaningful order in all of this anyway?

> If you can master nonsense as well as you have already learned to master sense, then each will expose the other for what it is: absurdity. (Hill and Thornley 1965: 79)

If so, it might be helpful indeed *not even to try understanding* individual examples of erratic acts, while understanding them as specimens of a larger tribe of events and entities. The aesthetics and the general practice of the speculative, the contingent, the inconsistent, and the discontinued, might lead a certain way. But does this vast corpus of the inconsistent already constitute an actual artistic, maybe even an academic research practice? To what could one refer in aesthetics? The erratic writings of the subcultural and irresponsibly gleeful *Principia Discordia* (1965), mentioned earlier, might lead a certain way:

> From that moment of illumination, a man begins to be free regardless of his surroundings. He becomes free to play order games and change them at will. He becomes free to play disorder games just for the hell of it. He becomes free to play neither or both. (Hill and Thornley 1965: 79)

Obviously, even in the frantic *infinite jest* of these writings, the *Californian Ideology* (Barbrook and Cameron 1996) of *skillful disruption as liberating method* is very lively and present. Though, admittedly, in this case the activities implied are definitely neither supportive of a nation state nor of a specific research culture or business development. Still, these practices of the disruptive are effectively erratic. They do not build anything; they do not draw from anything; they do not even show the least intention of generating anything orderly and at least somehow intelligible or semantically of higher consistency (aside from fervently praising and promoting inconsistency):

> Remember:
> KING
> KONG
> Died For
> Your Sins! (Hill and Thornley 1965: 725)

Such a discordian and thoroughly erratic practice of thinking and acting considers a senseless and nonsenseless way of performing as equally interchangeable:

> And as the master of his own games, he [the discordianist; HS] plays without fear, and therefore without frustration, and therefore with good will in his soul and love in his being. (Hill and Thornley 1965: 79)

Hence the alien tribe of humanoid *discordians* negates any primordial order—be it biological, genealogical, merito- or plutocratic, be it epistemological or logical. Not even primordial disorder is effectively preferred. *Why should there be any order in* "The World"—*as long as there could as well be disorder?* It would qualify as an anthropocentric narcissism to assume "This World" had essentially been provided in order to please and to inspire humanoid aliens like you or like me. Aesthetics and pragmatics of discordianism—and thus of erratic heuristics—are essentially guided by a compositional core principle of anti- if not *postanthropocentrism*:

> A.A.A.F.N.R.A. Anything Anytime Anywhere—For No Reason At All (Zappa 1989: 163)

With this notion, Frank Zappa, surely the most famous *pre-Socratic of popular culture*, made an effort to sketch the foundations of his musical and performative aesthetics. This notion is not a mere pun or an entertaining reply in an interview, ready to be quoted as soundbite; yet, it is effectively the driving *generative principle* of his works: to juxtapose the unexpected with the not-to-be-expected—and to choose particularly the largest contrast in coherence and cohesion as a principle for selecting musical phrases, motives, instrumentations, and rhythmic patterns. The work of Zappa is full of examples of this erratic aesthetic practice: beginning with his appropriation of then-contemporary Boyband aesthetics (*Ruben and the Jets*), over electroacoustic works (*Lumpy Gravy*), electronica-pop (*Jazz From Hell*) to grotesquely inflated parodies of concept albums (*200 Motels, Joe's Garage, Thing-Fish, The Yellow Shark*) that turned out to be his trademark. The album *Uncle Meat* (1969) surely provides one of the broadest variety of erratic tracks and pieces. As musical forms are already jumping quite erratically between jazz-rock, accelerated guitar solos, electronically syncopated staccati, bombastically overproduced mainstream riffs, electroacoustically deformed grunting to pseudo-dialogues staged in an exalted manner ("The Voice of Cheese"), and original footage of backstage dialogues. In the same way, the verbal registers and semantic fields touched by the singers jump from family relationships to selected groceries, rituals of food intake, environmental pollution, animal diseases, sexual activities (regarded as deviant or heteronormative at the time), and preservation methods to public transport. Even the vocal persona of the speaker or singer changes and jumps between differing personae, stages of life, social and educational strata, even nationalities, ethnic, and religious backgrounds. Not even the formal structure of the various pieces provides continuity as they vary between long and elaborated suites, brief and mischievous jingles, and generic pop songs. The disturbing and disorienting, the erratic contrast, hence, is not generated merely in one area of the artifact—be it language, instrumentation, metaphors, sonic textures—but the playground of erratic movements itself is constantly shifting, changing, erratically stopped and newly selected: *Infinite Jest*.

Such erratic movements are not restricted to the aesthetic realm. Erratic moves can easily jump out of this frame and enter an everyday discourse on politics, on power structures, on cultural and social relations, as well as on technological reliabilities. Effectively, an erratic move is the appropriate next step to be taken as soon as a structure of discourse and of pragmatics seems to be solidified to a sclerotic, immobile, prison-like, suffocating cocoon. The break-out an erratic move performs is then direly needed. A transformation of a suffocating structure is realistically probably only possible by such an erratic move. Discordianism provides a helping hand: It is the performative defibrillator against sudden cardiac death of concept. *Coincidence* (Lippe 1985) is challenged in a humble and highly responsive way: Your idiosyncratic obsessions guide you probably better than any safe, sane, and consensual superstructure provided by normalizing desires. Actions find their ground in the *bodily felt sense*, and hence the *sensory corpus* provides the best *heuristic* (Schulze 2005), the best problem-solving strategy. Sonic traces in *this* given situation might lead you into erratic and disturbing urges and thoughts, desires and goals—but couldn't it be: they are the only necessary and desired activities in this very situation? It could be that erratically disturbing, even partially destroying the given socio technological dispositive is the best one could do in relation to it. Some dispositives desperately ask for their own annihilation.

> There's an experiment I did. . . . I had taken a DAT recorder to Hyde Park and near Bayswater Road I recorded a period of whatever sound was

there: cars going by, dogs, people. . . . I put it in SoundTools and I made a fade-up, let it run for 3 1/2 minutes and faded it out. I started listening to this thing over and over. (Brian Eno in: Toop 1995: 25)

Generativity and disruption are—as in this example—performed by randomization, by *aleatorization* (Schulze 2000). Erratic interventions—like in the earlier examples in this section—stress the contingency of a situation and an artifact; and by doing so they equally multiply the options for coincidences. From a close and narrow, all too familiar and all too foreseeable framework of activities, trajectories, and outcomes—into the unknown plentiful, the disturbing overload, a surprising and sometimes unsettling amount of items and issues. Out of which a hitherto unexperienced form of consistency might as well take shape:

> Something that is as completely arbitrary and disconnected as that, with sufficient listenings, becomes highly connected. You can really imagine that this thing was constructed somehow. (Brian Eno in: Toop 1995: 25)

The author's joy in finding structures and consistencies, construction principles in the supposedly unstructured, is obvious here. Still, the affirmative character of Brian Eno's statement is equally obvious. He seems to be content with generating such new consistencies. As a form of resistance, it remains in the realm of artistic production of artifacts, in the immanence of the media formats and expectations by distribution companies. What needs to be qualified as a necessarily strategic and appropriate behavior in the context of artistic production demands nevertheless a stricter form of opposition as soon as one speaks about processes of political protest, erratic interventions, and social generativity. It is not sufficient just to randomize aesthetic entities apt for a reinvention of their own consistency. The contrary is needed: to randomize entities in the social realm, in the political realm—in order to reorder, to rethink, to reinvent generative relations. One leaves the discourse: One enters the public square (and re enters into discourse, yet differently, in doing so).

Noise as presence

An immense ocean of people. Hundreds, thousands of them. Hundreds of thousands. They are just standing there, moving slowly, progressing somewhat; they are making noise—as humanoid aliens tend to do. Aliens are never silent. You need to silence them forcefully if you want them to emit no sounds. But why should you? Who are *you* anyway to demand such a paralyzed behavior from some stranger? In this special case, they actively engage and indulge in making noise. In clapping and chanting; in a rhythmic vertigo. They enjoy this, this form of protest.—Wait: *Is* it a protest? Does it not seem way too joyful for a form of political resistance and earnest objection? They seem so content and self-sustainable. Are they cheering too voluptuously? Are they enjoying this form of political protest too much? Or *is* indeed any form of protest essentially a more profound way of performing and perceiving an intrinsic and idiosyncratic *jouissance*? As soon as I listen to forms of protest, do I not effectively hear the joy of representing one's needs and desires, one's demands and one's discontent? *To fan the fires of discontent* (Refused 1996). These protests (as mentioned earlier in Chapter 4: "In Auditory Dispositives"), these marches and temporary tent cities have in recent years become a core item of contemporary political activities, activities of citizens and the rejected, refugees and the precarious, scared and the aggressive. This happened not only in major cities and agglomerations but even more so at the borders of Fortress Europe: It happened at the fortified borders of various nation states in drag in the early twenty-first century. Whereas the actually addressed social and institutional conflicts in all their historical genealogies and underlying agreements, treaties, their associations or secessions are highly diverse and hardly comparable in most of their issues—ranging from libertarian and liberal to more nationalist, up to racist and xenophobe motivations, to reformist and ecological issues, demanding more participatory forms of democracy or even overthrowing the current government and installing an authoritarian regime of their own preference—there is one *sensorial* aspect that is not to be ignored in all of these urban and pre-urban rebellions (Harvey 2012): this multitude of bodies is not without agency. It is present, it acts, it moves, and it gestures; it sounds and it resonates. It is—if you will—a moving body of resistance. *It* is a *They*: Those aliens are there. They exist. They demand attention, recognition, and focus. As listening and sensory bodies, collective corpuses. A multitude of focuses, of lives and forms of existing, of biographies, desires, habits, and idiosyncrasies. Yet what these aliens do, what humanoid aliens do, is definitely not arbitrary and not private. Before this still young century started, Jean-Luc Nancy predicted the activities of these resisting bodies:

> What's coming is *whatever images show us*. Our billions of images show billions of bodies—as bodies have never been shown before. Crowds, piles, melees, bundles, columns, troops, swarms, armies, bands, stampedes, panics, tiers, processions, collisions, massacres, mass graves, communions, dispersions, a sur-plus, always an overflowing of bodies, all at one and the same time, compacted in masses and pulverizing dispersals, always collected (in streets, housing-projects, megapolises, suburbs, points of passage, of surveillance, of commerce, care, and oblivion),

always abandoned to the stochastic confusion of the same places, to the structuring agitation of their endless, generalized, *departure*. (Nancy 2008: 39)

Such mass congregations of protesting bodies in public places—as Nancy projected them in the early 1990s—seem indeed to constitute a major signature of international public affairs in recent years and months. Riots and uprisings, insurrections and demonstrations in resistance and in refuge, as well as minor and major forms of protest were and are becoming more and more a regular form of expressing an opinion in public: a cultural form of political commitment that state governments or administrations more often seem not to be too comfortable with (Clover 2016). As part of an ongoing process of globalization, of mediatization, and—not the least—of decolonization, this intensified presence of protesting bodies has been analyzed by Nancy. It is an effect of *globalization*, as manifold diverging concepts of the body and of corporeal performativity forcefully demand recognition which they might have been hitherto deprived; it is also an unexpected effect of *mediatization*, as the now common practices of individual articulation in manifold media outlets, platforms, and channels, under various avatars, speech roles, and codes suddenly seem to be translated into comparable practices of presence, articulation, and protest on the streets and in public squares; finally, it is an effect of *decolonization* (Fanon 1967) as more and more cultures of humanoid aliens effectively participate in the processes of globalization and mediatization and hence become visible, relevant, and demanding actors of discourses more and more relieved of their former hegemony. These three processes coalesce into moments of protest: into events of publicly staged performances of resistance.

This form of expression rather bluntly bears its roots in the long tradition of public protest and public mourning marches, the parades and public screenings arranged for in earlier decades and centuries; probably culminating in various events of the 1990s as an impressive starting decade of global mediatization and digitization. Did all those celebrating bodies as part of then so-called *Love Parades*, of *Streetraves*, of *Public Screenings* and *Public Mournings*, not contribute and prepare the emergence of resisting bodies in public? A collective exercise in how to perform collective affects in public spaces? Or are these bodies actually *still* celebrating their mere existence in public—though with another agency, and with other sensory corpuses and their particular physical performativity? A sonic agency in disseminated corpora? You and I, we are standing on this square. You are standing there and you are representing a form of discontent, of negation, of resistance. You *are* in denial. And as you are standing on this public square, your mere upright standing position becomes a massive form of resistance. Your bodily presence in this place is not only symbolizing resistance by some magical semiotic trick of denotation: your bodily presence *as such* in this location, on *that* time of the day, together with *those* other human bodies *is resistance* in all its materiality. *Just being there*. In precisely this rather extensionless point in time and space. In this *plane d'immanence*. This *epoché*. And you can sense it: your bodily response to being exposed in such a public square under all of these premises is quite obvious. You feel exposed, you feel uncomfortable, you feel hot and cold, tense and powerful, yet vulnerable and weak at the very same time. *You are*. And you like this. It is joy, and you are indulging in this deep pleasure of existing *right here, right now* (Fatboy Slim 1998: track 1). You feel and you enjoy this tension of being exposed, the tension of a thorough and almost total attention of all of the people around you. This *Aufmerksamkeitsspannung* (Schulze 2012: 77–83), this *tension of attention* seems to be holding you tight, it seems to keep you in place: Do you feel as if you could not move an inch now? Are you fixed and chained to this very location, into this very posture you took right now? Into this moment, and second, this instant—this now? Right now? *Epoché*.

In this very moment, you are occupying this space in a physical location precisely describable; you are not isolated in it, and you are not alone. It might seem as if all the resistance and all the energy needed to stand up against this environment that acts so hostile toward you leaves you quite alone in this situation. But actually, you sense quite the contrary. You might sense that all this attention around you—be it by your fellow protesters, by indolent citizens, by animals passing by, or even by the militarized police soldiers or security robots ready to attack or expel you—it seems to you that all of this attention reaches you foremost as an intensification of the relations between you and these manifold actors in situ. You feel somehow even more related to all these aliens with and around you. *Être Singulier pluriel*, as Nancy named such existential moments (Nancy 1996). But you do not stay like that: As soon as this moment of *singular resistance in plural* is forced to move, as soon as your standing here is proven to be not so appropriate and desired by some other humanoid aliens and their police soldiers concerning the actual daily procedures and implicit social rules—the dispositive in charge of this square—you will be forced to follow external forces other than those joining in this bodily manifestation of resistance. As soon as this very instant of physical conflict happens, of extreme repulsive violence with a distinct proclivity to annihilation: then all the energetic load, all the built up and the stored power, all the tension present in your body and in the many bodies of your comrades and also your antipodes, shows in all its raw anger, fear, and bloody, fleshy, voluptuous atrocity. Your all-encompassing tension, your *soul*—as defined by Nancy as a body in vital tension (Nancy 2000: 134)—is on open display. The whole congregation of resistance gets activated and aggressive and is massively reconnected to form an aggregate of aggression in unison with the antipodes and their attacking forces. Loud and noisy and hurtful and ear-deafening aggression breaks loose. This noise of a present conflict distorts the supposed connection of all to all, it disrupts this all too harmonious desire (a hegemonic desire, greedy for power)—with yet another desire: the desire to divide and to state a decision. To articulate a distinction and a difference:

> Noise is violence: it disturbs. To make noise is to interrupt a transmission, to disconnect, to kill. It is a simulacrum of murder. Music is a channelization of noise, and therefore a simulacrum of the sacrifice. It is thus a sublimation, an exacerbation of the imaginary, at the same time as the creation of a social order and political integration. (Attali 1985: 24)

Noise is presence. Noise realizes present differences and conflicts in their most hurtful, disruptive, and erratic appearance. It sets in with a certain *bodily felt sense* (Gendlin), a corporeal tension—"Un corps, c'est donc une tension" (Nancy 2000: 126)—turning into a thorough corporeal state of existence in aggressive tension: a sort of aggression to represent your individual place, being, and life—combined with a quite scared form of insecurity concerning who will let you be in this situation. This quite disturbing amalgamation of moods, emotions, individual stances, political assumptions, and projects, as well as long-lasting convictions, takes shape in such an instance as an explosive matter—*ready to detonate!* This is not a "mere" mental or "only" emotional state. It is a *corporeal state*. It is not noble or elegant or glorious. It is definitely and thoroughly destabilizing, if not destructive. It is disruptive in its deepest sense. No buzzword—a swear word, a curse.

Corporeally noisy tensions anticipate—No. Here I correct myself: Corporeally noisy tensions *precede* a disruption in one's individual habit of action, in our performative persona. Out of such a conflict, out of such a hurtful confrontation with often frightening forces of irritation and destabilizing tension, out of this vortex, this *magma* (Castoriadis 1975), this ἔκστασις (ecstasy) of resistance—a transformed person might emerge. One might emerge. The generative force of a *sinuous situation* implies our next step:

> Any situation, any bit of practice, implies much more than has ever been said. (Gendlin 1992: 201)

This highly reactive corporeal tension constitutes a major though clearly frightening and dangerous generative force. According to Eugene T. Gendlin, such tensions are sensory articulations of a meaning—just before one might try to translate this *bodily felt sense* into action, maybe words. Feeling lost or attacked, feeling angry or bored, might then pave the way to getting into action, into generating yourself as a persona, a transformed one. Following

Deleuze and Guattari (and with a little sidestep to Lacan), especially their concept of the term *percept* (Deleuze and Guattari 1991: 166), a specific *perceptual energy* vibrates through all matter in all locations and in all moments. The color, the sound, the heat, the smell, or the motion of anything is propagating and extending its particular energy into the corporeal area of you or me. Such it is—following Deleuze and Guattari—not at all correct to say: *I see* a color or *I hear* a sound. These sentences represent only the fallacies in hegemonic perceptual models. Yet, it would be more correct to say: *I am (full of)* these sounds. *I am (full of)* these colors. According to this Spinozist perceptualism, humanoid aliens are—in contrast to major semiotic theories of the last decades—effectively *not decoding or recoding* signals. They are instead continuously assimilating the percepts around. You are resonating with it. You are its *areal* (Nancy 2000): the corporeal volume in which these percepts are actualized. This process of assimilation is thought of as being radically *non-mediated*. In this concept of permanent immanence, the effect of resonance is never stopping, never pausing, never interrupted in the *chaosmos*—neither on levels of propagating waves nor concerning movement of individual molecules. *Only* this individual, material-physical, and actually experiential perspective onto a situation is real. This incessant dynamic is the real. Everything else (what was to be, what will, what should be happening) is mainly a culturally fueled, a widely symbolic imagination. Nothing real (according to Spinoza, Deleuze, and Guattari); just an idle play instrumentalizing the symbolic order for the sake of power games and territorial wars (or is this not the sole *raison d'être* of any symbolic order: being of use in power games?) Not a resonating sensory corpus—albeit more rigidly fixated and quantified symbolic orders, engraved and arranged by force of the law: a shiningly polished rigidness of a never insecurely reacting system, always self-assured. In moments of vast and highly tense resistance, this symbolic order is questioned, it is disturbed, it is severely disrupted. The corporeal presence of a multitude of resisting bodies questions this rigid symbolic order—and puts it in harsh opposition to particular sensory corpuses. The power and its imaginary is confronted with the real of life. The mere presence of resisting corpora questions the harmonizing power structure. *This presence is resistance*. It is material resistance, a physical and situated resistance. A resistance that is not directed toward deconstruction of a superstructure or a powerful dispositive alone. Resistance in this existential and corporeal sense aims at material transformations, at a materialist correction of individual lives and biographies. A non-responsive environment generates these noisy disruptions: Violent resistance demands an irrefutable response:

> There can be no retreat into the superstructures when there is no food, shelter or safety. (Wark 2015a)

Persona resista

You are sitting amid a web of tracks in a network of mediation. You have been implemented in this network. You are considered to be a fully functioning and a well-trained node in this vastly extended web. *Are you?* One might be surprised when actual persons do effectively emerge from this mesh, these woven and bound threads. *Yet they do.* Out of the multitude of protesting and resisting bodies, it is exactly a tense and corporeal situation of forced action, of forced confrontation, and of forced exposition that generates a specific person as such. It is in this confrontation between the corporeal alien, a bodily multitude in all its erratic and idiosyncratic inclinations, anxieties, dreams, obsessions, and hopes on the one side—and an externalized apparatus on the other side that tries to impose its principles, its goals, its structural phantasmata onto this body of resistance—in this situation of experienced violence—hurtful, physical, deforming, potentially annihilating—it might happen that a person does emerge. *A persona, a sensory persona.* It emerges, *I emerge,* out of the pressure and the tension created by an apparatus: an apparatus that might still seem invincible, impermeable, merciless, evermore static and changeless. Or in other words, the words of a contemporary persona of resistance, Edward Snowden:

> When all of us band together against injustices and in defense of privacy and basic human rights, we can defend ourselves from even the most powerful systems. (Snowden 2013)

Can we? How could resistance effectively be possible? In the end, a singular individual humanoid alien—following the apparatus theory—could never simply exchange or destroy a whole dispositive; as it is so deeply engraved and implemented into the whole of a culture. An individual alien would at best serve as an example—be it a bad or a good one—and as such it is easily removable from collective memory. Moreover: if it would be the case that single humanoid aliens could immediately transform the whole of a cultural continuum, one might never actually experience any continuity and stability in this cultural continuum. Perhaps this could be a desirable state? Yet, maybe this would be possible only in an inherently different lifeform and cultural discourse. How would a more fluid culture of humanoid aliens actually proceed, operate, and—exist? Do I need a sonic fiction to explicate this (maybe in the next, the ninth and last chapter of this book: "Generativity")? Aside from this imaginary, it is one's individual sensibility, one's individual empathy, that is at stake here: how do I, how do you— individually, personally—deal with such massive pressures of an apparatus? A dangerous and a more pathological way to deal with this is by following the guidance of the apparatus; by becoming an *Untertan*, a citizen merely serving and supporting the apparatus—with no guts; or as Klaus Theweleit stated in an interview from 2013:

> Exercise of power is a form of idiocy and always points to destroyed bodies; it testifies the destroyed bodies of people without supportive relationships of any kind. (Theweleit 2013; transl. HS)[1]

But as a humanoid and an alien, one exactly needs those *tragende Beziehungen* of which Theweleit speaks: to develop a persona that is more dynamic and more personal than just representing a static and perfectly polished image—a persona that is a resonating, a truly sensible, a *sensory persona*: a sonic persona incorporating an array of various, sensible personae. As a persona you are, I am, in a state of permanent tension, weakening and intensifying: a tension between, on the one hand, all the various *affordances* (Gibson 1979) and *appéllations* (Althusser 1970) of various *sensologia* (Perniola 1991) and *auditive Dispositive* (Großmann 2008), as well as many humanoids engaging in supporting this all-encompassing (if you will, *Empire*-like) apparatus; and on the other hand, there are still and quite surprisingly unremitting all those deeply idiosyncratic desires and wishes, one's anxieties and daydreams, fears and *dérives* (Debord 1958), the primary process of an alien that is an inherent part of one's individual body, one's *corpus* (Nancy 1992), one's *Leib* (Schmitz 1990). It is this existential and incessant tension, between the desiring *magma* and the containing *apparatus*, that forces a humanoid alien like you *not simply* to decide for one of the sides, speaking in dichotomies; yet it forces *you*. It forces *me*. As aliens and lovers, warriors and managers, craftsmen and poets, engineers and artists—it forces us to take action. *Personae in resistance: personae ex apparatus: personae ex machina.*

This is a utopia, no doubt. This is a sensory fiction, not the least. As such, it is obviously easy prey for any malevolent rejection as well as for any clever instrumentalization. Recent riots and public protests, all the marches and occupations, even more so the violent opposition to contemporary politics are surely no exception; future historians and analysts of the late twenty-first century, and surely the academics in the twenty-second century, will extract at least some of the oligarchic and manipulating power strategies at play in maybe all of these forms of articulating discontent. Nevertheless, one major consequence for one's individual way of performing actions of consent or dissent is one of a personal reflexivity. In your and my everyday work—be

---

[1] "Machtausübung ist eine Form von Idiotie und deutet immer auf zerstörte Körper; deutet darauf hin, dass dies Leute sind, die keine vernünftigen, keine sie tragenden Beziehungen haben." (Theweleit 2013)

it (from the professions possibly daring to read these lines) as researcher, as writer, as journalist, as musician, as engineer, as programmer, as historian or politician—there are a number of administrative actions in or for the institutions for which we work that might require certain activities you or I might not agree with. This is where actually a *critique in actu* takes place. A sensory critique of these administrative actions is not a philological or political critique ex post, it is a critique that operates as syrrhesis in the way that it actually makes severe efforts to transform these practices bit by bit. These transformations take place in every single, even the tiniest, most minor and maybe irrelevant actions. Such a transformation will never be infallible or permanently correct, but it might provide an extra layer of reflection and of ongoing critique of what actually to contribute or not to contribute to a mercilessly operating apparatus as part of which one works. All working environments, all individual project meetings, all announcements for job positions or calls for proposals or for contributions in which humanoid aliens are mainly treated and regarded as invulnerable and static objects that need to be compliant within a given framework, no matter how it would be constructed and no matter how the individual sensory corpus is living. This is not an esoteric or escapist fantasy. It is a guideline for everyday activities, for daily professional—and in thoroughly economized cultures, also implicitly personal—practice.

A practice of personal resistance generates the *persona resista*. A persona that is not polished and fixed in its self-presentation. A persona that is responsive and sensible to requests and activities, to doubts and ambiguities, to moments and reflections. A *persona resista* does not resemble the armored and tank-like militarized bodies which Klaus Theweleit found as a symptom of devastated men in Germany after being defeated in the First World War. Such phantasms of perfect orderliness and clean, symmetric systems are after all to be understood as fearful symptoms of deeply insecure humanoids. The militarized and perfected body is the body of fascist ideology. You can spot it as soon as perfection and optimized combat activity is demanded with a deeply moralist excitement; in a national army, as part of a guerilla squad; in business or management consultancy; in musical or non-musical entertainment productions, or in any educational facility. If perfection is mercilessly demanded with no respect for the idiosyncratic and vulnerable sensory corpus, then there is actually a militarized and invulnerable robot demanded: an obsessive and excessively idiosyncratic fiction from the empire of the *Bachelor's Machine* (as scrutinized in Chapter 4: "In Auditory Dispositives"). These desired robotic soldiers are the original *Männerphantasien* (Theweleit 1977), *Male Fantasies* of the twenty-first century.

For deviant activities outside of the realm of self-militarization and self-robotization, a sensible starting point might be found (as already mentioned in Chapter 6: "A Sensory Corpus") in the works of Hildegard Westerkamp. In her germinal text on *Soundwalking* from 1974, she proposes a form of sensory and sensological *critique in actu*, as a syrrhesis of walking:

> Start by listening to the sounds of your body while moving. They are closest to you and establish the first dialogue between you and the environment. (Westerkamp 1974)

Here, Westerkamp proposes a realistic and reflexive method to undertake a performative and thus sensory critique of bodily activity. This critique by Westerkamp proceeds by a miniscule perceptual exercise—extending into the emergence of further, even more deviant perceptual practices:

> Try to move
> Without making any sound.
> Is it possible? (Westerkamp 1974)

As reader and performer—you become one in no time: *while reading*—you explore and you listen. You sense.

> Which is
> the quietest sound of your body? (Westerkamp 1974)

Maybe some ephemeral neural activity? Some intrinsically cellular and hormonal activity? The sound of your cells multiplying?

> Lead your ears away from your own sounds and
> listen to the sounds nearby.
>
> What do you hear? (Make a list). (Westerkamp 1974)

Traffic noises outside the window, a TV set in the living room. Some news channel voices are agitatedly discussing—no: it was a shopping channel, unsettlingly. Clearly, again and again, the hard drive of this laptop; potatoes cooking in the kitchen.

> What else do you hear?
> Other people
> Nature sounds
> Mechanical sounds
> . . .

Can you detect
Interesting rhythms
Regular beats
The highest
The lowest pitch. (Westerkamp 1974)

Essentially, these intimately sensory practices might be closer to personal practices than any professional adherence to execute the precise demands of an apparatus. These practices indeed demand a highly refined *precision of sensibility* to execute them accordingly:

Do you hear any
Intermittent or discrete sounds
Rustles
Bangs
Swishes
Thuds? (Westerkamp 1974)

When following Westerkamp's requests, one actually might be approaching one's own, individual requests, desires, quirky preferences. "What are the sources of the different sounds? What else do you hear" (Westerkamp 1974)? One enters this situation right here, right now. One enters thus also the material percept of this situation—aside from imaginary accounts to represent concepts of a certain symbolic order and its power struggles (though obviously entering the symbolic order of sound art practices and of the discourses of sound studies). Moving away from conceptual idealisms of various origins—and toward a radical, extremely individualized empiricism as a new sensory materialism.

Lead your ears away from these sounds and listen
beyond—into the distance.
What is the quietest sound?
What else do you hear? (Westerkamp 1974)

If one takes steps directly into this specific situation right here, right now, one moves into a zone of conflicting resonances between the collective, highly imaginary, and quite psychotic dispositive and the many individual, idiosyncratic and sentient, vulnerable and pliable bodies. "What else? What else" (Westerkamp 1974)? Your sonic persona is situated right at this intersection: It is personal generativity. *Rebellious epoché.* "What else? What else" (Westerkamp 1974)? Or in the famous words by

Stéphane Hessel, son of German writer, poet, and thinker of the *flânerie*, Franz Hessel:

> Créer c'est résister, résister c'est créer. (Hessel 2010: 22)

I can sense now how my writing already has entered (or enters right now?) the realm of sonic fiction: *Generativity.*

CHAPTER NINE

Generativity

Cohesion

In the last few days I was recurrently listening to the *Sechs Stücke für Orchester* (1909) by Anton von Webern as skillfully produced, sonically sculpted, and effectively reinvented by Photek, the alias of Rupert Parkes (Parkes 2054). These six pieces provide a sensory generativity transcending most of the well-known auditory dispositives of these times, taking a breathtaking leap into the unknown. Depending on your individual corporeal experientiality with this form of visceral resonance, you might perform this piece in a timespan around the 12 minutes von Webern had coded it for. In the words of the philosopher:

> Ihren Klang. Ich verstehe die Sprachen. Ich verstehe die Sprachen nicht. Ich höre nur ihren Klang. (Anderson 1982: B2)

Their sound. I understand the languages. I do not understand the languages. I only listen to their sound. Their sound I am and you would be listening to, this sound is a flux of *cohesion* (Halliday and Hasan 1976): it provides a thoroughly idiosyncratically shaped, intensely materially dynamic of tension and release—while it performs various interlocking, protruding, retracting levels of sensory experiences. A material flux.

The six pieces are resonating through my body, in this hot early summer, here on the Martian colonies in the year 2145. My soma is the sole arena of these sound events. In listening to this piece, there is no piece of technology involved that was common in the twentieth century. The sound and the music appear in my corporeal area. They emanate from a sound source that lies actually *in* me. I hear it—and *I am* the actual source of these sounds as well. I am part of these events, their breaks and ruptures, syncopes and drones.

Their streams move like bodies, connecting and disconnecting in various ways, both collectively and individually, each in their idiosyncratically shaped rhythms and steps. My body, its fragments and streams, move and disconnect in these ways. The creatures in this stream, the entities and the particles, their trajectories and their gravitational fields, are neither radically disconnected nor are they absolutely dependent on each other. They are in a constant vibratory reordering. This permanent sensory reordering is, you could argue, a permanent revolution of entities. It is a total and radical, an almost unthinkable utopia. This is the reason I am writing about these pieces. For this utopia is an accurate description of physiological, physical, and chemical processes taking place in the known world, in the known chaosmic continuum one might live to tell. It would not be too far-fetched, it would not even be remotely esoteric or idiosyncratic, to argue that this utopian description of a listening situation is an accurate materialist description of this very moment. This utopia is immanence.

> Here, there are no longer any forms or developments of forms; nor are there subjects or the formation of subjects. There is no structure, any more than there is genesis. (Deleuze and Guattari 1987: 293)

This utopia is realism: corporeal realism. It is: *hypercorporealism* (Schulze 2007). In this piece by Photek, a.k.a. Rupert Parkes, the reference to Anton von Webern is a remote ground, not even a material substance, more a codified and written source within which the composer operates and acts. The compositional structure of Webern's piece is still present, albeit transformed and teleported into yet another material and technological dispositive: the auditory dispositive of these present times. After Parkes had undergone his spectacularly staged transformation into a regenerated lifeform of a fifth gender and of a variable set of mental storage silos, it has become quite clear: *plus ça change, plus ça c'est la même chose*. Photek's pieces after its crucial transformation have rather surprisingly reenacted and *recreated* some of its earlier works, most of them are surely now forgotten. In his 20s, Photek was one of the protagonists of a musical style that lingered between traditionally digital *breakbeat* and a first foreshadowing of what today one would call *expanded site-specific rhythmanalysis*. The author of these lines, admittedly an aficionado of these earliest works by names such as *Ni Ten Ichi Ryu*, *K.J.Z.*, or *The Hidden Camera*—frankly speaking—never expected this artist to make such a major step into truly uncharted territory without any actual territory. In this respect, the Parkes/Webern-production completes a long-lasting historical process that started out with the earliest quantifications of sound, setting in with research by Hermann von Helmholtz, Harvey Fletcher, or Leo Beranek between the mid-nineteenth and mid-twentieth centuries (as explored in Chapter 1 of this book: "Quantifying Sound"). Their adherence to a laboratory conception of research in combination with an almost obsessive yearning for the mathematization of sound and listening finds one of its late and unsuspected climaxes certainly in these *Six Pieces*. This Parkes achieves by shifting the material listening experiences of these rather timid, extremely short, and excessively weird and quirky pieces to the almost invisibilized technological apparatus of the late twenty-first century—anticipating technology of the early twenty-second century. The composer here takes up the materialization of listening that was first artistically explored in the various avant-garde movements with their efforts to expand hearing habits and listening practices in the early and mid-twentieth century; he also connects his self-confident joy of *spatial experialism* to the invention of harshly disruptive and deconstructivist artistic and technological practices of the late twentieth century (as explored in Chapter 2: "Materializing Listening"). Parkes turns Webern into a situationist performer as hacker and hauntologist at the same time. Webern's music hence performatively questions and sonically disassembles the concept of spatial listening experiences as they have been established by acousticians like Leo Beranek, as well as by architects or composers like Le Corbusier, Edgard Varèse, or Iannis Xenakis. After this disassembly, the bodies of its listeners, its performers, and its score are not the same. A critique has taken place that alters sensory relations and material qualities. The corporeally realized musical composition, *Sechs Stücke*, undertakes, therefore, a sensological critique by means of a breathtaking syrrhesis.

The publishing date of all recordings and all files related to these pieces is lost. Whether a malevolent archivist erased all the metadata, or the assumed producer himself took deep joy in confusing and offending any future listeners, we may never know. Albeit, by its intricate strategies of sound generation, its individual detours concerning time-bending, as well as its spatialized sonic aesthetics, its disturbing *Sonario* (Gampe 2014) and its experientially quite evident reference to the discourse of *Sonische Zeitfragen* (Ujita 2028), one can narrow down the production period of these pieces to the late and quite surprising phase of proto-*expanded site-specific rhythmanalysis* works Rupert Parkes published again under his youth-alias of Photek in the 2030s. Now rereleased in a special edition by the noble Congolese Academy of the Arts in Kinshasa, the specifically intriguing *cohesion* of these pieces can be experienced in the very sensory corpus one might share these days. This cohesion in the *Sechs Stücke* is the main generative aspect that drew me as listener into it: it implies a utopia of understanding by listening. Whereas the limits of sensory and sonic critique have been explored ad nauseam in recent decades, the growing assumption that sonic critique and sensological analysis could explicate any articulation of humanoid aliens is apparently misleading. This position of *sonic totality* is impossible to perform with reference to any theoretical framework imaginable; to take this position of totality as a starting point for sensible reflection in research has proven to be unfeasible. Any sensory critique operates thus as a selective referential model, an ideal, imaginary position, a quite educatedly imagined outline: a theory. Yet it is possible to take this as the starting point of a *Gedankenspiel*, an imaginary scenario: *seriously playing with thoughts*. Playing with thoughts leads to possible worlds—what Parkes and Voegelin (Voegelin 2012) alike introduced us to: *hearing the continuum of sound* as constituted out of a multitude of possible, imaginary continua. Tenderly is *Jynweythek* being played, in the back of my neck, like whilom 2001.

They exist, these sensorially material worlds. In one's sensory area, in my sensory corpus—or in hers, in yours, in its, in his. It is a relational utopia that Webern and Parkes, Voegelin and a load of other artists and poets, theorists and engineers, have generated in recent decades of the twenty-first and the twenty-second centuries. There is no radical *tabula rasa*. The desire to start anew, completely, with a profound set of self-containing and essentially non-related elements, is an understandable obsession, albeit a futile one. It is such an inspiring one—even though materially falsified. The vibrational nexus (Goodman 2009) responds, and it emerges.

> It represents nothing, but it produces. It means nothing, but it works.
> (Deleuze and Guattari 1972: 109)

Im Erwachten Garten

This place is rather silent. Rarely a crackle is to be heard. Though—is it a *place*, actually? What kind of material constellation is this really? Where *are* these sounds actually happening right now? It feels as if I could not any longer actually be near you, dear reader. In this listening situation, my sensory corpus is teleported into a different, diverging state of confluence. It is a state of conviviality that dominates in this *sonario*. Am I listening? Actually, I do not listen at all. *I sense*. I sense the sounds, the repercussions and resonances from lucent entities around me. What entities are there? No anthropoid alien can I sense here at all. Other aliens, yes, I might—well—*recognize* (to say the least). I recognize sorts of aliens more like animals, others more similar to plants—albeit both kinds essentially resembling decisive characters, agents, persons. *Sonic personae* of a different kind? Apparently I am situated in a garden now: in a garden that just awakened—*Im Erwachten Garten* (Dath and Kammerflimmer Kollektief 2009). Joyfully indulging in drinks and sensations, I am teleported into this very continuum of sensory connectivity. It was German author Dietmar Dath (already introduced in this book with his and Barbara Kirchner's interpretation of the *implex* in Chapter 5: "The Sonic Persona," section Idiosyncratic Implex) and the band collective Kammerflimmer Kollektief who proposed this sensory fiction. It refers to a germinal yet unpublished chapter of Dath's novel *Die*

Abschaffung der Arten (Dath 2008), *The Abolition of the Species* (Dath 2013). In this post-anthropocentric fiction, a decidedly Marxist as well as radically libertarian, a postapocalyptic society, is maintained foremost by non-humanoid aliens as lifeforms between mushrooms, plants, insects, and vertebrates. This social utopia is a sensory and biological utopia—a *technobiological* future: the garden in this sensory fiction has come to life. It is an effectively networked society made out of trees and bushes. Keyboarder Heike Aumüller, drummer Christoph Brunner, Dietmar Dath as narrator, and guitarist Thomas Weber generate a sound piece that audioports one into this sonario of a far future plantculture. The spoken word and the resonating tones do not illustrate each other like you would expect in a traditional, more narrative and theater-oriented radio drama. Instead, this piece follows more the long and strong tradition of experimental radio dramas that are *no drama* at all. They adhere more closely to the tradition of *postdramatic theater* (Lehmann 2006), interpreted as a combination of sound poetry with freeform sound performances. In the garden that just awakened, one encounters a political utopia: The sensory aliens of this utopia exist in mutual exchanges of substances, of touch, and of material effects—way more than in the transport of symbolic strings of characters. The culture presented here in *Im Erwachten Garten* as just emerging is the one fully evolved in *The Abolition of the Species:* a culture in which the materiality of existence dominates, in bodies and fluids, in particles and touches, in agglomerations that are edible, drinkable, digestible, and appealing to touch, to caress. This true material culture does not evade into artifacts as a means not to stay in touch and not to stay in constant and deep exchange. This culture definitely indulges in an incessantly intense and mutually devouring flow of intake. For any humanoid alien outside of this culture, this must definitely read as a scary, maybe lethal, and all in all not very appealing cultural habit. This fear of being digested results from the fact that this imagined alien culture seems to be so much closer to supposedly less culturally and legally regulated practices of exchange as observed in animal and plant populations. This post-anthropocentric culture is closer to biological, chemical, and physical forms of processing, transforming, annihilating, and generating than to scriptural, arithmetic, financial, and military forms. The sensory corpora of all the aliens substantiating this networked society in this sonic fiction trump the technological dispositive known in the networked societies you or I might have been introduced to in recent decades as part of the military-industrial-communication-entertainment complex (as explored in Chapter 3: "Corporealizing The Senses").

The technology of this present continuum around us not represented in this sonic artifact is part of a dispositive that excels in detaching itself from any instability and plasticity of biological, physiological, and geological processes (as explored in Chapter 4: "In Auditory Dispositives"). Recent developments in the sciences, in technology, and also in theory connect these seemingly non-vital and largely semiotic approaches more and more to vital, continuous, and material processes in plants and animals, bacteria and fungi. Starting with the individual bodily constitution, the outstretch and the intensity of connections in the body-wide nervenet, not ending with the training, the strengthening, and the weakening of specific areas and constituents of a humanoid's sensory corpus: muscles, bones, intestines, fascies, extremities, the highly resonant web of sensory organs as they are occupying idiosyncratically each bodily configuration (as explored in Chapter 6: "A Sensory Corpus"). In this close-up of corporeality, the simply sketched outline of a body, its organs and its internal connectivity may resemble a more complex electric circuit that has been transformed into an almost strangely mixed work of some weird approach to bricolage sculpture. Humanoid aliens are a factual assemblage made out of hairs and liquids, skinbags and plastic threads, pulsating agglomerations of tiny cells in various materials, multiple sizes, and highly differentiated dynamics. For living aliens, the shape and dimension of their bodies, their corporeal shape and internal structure, is fundamentally not limited to a once given outline. In contrast, *plasticity, transformability, and generativity* are crucial properties to one's sensory existence. *Im Erwachten Garten* unravels such a divergent reality of corporeal life. A revolution in technology that results in a biological, a social, a political, and an existential revolution.

This form of corporeal technology, of true *techniques du corps* (Mauss 1936), does not limit its activity in corporeal operations on a macro-level of actions, but also on minuscule adjustments, transformations, and transmutations on a micro- and even nano-level. Such operations transform the operating bodies continuously—and not only selectively—in their actual shapes, structures, and dimensions. Is there *A corpus techné*? A corpus as a means of technology—not merely enhanced, equipped, and connected to technology, but technologically operating in its own way? The highly industrialized branch of biotechnology seeks for such a *corpus techné*. Therefrom, researchers of many disciplines and approaches are truly intrigued (and equally slightly scared) by any development in this direction. One can sense this certain hope, this tiny glimpse of a perspective, that in exactly this field of the sciences and of engineering a thoroughly new form of technology and future cultural practice might possibly be evolving. Alien humanoids could be witnessing—in a not too distant future—the emergence of a new strand of technology that can actually on many unforeseen levels be called *vital, living, transforming*. It might scare us. As it is not so much different than humanoid aliens as such—but a new existential and ontological category on their sides. These technobiological aliens would not be a new class of slaves or servants as electromaterial robots are often conceptualized in fiction, in the sciences, or in politics. In contrary, they would act as true companions, collaborators, as competition. A new breed of alien humanoids of yet another kind. *Im Erwachten Garten* introduces you in this new continuum of a social and biological utopia through sound and narration, through sonic fiction. Two decades earlier, Dietmar Dath translated Kodwo Eshun's *More Brilliant than the Sun* (Eshun 1998) into German: *Heller als die Sonne* (Eshun 1999). Dath is well aware of the intersections between narration and sound, as well as of the sensory generativity that a sonic experience is capable of triggering. As soon as the garden awakens, the sonic performativity awakens as well in this piece. A sonic fiction is generated from the syrrhesis between a literary narration on which it is founded and the musical emanation radiating from it in the form of a collective performance between Kammerflimmer Kollektief and Dietmar Dath. Post-humanoid aliens occupy this sonic fiction. Theoretical ramifications complexify the projected rhythmanalysis inherent in this sonario. These aliens constitute the garden, the consciousness of this garden: one selected alien shared a body with another and they share and diverge in their experiences. Divergent historical continuations are being discussed, and out of this discourse—presented as part of the sonic artifact—the new continuum emerges and oozes out the musical performance by Heike Aumüller, singing and evoking this garden as leaving its sleep, a multiplicity of just awakened non-humanoid aliens. A society of convivialist non-humanoids. The four alien humanoids of the musical group perform hence a postcolonialist, a postimperialist, and a postexperialist study of species and of things. Traditional gender roles and social constitutions of gender emerge from the so-called *Gente*, the new genera, new tribes, new packs in this sonic fiction:

> Denn bei der regelrechten Liebe machen nicht die Regeln die Liebe—sondern die Liebe macht die Regeln. (Dath & Kammerflimmer Kollektief 2009: track 4)

Because in regular love, the rules do not make love—but love makes the rules. This utopia starts with the sensory corpus, it starts with the magma of desire, the mingled situations between non-humanoid aliens, transforming, emerging, radiating, changing. This embracing of the multiplicity of emerging experiences and sensibilities is the one and only meaningful starting point for *a non-anthropocentric anthropology of sound*. Any narrower or more focused starting point would miss the point. *Flowers can argue, laugh, and grumble* (ibid.: track 2, 22:02–22:05; transl. HS—as all following quotes). With my comrades, the non-humanoids, I dive into the *first thinking rose garden; enfibbed [sic—an invented word—also in the German original: umflunkert] by fragrances like tea, freshly cut grass, and bananas, I caught new ideologies, fears, infatuations, and thorn scratches* (ibid.: track 2, 23:13–23:23). *Stoned and exuberantly happy* (ibid.: track 2, 23:29–23:33), my bodily material becomes their playground. These plant-animal-aliens invite me to inhabit their garden, to co-perform and to co-receive their sensory acts.

Anecdotes about worm cake (ibid.: track 2, 23:02–23:03). *The joke about my ears* (ibid.: track 2, 23:06–23:08). The longer I dare to stay and dare to play with these, the longer I seem to be capable of assimilating, of integrating, of understanding their way of exchanging and communicating impressions, statuses, intentions, and habits. Their tensions become my tensions. I indulge in dissolving myself into their tensions and intentions. *In the necessary receptivity for the whispering of the many languages of fragrance.* (ibid.: Track 2, 22:44–22:48). More and more, the tension in these animal-plant-aliens extends into my listening body, into my sensory corpus, until they effectively inhabit me while listening. The techniques applied by this garden and its *plantoid aliens* are corporeal techniques. They provide access to a world touching the body of the plants and my body not via apparatuses, yet via an actual extension of mutual bodily actions. The garden is sound. My skins, my nerves, my hairs, are resonating in touch. Touching is the pervasive mode of attachment and connectivity. A *distributed subjectivity* (Kassabian 2013). This network is in tension. Radiating. Present.

I leave the thinking garden. I might leave the location—yet I won't leave the sensory and the reflective experiences I was an arena for in this location. Being a sensory arena for another plantoid alien is *refreshing*, to say the least. Transforming, it is. Being reborn this way. A re-corporealization of the senses. A sensory technology was raised and educated in this awakened garden. It is not a lifeless, dumbed down version of a humanoid alien as a stubborn impostor. In these plants another continuum could begin: in their sensing and thinking, their sensibility and caressing, their love. I went out and got back in. Then I watered the little lime tree on our balcony.

Sensory syncope

Nostalgically, you and I might remember this pivotal piece of the 2010s. You remember the deep and ever deeper pitched vocal twists and shouts by a younger female alien anthropoid. It seems to indulge in this state of being processed toward a darker, deeper, lower register of its lifeform. It is transforming itself in this vocal arrangement. It is aspiring and acquiring—after a first vocal entry in the first fractions of its tenth second—then a thorough transformation in the five seconds from no. 17 to no. 22: A reformation that none of us, not a single, sensible alien could have foreseen. The vocal emission is pushed toward a deeper stance; it is drilled into its own ground of vocal substance. It is this *substance of listening* (Sowodniok 2012a) that is being performed right here—calculated, reiterated, stored, and transmitted. And then it gets drilled even deeper in the ground. The *sensory corpus of the vocal performer* is being transformed and deformed, upcycled and downsized. The voice is being remolded and ensounded differently, differing and differentiatingly. The performer has become bass. A deeper, more visceral bass taking place in the groin, in the guts, and in the fascies of the *sonario* (Gampe 2014) that is, again, your or my corporeal arena for instance. The corpus of this voice has been skipped and scratched, tracked and clicked, sampled and reconstructed, remodeled. Miley Cyrus is this *sensory syncope*. The persona of Miley Cyrus has undergone a thorough remodeling—yet only taking place in these very humble seconds, somewhere close to the midpoint of this whole recorded work. *Fuckin Fucked Up* is the name of this work (Cyrus 2015: track 6). It drives my area, the area of my body as a corporeal auditory dispositive, beyond a hitherto known border of experiential depth. And then it ends. Wimpy. Quirky. Ridiculous. These fifty seconds should contain all of this? Why do I feel urged to even write about some measly fifty seconds?

These fifty seconds are a manifesto. A manifesto of non-narrative, post-hero, post-gender, post-stability, post-symmetrical, neo-generative performativity. They are an opera. As they seem to take one only from a previous, highly affective and addictive sonario—track 5: *Space Boots*—to yet another one, equally as addictively affectionate—track 7: *BB Talk*—effectively they are some truly seductive Odyssey in themselves: *A Northwest Passage* of sound and the senses. Fuckin' fucked up is the generative nucleus of this piece. As the *Six Pieces* by Photek and von Webern—explored in the starting section of this chapter—being fucked up is a fundamental and seriously affective, thoroughly aesthetic quality to a sonario. As a sonario, following Johanna Gampe (Gampe 2014), it is necessary to take into account that the whole sensory and experiential situation in all its entanglement, its complexity, and its erratic generativity, is contributing to a sonic experience. The state of being fucking fucked up now relates to, it addresses, and it even attacks numerous affective states in an experiential area that you or I might actually be and perform in at a certain moment: it is a highly contingent, an intensely ambivalent, and—not the least—a deeply craved, admired, feared, and desired state in an alien humanoid, a monster like me and you. It is a state in which a corporeally intense and on some level devastating experience has been made by one alien humanoid, presumably in relation to a series of (more or less) other and (at least in some aspects) differing monsters and humanoids. This being fucked up is not seldom executed by the use and application of various techniques, apparatuses, and chemical substances, preferably in the aggregate state of liquid or gas. One indulges in the excess of these substances, in related performativity, in situative drifts and *implexes* (Dath and Kirchner 2012) into a shared yet infinitely different sensory corpus emerging out of this collision of alien humanoids: a joyful collision—as joyful as a mutual play with generative software or musical instruments, with transgressive desires and evolving interwoven practices of intimacy and self-reflection or with the persona, the sensory persona one could be, will be, intends to be. A beautiful struggle. In this colliding state in flux, the process of fucking one another or oneself up takes place. It is definitely not only a thoroughly agreeable activity in which one would engage before being thoroughly fucked up. But there is joy in violence, joy in heightened states of being hurt and used, being abused, there are moments in an alien-collision when the intensity of being violently treated following one's own will and desire is incredibly high. Or simply: the exchange of intensity transcends common limitations of behavior between rather civilized and educated alien humanoids. *We transcend ourselves.* You and I, we hand ourselves over to one another and to the mutual exchange taking place with energy, greediness, horniness, urge, and will. The common monsters like you and me seem to enjoy this a lot. One actually seems to need this, now and then. This incredibly dangerous, scary, and lustful passage from known territories into transgression:

Je cherche le passage entre la science exacte et les sciences humaines. (Serres 1980: 15)

This *passage between the exact sciences and the humanities* has been produced and it is being experienced in *Fuckin Fucked Up*: a passage from the overly explicit exactitude of measuring, and its resulting analytical and technological dispositives—to a more complexly implied precision of sensibility and its sinuously syrrhetical reconfigurations and reinventions of a sensory corpus. This passage, this struggle between secure and known territories to lesser or unknown states and situations, moves through a scary and often unsettling zone of ambiguity, transformation, and plasticity. Exactly this liquid state terrifies alien humanoids to a surprising degree: As the comfort in familiar dispositives is almost lost—and a contrasting comfort in yet another stable concept, for instance in a new sonic persona, is not yet found. In this state of in-between, one moves across the sensory corpus that is never fixed and stable, but reacting and responding, malleable and soft, vulnerable and doubtful. An existence consisting largely of resonances and situations, tactical and impulsive instead of an often desired existence consisting of fixed and definite attributions by a hegemonic apparatus in power, with clear benefits and future gains. The singer and producer of this piece is moving through this passage, in her whole album and also in this selected, brief skit between tracks 5 and 7. From a technologically crystallized concept of commodified sound, she takes you and me into an anthropological understanding of sonic experiences: From the dissolution of a dispositive (as explored in Chapter 4: "In Auditory Dispositives") into the generation of a new sonic persona (as explored in Chapter 5: "*The Sonic Persona*").

The dissolution of the dispositive is prepared and established in the previous track, *Space Boots*: the track is still a rather common pop song, a slow and low one, a crooner and a slow jam before it enters more generic pop song territory. The *dispositive of pop* is present here in the harmonic and percussive structure as well as in the melody and the hookline. Already the singer as sonic persona is being partially dissolved—a transformation that is often seductively introduced into pop as forms of sonic distortion and performative disruption; yet it is seldom executed in a radically extreme way. So it is here as the song remains the same after all, even after distorting the singer's voice now and then, after introducing transitioning sounds and deep and weird vocalizations as well as remote and nostalgic sounds punctuating this recording. The dispositive of pop remains unchallenged. I might indulge in the perfection of this tiny cosmos of four minutes and forty-nine seconds. Albeit after the rupture, the syncope of this little 50-second skit, the sonic persona of the producer and the singer is regenerated in the subsequent track: *BB Talk*. The persona has now been royally fucked up. Its language, its habitus, its strange ways of laidback pronunciation have been intrinsically transformed. She is not the same as she was just fifty seconds before. "I got no idea what the fuck I want, I guess" (Cyrus 2015: track 7, 0:54–0:57). In this track, the new persona has emerged. It has crystallized, and it intends to articulate its newfound, its newly generated, sensory corpus. The singer and her lyrics articulate a distinction from the *baby talking*, the *BB Talk* her lover and partner and significant other still seems to indulge in:

> I mean, you put me in these fucking situations where I look like a dumbass bitch and I'm not a fucking dumbass bitch. You know, like, I hate all that fucking PDA, I probably hate it more than your fucking friends do. You know, it's sweet and you couldn't be more opposite of my last dickhead but I don't know if I can get over the fucking goo. (Cyrus 2015: track 7, 1:52–2:14)

The sound of this track might sound less intriguing than the fifty-second skit; yet exactly this mainly looped and repetitive fundament of the track represents a major difference to the rather less flowing, more voguing, more snapshot-crystallized posture of a pop dispositive: The transformation happening between tracks 5 and 7 constitutes this *sensory syncope*. This syncope is a break, a rupture that connects and continues in transition: "I'm feeling like I'm gonna vomit" (Cyrus 2015: track 7, 2:31–2:34). As a transition, this continuity is being secured sensorially and sonically by a form of break and destruction of an earlier sonic persona and the generation of another: by a rising feeling of vomiting—of expulsion of one's earlier self. The new sonic and sensory persona goes, consequentially, through stages of self-denial and of self-loathing and externalized aggression—because of PDAs, *public displays of affection*: "Fuck me so you stop baby talking" (Cyrus 2015: track 7, 3:51–3:56). The baby-talking goes on regressively when listening to this track on the webpage specifically created for a free online streaming of this track: one sees there a gooey, sticky, viscid layering of sweets and liquids running over the face of the singer's persona—who consequently indulges in licking off, eating up, devouring these particles of utter indulgence. This visual depiction of regression in sweetness and liquids is nothing else than the detested *public display of affection*—though not toward another alien humanoid but toward some not-so-humanoid, alien, crunchy, viscid delicate liquid. Liquid sweetness all over us. As the German band Tocotronic sang in a song they released in the same year as Miley Cyrus's record:

Du bist aus Zucker, du bist zart
Du schmilzt dahin, du wirst nicht hart
Du bist zänkisch und suspekt
Du bist ein toxisches Subjekt (Tocotronic 2015: track 10)

You're made of sugar, you are tender. You are melting, you don't get hard. You are quarrelsome and suspicious: You are a toxic subject. Miley Cyrus performs here as exactly this indulging, quarreling, and toxic subject of which Tocotronic are singing: She performs her sweetness, her melting, and her never solidifying. Or, as Nikah Ujita writes in her *Sonische Zeitfragen VII*: "Das Sonische frißt seine Hörerinnen und Hörer" (Ujita 2028: 812). *The sonic eats up all its listeners*, of all genders, races, disabilities, and proclivities. The tenderness of Miley Cyrus's sweetness-performance devours all myths and brands and beauty practices—incorporating them, and as such transcending them as sexual practices:

Darling, Candy Parzival
trinkst Cherry Cola aus dem Gral
mit spitzen Fingern—Nagellack
Du bist ganz sicher too crunk to fuck (Tocotronic 2015: track 10)

Darling, Candy Parzival: drink Cherry Cola from the Grail with pointed fingers—nail polish. For sure you are too crunk to fuck: "Shit's 'bout to get real freaky I can feel it" (Cyrus 2015: track 8, 1:19–1:23). The freaky generates through sickness and through appetite. And even if— in an alternate, more repulsive universe to ours here in the year 2384, in the Kuiper Belt Colonies—this singer might in the years afterwards have changed its media, sonic, and stage persona in another direction, catering to listeners and consumers who indulge in more xenophobic, in gender-stereotyped and weirdly sexist performances, even if this should have been the case, the state of a temporary syncopated transformation can still be heard: perhaps interwoven with already suspicious sexist, abusive, racist stereotypes underneath and overtop. *You're made of sugar, you are tender. You are melting, you don't get hard*:

*Du bist aus Zucker, du bist zart
Du schmilzt dahin, du wirst nicht hart* (Tocotronic 2015: track 10)

Synaptic Island

A deep thrust, again, is throwing me down. There are movements in my head, in my lower intestines. There are barrels, ladders, steel tolls falling down a staircase—in my inner ear. They are multiplying in me. They fall and fall, all over again. These falls are layering on each other—and suddenly igniting. They ex- and implode into each other, they accelerate these eximplosions to incredibly expanded, stretched out and thinned out levels of firing—an ongoing dynamization, until they reach a point where they actually fuse: *A screaming comes across the sky, it has happened before. But there is nothing to compare it to now.* A white noise, again, in various layers until the previous sequence of exploding and imploding has turned into one continuous drone of fusing, just slightly intensified. This now goes on for quite some time. Longer than I had previously expected. Then me, my corporeal area, seems to be sufficiently prepared for yet another transformation: millions and millions of lasering needles, pinching with sinuswave-like precision, are taking their places in my body, in my listening organs, they pinch me, permutate and oscillate, they sing and coerce, they dissolve and they conflux. Again and again. And all over again. Now I am, finally, turned into some rather willing and open playground for all these sounds to take place. The sonic arena is my body. I indulge in these sounds eating me up (Ujita 2028: 812). My sensory corpus is the material flesh with which these sonic events play, from which these *eximplosions* take their perceptual substance. It is not a minor experience. It is an ongoing pressure and tension, an intensifying and decreasing ache, minuscule injuries attacking me, my hearing and sensing, my kinesthetic, my tactile, my proprioceptive and my enteroceptive senses. It is not easy to endure. As a listener, I need to recover again and again. I need to pull up my strength just to endure—and somehow even to enjoy in the end—this form of being devoured parasitically by this myriad of sonic performances in nanoseconds, raining onto my sensory corpus.

Maryanne Amacher, the inventor of this composition, operates in the physical material of a given location: the walls and the floors, the cables and the furniture, the alien humanoids lingering and working there, the appliances, machines, and computers connected to the electrical grid (cf.

Chapter 6: "A Sensory Corpus"). In Amacher's work, sound is not a category floating freely through gases and resonances from vocal chords to eardrums, from diaphragms in loudspeakers to diaphragms in microphones. On the contrary, sound is for Amacher a material emanation moving along the massive and rather stable yet resonating and oscillating materials in an edifice: Amacher is an outstanding artist of sonic materialism avant la lettre. Sound is aural architecture (Blesser and Salter 2007). The sonic materiality in her work, though, is massively extended into the listeners and their bodies. The aural architecture external to a listening and resounding alien anthropoid like you or me extends to exactly your or my corporeally viscous bricolage of your or my sensory corpus: material sound is connected to physiological sound—bypassing the hermeneutics of semiotics and aesthetics, of cultural history and media analytics (as also explored in Chapter 6: "A Sensory Corpus"). The nerves and fascies, the muscles and skins, the synapses and bones, are not essentially detached from any other material nodes in the sensory continuum. What alien humanoids can perceive is mainly what is materially present and impactful—here and now. The *Synaptic Island* in a humanoid's cranium is actually *not* detached from the *ocean of sound* (Toop 1995) engulfing it. Amacher's piece by the name of *Synaptic Island* (Amacher 1999: tracks 3 and 4) hence puts this supposed island back in its original and constitutional environment again: into the oceans out of which it emerged and in which it is situated. Oceans of the senses. My synaptic island is punctuated, it is penetrated, it is transfixed by sounds. Out of all the artists covered in this final chapter so far, Amacher plays the body of the listener most as an instrument. Miley Cyrus (teaming up with The Flaming Lips for this piece), Kammerflimmer Kollektief, and Photek operate on the sensory body of a listener equally in an intense and pervasive way. Yet they do not effectively cross the main barrier of psychoacoustics. They do not operate in the dangerous, scary, and bodily intrusive voids, in the tiny cracks and caverns, the abyss of hearing and sensing. Cyrus, Kollektief, and Photek operate still foremost—though with growing extensions and excess—on layers of the imaginary and the dispositive, on layers of sonic experiences and sensory imaginations that affect a whole listener's body; Maryanne Amacher is entering areas of blunt and excessive, subliminal and suprasensory listening. *Synaptic Islands* takes common notions of psychoacoustics, individual listening experiences, and the composer's own microsensory explorations into hearing. It expands those explorations into interventions on a neurosurgical level that constitutes an *expanded site-specific rhythmanalysis*—for which the site is effectively one's inner ear:

> When played at the right sound level, which is quite high and exciting, tones in this music will cause your ears to act as neurophonic instruments that emit sounds that will seem to be issuing directly from your head. . . .

> Produced interaurally, these virtual sounds and melodic patterns originate in ears and neuroanatomy, not in your loudspeakers. (Amacher 1999: booklet)

You, the listener, become the *dispositive of sound reproduction*. I am the instrument being played by a dead composer: a zombie's game console. This room, where I am listening now to a recording of Maryanne Amacher, *a room different from the one you are in now*, this room generates a concert hall between my ears, as a third ear emerging out of my factual ears:

> In concerts my audiences discover music streaming out of their head, popping out of their ears, growing inside of them and outside of them, meeting and converging with the tones in the room. (Amacher 1999: booklet)

These individual imaginations of what these listeners encounter are not phantasms to be ignored. These imaginations represent in the best way possible what is materially happening and experientially efficacious in their bodies. It is the best verbal account, the best sensory metaphor, the best sonic fiction for listeners to describe this sensory activity. It is a perfect example for subtle and sensible *sensory critique*—relying on the listeners' *precision of sensibility* (as explored in Chapter 7: "The Precision of Sensibility"). Such sensory imaginations are the direct effects on alien humanoids as soon as they encounter materially intense experiences:

> These virtual tones are a natural and very real physical aspect of auditory perception, similar to the fusing of two images resulting in a third three-dimensional image in binocular perception. (Amacher 1999: booklet)

The emergence of these tones generates a different, more physical, corporeally expanded, and unprecedentedly detailed listening. A listening that materializes and corporealizes the process of listening and its prerequisites, the corporeal dispositive of your or my, her or his or its body. The music by Amacher is heard as a music not only listened to by a humanoid's ears—but also being played on a humanoid alien's emitting listening organs. Maryanne Amacher serves you in growing another, a third ear: "*Third Ear Music*—when our ears act as instruments and emit sounds as well as receive them" (Amacher 1999: booklet). The body is performative while listening. Amacher composes "music which is produced by the listener" (Amacher 1999: booklet). The composer is hence one of the most progressive artists who almost predicted the musical and sonic aesthetics predominant since the mid-twenty-first century. Whereas for composers and artists in the twentieth century, it was almost unthinkable to operate effectively and directly in the sensory apparatus of alien humanoids—this was already the approach of Amacher. What the classical avant-gardes of the early twentieth century promoted and proclaimed, what later was praised and demanded from contemporary arts in Fluxus and other late avant-gardes, this was finally in sight and in sound for artists at the turn of the millennium. The technical apparatus that once was thought of as an armor, as a castle or fortress surrounding, securing, and shielding one, has step by step been implemented into the individual body, its sensory corpus and its various sensory practices. The listening corpus of today—over four centuries after the termination of Amacher's biography in 2009—is loaded and refined, connected and enhanced with practices and sensibilities, receptivity, and techniques that provide you and me with incessant experiences of sound occurring in your or my body. What Amacher once wrote as a provocative and then truly disturbing experience would these days only qualify as the usual critique of any musical performance between accelerated brandpop and pensive media constellations:

> Tones dance in the immediate space of their body, around them like a sonic wrap, cascade inside ears, and out to space in front of their eyes, mixing and converging with the sound in the room. (Amacher 1999: booklet)

The generativity of the sensory corpus is fully developed in Amacher's work. She confronts her listeners, performers, and interpreters with the fact that these three modalities of sonic experience cannot be separated. The generativity is taking place in your or my very own flesh. We discover: "[we] are producing a tonal dimension of the music which interacts melodically, rhythmically, and spatially with the tones in the room" (Amacher 1999: booklet). This situation, my corporeal idiosyncrasies, your biography of listening experiences and trained sensory techniques, becomes not the main, it becomes the *only* source for interpretation, for performance, for listening.

Generativity

Are you listening now? I am too tired to listen, it seems to me. Our four-year-old boy is lying next door, in the living room, in fever; I am half writing these sentences, half listening to his breathing, his movements on the couch, possible coughs or mumblings. His and my mutual sensoria are interlinked and temporarily molded. My sonic persona in this very moment is—as it is quite often—split into a writing and arguing, imagining and phrasing persona, and an ambient listening persona, noting and attentively listening to all the minor sound events around me, audible for me. I feel a sore throat myself, so my listening to the child is equally a listening to the coughing noises, the pinchy hurt I feel around my larynx, around my resonating and vocally projecting generator. The sun shines in from the right side, now and then it even blinds the screen on which I am reading and writing these words. It is late morning on a Tuesday in Berlin, a wee bit too warm for the beginning of February; I am preparing to take the plane to Copenhagen in a few hours.

Are you listening to what you are now hearing? Of course not. I would be paranoid—or a saint, or a demigod, to be capable of doing so. I am zoning in and zoning out, drifting and driving, focusing and defocusing my aural attention according to the shifting and reordering of my whole corporeal attention, scattered across the sensory spectrum. By the way: it might be that the scholarly distinction between listening and hearing is at stake. Corporeal listening as a form of hearing is on the rise, and it incorporates more and more aspects of attentive, pensive, focused, and close listening. The ongoing transformation of listening cultures also affects and effects a transformation of enveloping thinking figures and concepts, terms and distinctions. So, actually: Yes, I am listening as I am hearing. *Right here. Right now.*

Are you hearing while you listen? Well. Instead of responding to this slightly unpleasant interrogation of an inquisitive and truly decontextualized style—as is too often common in academia—I prefer to turn to present idiosyncrasies: to pressing yet erratic sensory and thought events in *this* actual situation of immanence that is the real ground for these writings. Briefly, I was in the kitchen to prepare lunch for us two, some potatoes, some fresh vegetables, some cooling cheese curd with loads of chive. On the radio they played the song *4 Degrees* by Anohni, alias Antony Hegarty. And I thought by myself: "Die vollendete Idylle des Schreibens der Seiten 227–31" (Schulze 2016). *The perfect idyll of writing pages 227–31.* "I wanna see them burn—it's only 4 degrees" (Hegarty 2015)! It is an incredibly cruel and insanely brutalist song; in utter and quite joyful conflict with the usual tone one might have expected from the transgender persona of Antony Hegarty: "I wanna burn the sky, I wanna burn the breeze" (Hegarty 2015). The boy got up, moaning, just went to the toilet; I'm looking after him now.

Are you listening while you are hearing? The evening has set in. After several phone calls with colleagues, after a visit to the doctor, reading a bedtime story to my little son, and after continuing the work on this section and another article due in two months' time, I feel exhausted and stuffed at the same time. My sensory corpus is numbed and thin-skinned now. I indulge in this moment of fulfillment and calm. In the afternoon I learned that the singer mentioned in the previous paragraph, Anohni, sings about the imminent climate change in a quite uncommon persona, joyfully and eagerly anticipating total annihilation of all wildlife. The structural death wish and thanaticism inherent in contemporary globalized, postindustrial, consumerist media culture is singing. The capitalizing apparatus itself—so to speak—sings: "I wanna hear the dogs crying for water. I wanna see fish go belly-up in the sea. All those lemurs and all those tiny creatures: I wanna see them burn—it's only 4 degrees" (Hegarty 2015). Outside it's raining now, quite comfy in the night. On media websites and on TV, they are discussing the results of the Iowa Caucus, one of the early primary elections en route to the election of the president of the United States, in 2016.

Do you remember the last sound you heard before these questions? No, I don't. I was too immersed and too entangled in all the discussions of the recent hours, the collective planning activities as well as refining and correcting my argument and my writing in the texts I was crafting. When I am involved in such activities, it is barely possible, only with a great deal of extra effort and specialized focus, to listen to sounds not connected to my main activity. At least for me. In general, one's sensibility for sensory or sonic experiences is never identical over time and space; it swivels and bops with the changing sensory intensity, constellation, and focus of one's various activities (as explored in Chapter 7: "The Precision of Sensibility"). However, if I let this request sink in for some minutes, I remember this sound: a certain high pressure on my right, but also—lesser, though—on my left earlobe. A pressure that translates into a medium frequency hum, maybe with the frequency of electricity oscillating, 50 Hertz. A deep bass, hardly to be undercut, the general bass of modern electric culture (60 Hertz in the United States, obviously). The sound of intense communication, of exchange, of transport. Media music. Sounds of the apparatus.

What will you hear in the near future? I will go to sleep now; tomorrow, early in the morning, I'll catch the plane to Copenhagen. I anticipate sitting in 14D, with comfortable legroom, and resting, contemplating for some time. Maybe reading *The Pale King* by David Foster Wallace. Later, I will be holding the first lecture of my course in Popular Music Studies this semester. Anticipating the flimsy, sometimes harsh noises and sonic traces of all the listeners in the lecture hall, around one hundred sonic personae with their individual listening biographies, their individual efforts to cultivate an appropriate precision of sensibility, their existence under the spell of thoroughly differently experienced apparatuses than mine; though our individual, over one hundred experiential sensory corpora surely touch each other, now and then, at selected moments of laughter, irritation, understanding, fear. Of joy.

Can you hear now and also listen to your memory of an old sound? After air travel and lecturing, lunch and meetings, I find the time now to continue answering these questions. It is obviously hard to remember a remote episode in one's life—and at the same time to be present in this very episode now. It requires a double effort. Here in Copenhagen, remembering sounds I listened to in earlier stages of my biography, there is one recurring experience that quickly comes at me: On many evenings as a child, I listened to fairytales and bedtime stories of my choice on an ancient, plastic record player with some mono-loudspeaker. Later, as a young adolescent, I remember meditating, sometimes zoning out, while listening to favorite albums, to sound art, experimental radio plays on German radio. And only a bit later I felt a deep joy and an almost universal freedom while sitting in a fine concert hall or some off-venue and letting New Music run and play through my body, through all my nerves, my sensing and reflecting. Moments of felt complexity and completeness. Moments of haunting bliss. *Being, nothing else, without any further definition and fulfillment.* It is early evening. At the department I prepare a lecture I will be holding later this semester. *Delusions of the living dead.* For this purpose I listen to the sound piece *Martial Hauntology* (Goodman and Heys 2014). Much later I prepare an abstract for a conference in a few months' time, a talk on the German group Deichkind. Headphones, they saved my life. A *sensory critique* of remembering and of presence.

What causes you to listen? Do I ever *not* listen? Apparently I do, as I insisted earlier in this section. Writing this paragraph here now, it seems to me as if I never was *not* listening, never could be *not* listening to what is happening around me; in my corporeal imagination, in selected, quite logocentric counterarguments by the imaginary parliament of friends, relatives, and colleagues commenting on this writing, for example. They are generative. These imaginary sounds constitute what I am—as a sonic fiction, as a sonic persona, fictionalized. These sounds of remanence and imagination, they drive my writing and thinking, sensing and sketching. *Du musst immer weiter durchbrechen* (Egoexpress 1999). *You need to break through—on and ever onwards.* An urgency in this sonic articulation, these sonic traces: This causes me to listen. No doubt about this.

Do you hear yourself in your daily life? I try to. Yet it never is easy. It can be very simple, though, as long as the environment and the surrounding people are only really interested in supporting one's individual well-being. What is obviously a rare if not excessively luxurious situation: the life of a baby, of an oligarch, of a manic entrepreneur believing in himself being a genius. Most of the time, for most of alien humanoids, the demands and dynamics, the mutual expectations and collective or partial interests, are summing up to an accelerated vortex of action in which one's individual desires or interests are just minor vectors in a complex calculation. My hearing is not included. I need to resist, I need to free a large chunk of time and space to grant myself to hear: to hear myself (as explored in Chapter 8: "Resistance and Resonance"), to hear for myself. It requires energy—and sometimes even arrogance. A sonic ego.

Do you have healthy ears? Audiologists or audiopietists, I am very sure, will object to what I am going to write now: If one seriously speaks of *healthy* ears, one implicitly dooms all others as sick, deviant, inappropriate, and outcast ears. *Health* is an intricately complicated and culturally grounded concept of bodily integrity and non-dysfunction. To state an alien humanoid is in a *state of health* relies on experienced, conventionalized, and highly selective interpretations of physiological irregularities (aside maybe from simply obvious injuries, lethal diseases, or corporeal decomposition). Most of the alien humanoids

I met and asked about common irregularities in their listening experience usually first denied having any. They subsequently often admitted to having listening differences in both ears, frequency ranges with lower sensitivity, and also often forms of ongoing tinnitus. The differential in sensory corpora is infinite. Isn't it more common to experience irregular forms of listening than regular ones? Is the idea of a standard listening capability nothing more than an idealist, abstract concept almost no alien anthropoid ever actually fulfills? Statuarian, symmetrical, and perfect listening is an ideal outside the reality of any actual sonic persona. There is, though, a situated and adequate form of listening capability. I aspire to approach any sonic experience with at least an approximately appropriate practice of listening. I like to learn new ways of hearing.

If you could hear any sound you want, what would it be? I would love to listen right now to actual everyday sounds of remote historical times, say Rome 54 B.C., Babylon 1721 B.C., Vienna 1732, Beijing 1843, Moscow 1987. "I'm going to prove the impossible really exists" (Björk 1996: track 10, 0:57–1:07). I would also love to listen to alien lifeforms on remote planets, their articulations and sonic traces: "Bowie leaves us—and then a 9th planet appears" (Bell 2016). Yet another sonic environment I would love to indulge in right now is evoked in these words by Theodor Wiesengrund, alias Adorno:

> Rien faire comme une bête, lying on water and looking peacefully at the sky, "being, nothing else, without any further definition and fulfillment," might take the place of process, act, satisfaction, and so truly keep the promise of dialectical logic that it would culminate in its origin. None of the abstract concepts comes closer to the fulfilled utopia than that of eternal peace. (Adorno 1974: 156f.)

Are you listening to sounds now or just hearing them? You probably recognized the piece: this final section of the book consists of a written performance of the *Ear Piece* (1998) by the great artist, composer, sonic thinker, and performer Pauline Oliveros (Oliveros 2005: 34). She asks thirteen questions in this piece to explore listening and sounding. Her questions guide my concluding reflections summarizing this anthropology of sound: "force, flow, and capture" (Cox 2011: 157).

What sound is most meaningful to you? Generativity is what constitutes a sonic persona. The tension between hegemonic auditory dispositives and idiosyncrasies of a specific sensory corpus unravels in sonic traces. The experience of these traces, their resistant implex, is articulated and challenged by sensory critique. "Hit. . . . Move. Travel lightly. Occur. Be *here*" (Wallace 1996: 612). Sound is cohesion. "Learn. Try" (ibid.). Dancing is a way of hearing; singing is a way of dancing: Singing is a way of hearing.

SOURCES

Abbate, D. (2016), "Sound Object Lessons," *Journal of the Americal Musicological Society* 69 (3): 793–829.
Adams, C. J. (1990), *The Sexual Politics of Meat*, New York: Continuum Publishers.
Adams, D. (2002), *The Salmon of Doubt*, Now York: Random House.
Adorno, T. W. (1951), *Minima Moralia. Reflexionen aus dem beschädigten Leben*, Frankfurt am Main: Suhrkamp Verlag.
Adorno, T. W. (1956), *Dissonanzen. Musik in der verwalteten Welt*, Göttingen: Vandenhoeck & Ruprecht.
Adorno, T. W. (1971), *Kritik. Kleine Schriften zur Gesellschaft*, Frankfurt am Main: Suhrkamp.
Adorno, T. W. (1974), *Minima Moralia: Reflections from a Damaged Life*, translated by Edmund Jephcott, London: New Left Books.
Ahmed, S. (2006), *Queer Phenomenology: Orientations, Objects, Others*, Durham, NC: Duke University Press.
Altman, R. (1992), *Sound Theory, Sound Practice*, Now York: Routledge.
Amacher, M. (1999), *Sound Characters (Making The Third Ear)*, New York: Tzadik Records.
Amacher, M. (2008), *Sound Characters 2 (Making Sonic Spaces)*, New York: Tzadik Records.
Anderson, L. (1982), *Big Science*, New York: Warner Bros. Records Inc.
Artaud, A. (1947), *Pour en finir avec le jugement de Dieu: émission radiophonique enregistrée le 28 novembre 1947*, Paris: ORTF.
Artaud, A. (1992), "To Have Done with the Judgment of God," translated by Clayton Eshleman, in *Wireless Imagination: Sound, Radio and the Avant Garde*, edited by Douglas Khan and Gregory Whitehead, Cambridge, MA: The MIT-Press.
Attali, J. (1985), *Noise: The Political Economy of Music*, translated by Brian Massumi, foreword by Fredric Jameson, afterword by Susan McClary, Minneapolis & London: University of Minnesota Press.
Augoyard, J.-F. and Torgue, H. (2005), *Sonic Experience. A Guide to Everyday Sounds*, translated by Andra McCartney and David Paquette, Montreal and Kingston: McGill-Queen's University Press.
Auinger, S. and Odland, B. (2007), "Hearing Perspective (Think with Your Ears)," in *Sam Auinger. Katalog*, edited by C. Seiffarth and M. Sturm (Hg.). Wien: Folio.

Auinger, S. and Odland, B. (2006): *Innsbruck 6020*. Online: http://samauinger.de/de/timeline/innsbruck-6020/
Auinger, S. and Odland, B. (2011): *Sonic Vista*, Frankfurt am Main.
Balzacq, T. (ed.) (2011), *Securitization Theory: How Security Problems Emerge and Dissolve*, Oxford: Routledge.
Barbrook, R. and Cameron, A. (1996), "The Californian Ideology," *Science as Culture* 6 (1): 44–72.
Baudry, J.-L. (1970), "Effets idéologiques produits par l'appareil de base," *Cinéthique* Nr 7–8: 1–8.
Baudry, J.-L. and Williams, A. (1974/75), "Ideological Effects of the Basic Cinematographic Apparatus," *Film Quarterly* 28 (2): (Winter): 39–47.
Baudrillard, J. (1976), "The Hyperrealism of the Simulation," in Baudrillard, J. (1988), *Jean Baudrillard: Selected Writings*, edited by Mark Poster, 143–47, Stanford: Stanford University Press.
Bell, S. [atstephenbell] (2016, January 20), bowie leaves us and then a 9th planet appears, i don't need to read your science article [Tweet]. Retrieved from https://twitter.com/atstephenbell/status/689926009953587200
Beranek, L. (1954), *Acoustics*, New York: McGraw Hill.
Beranek, L. (2004), *Concert Halls and Opera Houses: Music, Acoustics, and Architecture*, New York: Springer Publishing.
Berardi, B. (2009), *The Soul at Work: From Alienation to Autonomy*, translated by Francesca Cadel and Giuseppina Mecchia, with preface by Jason E. Smith. Los Angeles, CA: Semiotexte.
Berker, T., Hartmann, M., Punie, Y. and Ward, K. (2006), *Domestication of Media and Technology*, London: Open University Press.
Biddle, I. and Thompson, M. (eds.) (2013), *Sound, Music, Affect. Theorizing Sonic Experience*, New York: Bloomsbury.
Bijsterveld, K. (2008), *Mechanical Sound. Technology, Culture and Public Problems of Noise in the Twentieth Century*, Cambridge, MA: The MIT-Press.
Bijsterveld, K., Cleophas, E., Krebs, S. and Mom, G. (2013), *Sound and Safe: A History of Listening Behind the Wheel*, Oxford: Oxford University Press.
Bijsterveld, K. (2018), *Sonic Skills. Listening for Knowledge in Science, Medicine and Engineering, 1920s-Present*, London: Palgrave Macmillan.
Björk (1995), *Post*, London: One Little Indian Records.
Bolter, J. D. (1991), *Writing Space: The Computer, Hypertext and the History of Writing. Hillsdale*, New York: Lawrence Erlbaum.
Burroughs, W. S. (1961/66), *The Soft Machine*, Paris: Olympia Press.
Burroughs, W. S. (1962/67), *The Ticket That Exploded*, Paris: Olympia Press.
Burroughs, W. S. (1964), *Nova Express*, New York: Grove Press.
Blesser, B. and Salter, L.-R. (2007), *Spaces Speak, Are You Listening? Experiencing Aural Architecture*, Cambridge, MA: The MIT-Press.
Brabandere, N. and Flett, G. (2016), "Hearing on the Verge: Cuing and Aligning with the Movement of the Audible," *Fluid Sounds,* Copenhagen: Seismograf (online: http://seismograf.org/fokus/fluid-sounds/hearing-on-the-verge)
Brauns, J. (2003), *Schauplätze. Untersuchungen zur Theorie und Geschichte der Dispositive visueller Medien*, PhD, Bauhaus Universität Weimar.

Bressan, P. and Kramer, P. (2015), "Humans as Superorganisms: How Microbes, Viruses, Imprinted Genes, and Other Selfish Entities Shape Our Behavior," *Perspectives on Psychological Science* 10 (4): 464–81.
Brooker, C. (2011), *Black Mirror—Season 1, Episode 2: Fifteen Million Merits*, London: Channel 4.
Bull, M. (2003), *Sound Moves. iPod Culture and Urban Experience*, London: Routledge.
Burkhalter, T., Grab, S. and Spahr, M. (2013), *Sonic Traces: From The Arab World*, Bern & Solothurn: Norient & Traversion.
Burns, T. (1961/62), "Micropolitics: Mechanism of Institutional Change," *Administrative Science Quarterly*, H. 6: 257–81.
Buzan, B., Wæver, O. O., Wilde, J. de(1998), *Security: A New Framework for Analysis*. Lynne Rienner: Boulder.
Caffentzis, G. (2013), *In Letters of Blood and Fire: Work, Machines, and Value*, Oakland: PM Press.
Cage, J. (1979), *Empty Words*, Middleton, CT: Wesleyan.
Cahan, D. (ed.) (1994), *Hermann von Helmholtz and the Foundations of Nineteenth-Century Science*, Berkeley: University of California Press.
Calix, M. (1996), "Humba," *Blech II: Blechsdöttir*, Sheffield: Warp Records, Track 16.
Captain Beefheart (1969), *Trout Mask Replica*, Los Angeles: Straight Records.
Carrouges, M. and Duchamp, M. (1976): *Les Machines Célibataires*. Paris: Editions du Chêne.
Castoriadis, C. (1975), *L'institution imaginaire de la société*, Paris: Le Seuil.
Chandler, D. (1994), "The Transmission Model of Communication" http://visual-memory.co.uk/daniel/Documents/short/trans.html.
Châtelet, G. (1998), *Vivre et penser comme des porcs. De l'incitation à l'envie et à l'ennui dans les démocraties-marchés*, Paris: Exils.
Classen, C. (2012), *The Deepest Sense: A Cultural History of Touch*, Champaign: University of Illinois Press.
Clover, J. (2016), *Riot. Strike. Riot. The New Era of Uprisings*, New York: Verso Books.
Cobussen, M., Vincent M. and Schulze, H. (2013), "Towards New Sonic Epistemologies. Editorial," *Journal of Sonic Studies* 1. http://journal.sonicstudies.org/vol04/nr01/a01.
Cox, C. (2011), "Beyond Representation and Signification: Toward a Sonic Materialism," *Journal of Visual Culture* 10 (2): 145–61.
Cressman, D. M. (2012), The Concert Hall as a Medium of Musical Culture: The Technical Mediation of Listening in the 19th Century, PhD, Vancouver: Simon Fraser University.
Cressman, D. M. (2015), "Acoustic Architecture before Science: The Case of Amsterdam's Concertgebouw," *SoundEffects* 5 (1), http://www.soundeffects.dk/article/view/23304/20352.
Cyrus, M. (2015), *Miley Cyrus & Her Dead Petz*, Nashville: Smiley Miley, Inc.
Dath, D. (2014), *Klassenkampf im Dunkeln. Zehn zeitgemäße sozialistische Übungen*. Hamburg: Konkret Verlag.
Dath, D. and Kirchner, B. (2012), *Der Implex. Sozialer Fortschritt: Geschichte und Idee*, Berlin: Suhrkamp Verlag.

Dath, D. and Kollektief, Kammerflimmer (2009), *Im erwachten Garten*, Berlin: Staubgold.
Dath, D. (2008), *Die Abschaffung der Arten. Novel*, Frankfurt am Main: Suhrkamp Verlag.
Dath, D. (2013), *The Abolition of Species. English Translation by Samuel P. Willcocks*, London: Seagull Books.
Debord, G. (1958), "Théorie de la dérive" *Internationale situationniste*, Numéro 2, Paris Décembre 1958.
Debray, R. (2000), *Transmitting Culture*, New York: Columbia University Press.
Debray, R. (2006), "Effet Jogging," *Conférence à Séville*.
Deleuze, G. and Guattari, F. (1991), *Qu'est-ce que la philosophie?* Paris: Les Editions de Minuit (engl. Translation 1994: What Is Philosophy? Translated by Graham Burchell and Hugh Tomlinson, New York: Columbia University Press).
Deleuze, G. and Guattari, F. (1972), *L'Anti-Œdipe. Capitalisme et schizophrénie*. Paris: Éditions de Minuit.
Deleuze, G. and Guattari, F. (1987), *A Thousand Plateaus*, Minneapolis: University of Minnesota Press.
Deleuze, G. (2005), *Pure Immanence. Essays on a Life—Introduction by John Rajchman, translated by Anne Boyman*, New York: Zone Books.
Derrida, J. (1985), *Margins of Philosophy -- Translated, with Additional Notes by Alan Bass*. Chicago: University of Chicago Press.
Egoexpress (1999), *Weiter*, Hamburg: Ladomat 2000.
Eickhoff, H. (1993), *Himmelsthron und Schaukelstuhl: Die Geschichte des Sitzens*, München: Carl Hanser Verlag.
Eickhoff, H. (1997), *Sitzen. Eine Betrachtung der bestuhlten Gesellschaft*, Frankfurt am Main: Anabas-Verlag.
McEnaney, L. (2000), *Civil Defence Begins at Home: Militarization Meets Everyday Life in the Fifties*, Princeton: Princeton University Press.
Eno, B. (1978), *Music for Airports. Ambient 1*, London: E. G. Records.
Erlman, V. (2010), *Reason and Resonance: A History of Modern Aurality*, New York: Zone Books.
Ernst, W. (2003), "Medienwissen(schaft) zeitkritisch. Ein Programm aus der Sophienstrasse." Antrittsvorlesung (inaugural lecture): Humboldt University of Berlin, October 21.
Ernst, W. (2002), *Das Rumoren der Archive: Ordnung aus Unordnung*, Berlin: Merve Verlag.
Encyclopaedia Britannica (2003), "Sound."
Eshun, K. (1998), *More Brilliant Than The Sun. Adventures in Sonic Fiction*, London: Quartet Books.
Eshun, K. (1999), *Heller als die Sonne: Abenteuer in der Sonic Fiction. Aus dem Englischen von Dietmar Dath*, Berlin: ID Verlag.
Fanon, F. (1967), *The Wretched of the Earth*, New York: Grove Press.
Fatboy Slim (1998), *You've Come a Long Way, Baby*, Brighton: Skint Records.
Feld, S. (1982), *Sound and Sentiment: Birds, Weeping, Poetics, and Song in Kaluli Expression*, Philadelphia, PA: University of Pennsylvania Press.
Fisher, M. (2015), "Abandon hope (summer is coming)" *k-punk*, London May 11, 2015 Online: http://k-punk.org/abandon-hope-summer-is-coming/
Fisher, M. (2009), *Capitalist Realism: Is there no Alternative?* London: Zero Books.

Fleck, L. (1980), *Entstehung und Entwicklung einer wissenschaftlichen Tatsache. Einführung in die Lehre vom Denkstil und Denkkollektiv*, Frankfurt am Main: Suhrkamp Verlag.
Fletcher, H. (1929), *Speech and Hearing*, New York: Van Nostrand.
Flückiger, B. (2001), *Sound Design. Die virtuelle Klangwelt des Films*, Marburg: Schüren.
Gallagher, S. (2005), *How the Body Shapes the Mind*, New York: Oxford University Press
Gampe, J. (2014), *On Digital Aesthetics. Changes arising from the Digital Revolution. A Media, Sound Art and Philosophy Perspective*, PhD Université Sorbonne Paris 2014.
Gendlin, E. T. (1962/1997), *Experiencing and the Creation of Meaning. A Philosophical and Psychological Approach to the Subjective*, Glencoe, IL: Free Press of Glencoe (reprinted: Chicago: Northwestern University Press, 1997)
Gendlin, E. T. (1992), "The Wider Role of Bodily Sense in Thought and Language," in *Giving the Body its Due*, edited by Maxine Sheets-Johnstone, 192–207, Albany: SUNY Press.
Gibson, J. J. (1979), *The Ecological Approach to Visual Perception*, Boston: Houghton Mifflin.
Gillis, J. R. (ed.) (1989), *The Militarization of the Western World*, New Brunswick: Rutgers University Press.
Goetz, R. (2000), *Dekonspiratione. Erzählung—Heute Morgen 5.3*, Frankfurt am Main: Suhrkamp.
Goodman, S. (2009), *Sonic Warfare: Sound, Affect, and the Ecology of Fear*, Cambridge, MA: The MIT-Press.
Goodman, S. and Heys, T. (2014), *Martial Hauntology*, London and Manchester: AUDINT Records.
Gopinath, S. and Stanyek, J. (2014), *The Oxford Handbook of Mobile Music Studies*, Oxford: Oxford University Press.
Gregg, M. and Seigworth, G. J. (eds.) (2010), *The Affect Theory Reader*, Durham, NC: Duke University Press.
Großmann, R. (2008), "Verschlafener Medienwandel," *Positionen—Beiträge zur neuen Musik* 74: 6–9.
Hacking, I. (1983), *Representing and Intervening*, Cambridge: Cambridge University Press.
Halffman, W. and Radder, H. (2015), "The Academic Manifesto: From An Occupied To A Public University" *Minerva* 53 (2): 165–87
Halliday, M. A. K. and Hasan, R. (1976), *Cohesion in English*, London: Longman.
Hansen, B. R., Plotegher, P. and Zechner, M. (2013), *Nanopolitics Handbook: The Nanopolitics Group*, Wivenhoe, New York and Port Watson: Minor Compositions.
Haraway, D. (2015), "Anthropocene, Capitalocene, Plantationocene, Chthulucene: Making Kin," *Environmental Humanities* 6: 159–65
Harding, S. (1987), *The Science Question in Feminism*, Ithaca, NY: Cornell University Press.
Hardt, M. and Negri, A. (2009). *Commonwealth*, Cambridge, MA: Belknap Press of Harvard University Press.

Harrasser, K. (2015), "Koine Aiesthsis Im Untergewebe taktiler Medialität," *Texte zur Kunst* 98: 105–18.
Harrasser, K. (2013), "Synthesis als Vermittlung. Innere Berührung und exzentrische Empfindung," in *Synthesis. Zur Konjunktur eines philosophischen Begriffs in Wissenschaft und Technik*, edited by Gabriele Gramelsberger, Peter Bexte, and Werner Kogge, Bielefeld: Transcript Verlag.
Hartmann, M. (2013), *Domestizierung*, Baden-Baden: Nomos Verlag.
Harvey, D. (2012), *Rebel Cities: From the Right to the City to the Urban Revolution*, London: Verso.
Hegarty, A. alias Anohni (2015), *4 Degrees*, London: Rough Trade.
Heider, F. (1926), "Ding und Medium," *Symposion: Philosophische Zeitschrift für Forschung und Aussprache* 1 (2): 109–57.
Helmholtz, H. V. (1863), *Die Lehre von den Tonempfindungen als Physiologische Grundlage für die Theorie der Musik*, Braunschweig: Druck und Verlag von Friedrich Vieweg und Sohn.
Helmholtz, H. V. (1885), *On the Sensations of Tone as a Physiological Basis for the Theory of Music*. Second English translation by Alexander John Ellis. London: Longmans, Green, and Co.
Henrich, J., Heine, S. J. and Norenzayan, A. (2010), "The weirdest people in the world?" *Behavioral And Brain Sciences* 33: 61–135.
Henriques, J. (2011), *Sonic Bodies. Reggae Sound Systems, Performance Techniques, and Ways of Knowing*, New York: Continuum Press.
Herbert, R. (2011), *Everyday Music Listening: Absorption, Dissociation and Trancing*, Aldershot: Ashgate.
Herzogenrath, B. (ed.) (2017), *Sonic Thinking. A Media Philosophical Approach— Vol. 4 of the book series Thinking Media*, New York: Bloomsbury Publishing.
Hessel, S. (2010), *Indignez-vous!* Montpellier: Indigène éditions.
Hill, G., Thornley, K. W. (1965), *Principia Discordia or How The West Was Lost*, Berkeley: Xerox Copies.
Hogan, M. (1998), *A Cross of Iron: Harry S. Truman and the Origins of the National Security State*, Cambridge: Cambridge University Press.
Hogrebe, W. (1996), *Ahnung und Erkenntnis. Brouillon zu einer Theorie des natürlichen Erkennens*, Frankfurt am Main: Suhrkamp Verlag.
hooks, b. (1994), *Outlaw Culture: Resisting Representation*. London: Routledge.
Howes, D. (ed.) (2006), *Empire of the Senses: The Sensual Culture Reader*, Oxford: Berg Publishers.
Howes, D. and Classen, C. (2013), *Ways of Sensing: Understanding the Senses in Society*, London: Routledge.
Ikoniadou, E. (2014), *The Rhythmic Event. Art, Music, Sound*, Cambridge, MA: The MIT-Press.
James, W. (1912), *Essays in Radical Empiricism*, New York: Longman Green and Co.
Joshi, S. T. and Schultz, D. E. (2001), "Call of Cthulhu, The," in Joshi, S. T. and Schultz, D. E. (ed.), *An H.P. Lovecraft Encyclopedia, Westport*, CT: Greenwood Publishing Group, 28–29.
Joyce, J. (1939), *Finnegans Wake*, London: Faber & Faber.
Jullien, F. (2004), *Detour and Access: Strategies of Meaning in China and Greece. Translated by Sophie Hawkes*, Cambridge, MA: The MIT-Press.

Kahn, D. (2013), *Earth Signal Earth Sounds*, Berkeley: University of California Press.
Kamper, D. and Wulf, C. (1984), *Das Schwinden der Sinne*, Frankfurt am Main: Suhrkamp Verlag.
Kamper, D., Trabant, J. and Wulf, C. (eds.) (1993), *Das Ohr als Erkenntnisorgan. Paragrana 2, H. 1–2*. Berlin: Akademie Verlag.
Kant, I. (1781), *Kritik der reinen Vernunft*, Riga: Johann Friedrich Hartknoch.
Kalof, L. and Bynum, W. (eds.) (2010), *A Cultural History of the Human Body. Volume 1-6*. Oxford: Berg Publishers
Kassabian, A. (2013). *Ubiquitous Listening: Affect, Attention, and Distributed Subjectivity*, Berkley: University of California Press
Kelly, K. (2010), *What Technology Wants*, New York: Viking Press.
Kish, D. (1982), *Evaluation of an Echo-mobility Training Program for Young Blind People*, MA thesis, University of Southern California.
Kittler, F. (1980), "Einleitung" *Austreibung des Geistes aus den Geisteswissenschaften: Programme des Poststrukturalismus. Edited by Friedrich Kittle*, Paderborn: Ferdinand Schöningh,7–13
Kittler, F. (1985), *Aufschreibesysteme 1800-1900*, München: Wilhelm Fink.
Kittler, F. (1986), *Grammophon Film Typewriter*, Berlin: Brinkmann & Bose.
Kittler, F. (2005), *Musik und Mathematik I. Hellas 1: Aphrodite*, Paderborn: Wilhelm Fink.
Kittler, F. (2009), *Musik und Mathematik I. Hellas 2: Eros*, Paderborn: Wilhelm Fink.
Kursell, J. (2006), *Epistemologie des Hörens, 1850–2000*. Research project, Max-Planck Institut für Wissenschaftsgeschichte Berlin.
Kytö, M. (2015), The soundscape here is composed by two cockerels, a flame thrower, kid on a trampoline, a nail gun, a müezzin, a circular saw and two wind chimes. [Facebook status update]. Retrieved from: https://www.facebook.com/merikyto/posts/10153805788589430
Laboria Cuboniks (2015), *Xenofeminism: A Politics for Alienation*, http://laboriacuboniks.net
Latour, B. (1993), *We have never been modern*, Harvard: Harvard University Press.
Latour, B. and Serres, M. (1995), *Conversations on Science, Culture, and Time. Trans. Roxanne Lapidus*, Ann Arbor: University of Michigan Press.
Lavender, J. (2015), "Objects, Orientations and Interferences: On Deleuze and Sound Studies," *Parallax* 21 (4): 408–28.
Law, R. and Wark, M. (2013), *W.A.N.T.—Weaponized Adorables Negotiation Tactics*, New York: Kickstarter.
Lehmann, H.-T. (2006), *Postdramatic Theatre. Translated and with an Introduction by Karen Jürs-Munby*, London: Routledge.
Lefebvre, H. (1992), *Éléments de rythmanalyse*, Paris: Éditions Syllepse.
Lefebvre, H. (2014), *The Critique of Everyday Life - Volume I: Introduction* (1947), translated by John Moore, with a preface by Michel Trebitsch, London: Verso Books.
Leibniz, G. W. (1765), *Nouveaux essais sur l'entendement humain*, Amsterdam and Leipzig: Jean Schreuder.
Link, J. (1997), *Versuch über den Normalismus. Wie Normalität produziert wird*, Göttingen: Vandenhoeck & Ruprecht.

Lippe, R. Z. (1985), *Sinnenbewußtsein: Grundlegung einer anthropologischen Ästhetik*, Reinbek bei Hamburg; Rowohlt (2nd edition in 2 volumes: Baltmannsweiler Schneider-Verlag 2000)

Lombardo, V., Valle, A., Fitch, J. Tazelaar, K., Weinzierl, S., Borczyk, W. (2009), "A Virtual-Reality Reconstruction of "Poème electronique" based on Philological Research," *Computer Music Journal* 33 (2): 24–47.

Lorusso, A. M. (2015), *Cultural Semiotics: For a Cultural Perspective in Semiotics*, New York: Palgrave Macmillan US.

Lovecraft, H. P. (1928), "The Call of Cthulhu," in *The Dunwich Horror and Others* (9th corrected printing ed.), edited by S. T. Joshi, Sauk City, WI: Arkham House

Lovecraft, H. P. (1927), "Supernatural Horror in Literature," *The Recluse* 1: 23–59.

Macarthur, S., Lochhead, J., and Shaw, J. (eds.) (2016), *Music's Immanent Future: The Deleuzian Turn in Music Studies*, Oxford: Routledge.

Maier (née Müller-Schulzke), C. J. (2012), *Transcultural sound practices: South Asian sounds and Urban Dance Music in the UK*, PhD diss., Goethe-Universität Frankfurt.

Maier, C. and Schulze, H. (2015), "The Tacit Grooves of Sound Art: Aesthetic Artefacts as Analog Archives," *SoundEffects*—An Interdisciplinary Journal of Sound and Sound Experience 7 (2).

Marx, K. and Engels, F. (1867/1968), *Werke—Band 23: Das Kapital, Bd. I (1867)*, Berlin: Dietz Verlag.

Mauss, M. (1936), "Les Téchniques du Corps," *Journal de Psychologie* XXXII, Nr. 3–4, 15 März – 15 April.

Merleau-Ponty, M. (1962), *Phenomenology of Perception* (1945), translated by Colin Smith, London: Routledge & Kegan Paul.

Miller, D. (ed.) (1998), *Material Cultures*, London: UCL Press/University of Chicago Press.

Miller, D. (2008), *The Comfort of Things*, Polity: Cambridge.

Miller, D. (2010), *Stuff*, Cambridge: Polity.

Mintzberg, H. (1983), *Power in and Around Organizations*, Englewood Cliffs, NJ: Prentice-Hall.

Moisala, P., Leppänen, T. Tiainen, M., and Väätäinen, H. (eds.) (2017), *Musical Encounters with Deleuze and Guattari*, New York: Bloomsbury Publishing.

Moore, J. W. (2015), *Capitalism in the Web of Life: Ecology and the Accumulation of Capital*, New York: Verso Books.

Moore, J. W. (2014a), "The Capitalocene, Part I: On the Nature & Origins of Our Ecological Crisis," unpublished paper. Department of Sociology, Binghamton University

Moore, J. W. (2014b), "The Capitalocene, Part II: Abstract Social Nature and the Limits to Capital," unpublished paper. Department of Sociology, Binghamton University

Mouffe, C. (2013), *Agonistics: Thinking The World Politically*, London: Verso.

Mountz, A. (2015), "For a Slow Scholarship," https://www.academia.edu/12192676/For_Slow_Scholarship_A_Feminist_Politics_of_Resistance_through_Collective_Action_in_the_Neoliberal_University

Musil, R. (1930), *Der Mann ohne Eigenschaften*, Berlin. Rowohlt Verlag.

Nancy, J.-L. (1992), *Corpus*, Paris: Editions Métailié.

Nancy, J.-L. (2008), *Corpus*. Translated by R.A. Rand, New York: Fordham University Press.
Nancy, J.-L. (1996), *Être Singulier Pluriel*, Paris: Edition Galilée.
Nancy, J.-L. (2000), *Being Singular Plural*, Stanford: Stanford University Press.
Neuberger, O. (1995), *Führen und führen lassen*. Stuttgart: Lucius & Lucius.
Ngai, S. (2012), *Our Aesthetic Categories: Zany, Cute, Interesting*. Cambridge: Harvard University Press.
Nietzsche, F. (1997), *Untimely Meditations*, edited by Daniel Breazeale; translated by R. J. Hollingdale, Cambridge: Cambridge University Press.
Oliveros, P. (1984), *Software for People: Collected Writings 1963-80*, Baltimore: Smith Publications.
Oliveros, P. (1998), *The Roots of the Moment*, New York: Drogue Press.
Oliveros, P. (2005), *Deep Listening: A Composer's Sound Practice*, New York: iUniverse, Inc.
Palasmaa, J. (1996), *The Eyes of the Skin: Architecture and the Senses*, London: Academy Editions.
Papenburg, J. G. (2008), "Hörgeräte. Zur Psychomathematik des akroamatischen Leibniz," in *Zeitkritische Medienprozesse*, edited by Axel Volmar, 369–83, (Berlin: Kadmos).
Papenburg, J. G. (2012), *Hörgeräte. Technisierung der Wahrnehmung durch Rock- und Popmusik*, Berlin: PhD, Humboldt-Universität.
Parks, R. a.k.a. Photek (2054), *Six Pieces*, Kinshasa: Academy of the Arts.
Parikka, J. (2015), *The Anthrobscene*, Minneapolis: Minnesota University Press.
Parikka, J. (2011), "Operative Media Archaeology: Wolfgang Ernst's Materialist Media Diagrammatics," *Theory, Culture & Society* 28 (5): 52–74
Perniola, M. (1991), *Del Sentire*, Turin: Einaudi.
Perloff, M. (1994), *John Cage: Composed in America*, Chicago: University of Chicago Press.
Petzold, C. (2010), "You Can Only Narrate Loneliness Acoustically. An Interview," in *Immediacy and Non-Simultaneity: Utopia of Sound*, edited by Diederich Diederichsen and Constanze Ruhm, 219–243, Vienna: Schleebrügge Editor.
Pink, S. (2009), *Doing Sensory Ethnography*, London: SAGE Publishing.
Pfaller, R. (2003), *Illusionen der Anderen*, Frankfurt am Main: Suhrkamp Verlag.
Polanyi, M. (1966), *The Tacit Dimension*, New York: Doubleday
Posner, R. (2008), "Kultursemiotik," in *Konzepte der Kulturwissenschaft. Theoretische Grundlagen—Ansätze—Perspektiven*, edited by Ansgar Nünning and Vera Nünning, Stuttgart: Verlag J. B. Metzler.
Pothast, U. (1988), *Philosophisches Buch: Schrift unter der aus der Entfernung leitenden Frage, was es heißt, auf menschliche Weise lebendig zu sein*, Frankfurt am Main: Suhrkamp Verlag.
Pothast, U. (2009), "Bewußtes Leben und Innengrund," in *Gespür. Empfindung. Kleine Wahrnehmungen. Klanganthropologische Studien*, edited by Holger Schulze, Bielefeld: Transcript Verlag.
Razcal, D. (2009), *Tongue n' Cheek*, London: Dirtee Stank.
Refused (1996), *Songs To Fan The Flames Of Discontent*, Stockholm: Startrec
Rieger, M. (2006), *Helmholtz Musicus. Die Objektivierung der Musik im 19. Jahrhundert durch Helmholtz' Lehre von den Tonempfindungen*, Darmstadt: Wissenschaftliche Buchgesellschaft.

Rodgers, T. and Sterne, J. (2011), "The Poetics of Signal Processing," *Differences: A Journal of Feminist Cultural Studies* 22 (2 & 3).
Roland, A. (2001), *The Military-Industrial Complex*, Washington, DC: American Historical Association.
Said, E. (1978), *Orientalism*, New York: Pantheon Books.
Schmidgen, H. (2013). "Eine originale Syntax Psychoanalyse, Diskursanalyse und Wissenschaftsgeschichte," *Archiv für Mediengeschichte* 13: 27–43.
Schmidt, G. (2012), *Klavierzerstörungen in Kunst und Popkultur*, Berlin: Reimer.
Schmitz, H. (1990), *Der unerschöpfliche Gegenstand. Grundzüge der Philosophie*, Bonn: Bouvier.
Schoon, A. (2012), "Unmerkliche Eindringlinge. Versuch über akustische Kontrolle," in *Das geschulte Ohr. Eine Kulturgeschichte der Sonifikation*, edited by Andi Schoon and Axel Volmar, 285–97, Bielefeld: Transcript Verlag.
Schrimshaw, W. (2017), *Immanence and Immersion. On the Acoustic Condition in Contemporary Art*, New York: Bloomsbury Publishing.
Schulze, H. (2016), "Der Klang und die Sinne. Gegenstände und Methoden eines sonischen Materialismus," in *Materialität: Herausforderungen für die Sozial- und Kulturwissenschaften*, edited by Herbert Kalthoff, Cress Torsten, and Röhl Tobias, 395–416, München: Wilhelm Fink.
Schulze, H. (2014), "The Medial Persona. Tectonics of the Medial Imaginarium," in *Communication of Love. Mediatized Intimacy from Love Letters to SMS. Interdisciplinary and Historical Studies*, edited by Eva Lia Wyss, Bielefeld: Transcript Verlag.
Schulze, H. (2013), "The Sonic Persona. An Anthropology of Sound," in *Exploring the Senses. South Asian and European Perspectives on Rituals and Performativity*, edited by Axel Michaels and Christoph Wulf, 181–91, London, New York and New Delhi: Routledge.
Schulze, H. (2013), "Adventures In Sonic Fiction A Heuristic for Sound Studies," *Journal of Sonic Studies* 4.
Schulze, H. (2012), "The Body of Sound Sounding out the History of Science," *SoundEffects—An Interdisciplinary Journal of Sound and Sound Experience* 2: 196–208.
Schulze, H. (2012), *Intimität und Medialität. Eine Anthropologie der Medien—Theorie der Werkgenese, Bd. 3*, Berlin: AVINUS-Verlag
Schulze, H. (2007), "Spatial Body Sound. An Anthropology of With," in *Sam Auinger. Katalog*, edited by Carsten Seiffarth and Martin Sturm, translated by Catherine Kerkhoff-Saxon, 75–87, Wien-Bozen: Folio Verlag.
Schulze, H. (2005), *Heuristik*, Bielfeld: Transcript Verlag.
Schulze, H. (2008), "Hypercorporealismus: Eine Wissenschaftsgeschichte des körperlichen Schalls," *Popscriptum* 16 (10).
Schulze, H. (2000), *Das aleatorische Spiel. Erkundung und Anwendung der nichtintentionalen Werkgenese—Theorie der Werkgenese, Bd. 1*, München: Wilhelm Fink Verlag.
Schulze, H. [mediumflow] (2016, February 2), Die vollendete Idylle des Schreibens der Seiten 354–9. [Tweet]. Retrieved from https://twitter.com/mediumflow/status/694478041502896132
Seitter, W. (1997), *Physik des Daseins: Bausteine zu einer Philosophie der Erscheinungen*, Wien: Sonderzahl.

Serres, M. (2014), "Réflexion sur l'homme et la ville," in *Agora 2014—Biennale d'architecture, d'urbanisme et de design,* Bordeaux: Adim Sud-Ouest 12. September 2014 (online: http://mydesiringmachines.wordpress.com/2014/10/19/michel-serres-on-architecture-urbanism-space/)

Serres, M. (2008), *The Five Senses: A Philosophy of Mingled Bodies. Translated by Margaret Sankey and Peter Cowley,* New York: Continuum Publishers.

Serres, M. (1985), *Philosophie des corps mêlés: Les Cinq Sens,* Paris: Éditions Gallimard.

Serres, M. (1980), *Hermes V: Le Passage du Nord-Ouest,* Paris: Les Éditions de Minuit.

Shannon, C. (1948), "A Mathematical Theory of Communication," *Bell System Technical Journal* 27 (July and October): 379–423, 623–56 (July, October).

Snowden, Ed. (2013) Letter to Brazil—online: http://www1.folha.uol.com.br/internacional/en/world/2013/12/1386296-an-open-letter-to-the-people-of-brazil.shtml [retrieval date: December 17, 2013]

Steup, M. (2012), "Epistemology," in *The Stanford Encyclopedia of Philosophy* (fall 2012 ed.), edited by Edward N. Zalta. (online: https://plato.stanford.edu/entries/epistemology/)

Stangl, B. (2000), *Ethnologie im Ohr. Die Wirkungsgeschichte des Phonographen,* Wien: Wiener Universitätsverlag.

Sterne, J. (2012), *MP3—The Meaning of a Format,* Durham, NC: Duke University Press.

Sterne, J. (2003), *The Audible Past: The Cultural Origins of Sound Reproduction,* Durham, NC: Duke University Press.

Stewart, S. (2012), "Listening to Deep Listening: Reflection on the 1988 Recording and the Lifework of Pauline Oliveros," *Journal of Sonic Studies* 2, nr. 1 (May 2012) (online: http://journal.sonicstudies.org/vol02/nr01/a12)

Stockfelt, O. (1997), "Adequate Modes of Listening," in *Keeping Score: Music, Disciplinarity, Culture,* edited by David Schwartz, Anahid Kassabian, and Lawerence Siegel, 129–46. Charlottesville: University of Virginia Press.

Sowodniok, U. (2016), "Voce in Libertà," *The Senses and Society* 11 (1).

Sowodniok, U. (2013), *Stimmklang und Freiheit. Zur auditiven Wissenschaft des Körpers,* Bielefeld: Transcript Verlag.

Sowodniok, U. (2012a), "Von der Substanz des Hörens," in *Gespür, Empfindung, kleine Wahrnehmung. Klanganthropologische Studien,* edited by Schulze, H., 167–99. Bielefeld: Transcript Verlag.

Sowodniok, U. (2012b), "Stimmklang und Bedeutung. Fünf Perspektiven auf den resonierenden Körper—oder: Was singt mir, die ich höre in meinem Körper das Lied?" *Zeitschrift für Semiotik* 34 (1–2): 67–90

Stewart, K. (2007), *Ordinary Affects,* Durham, NC: Duke University Press.

Supa, M., Cotzin, M., and Dallenbach, K. M. (1944), "Facial Vision: The Perception of Obstacles by the Blind," *American Journal of Psychology* 57 (2): 133–83.

Szepanski, A. (2014a), *Kapitalisierung—Bd. 1: Marx' Non-Ökonomie,* Hamburg: Laika Verlag.

Szepanski, A. (2014b), *Kapitalisierung—Bd. 2: Non-Ökonomie des gegenwärtigen Kapitalismus,* Hamburg: Laika Verlag.

Szepanski, A. (2015), "Immanent Non-Musicology: Deleuze/Guattari vs. Laruelle" *Non*, 31. Juli 2015. Online: http://non.copyriot.com/immanent-non-musicology-deleuzeguattari-vs-laruelle/

Supper, A. (2012), *Lobbying for the Ear. The Public Fascination with and Academic Legitimacy of the Sonification of Scientific data*, PhD University of Maastricht.

Theweleit, K. (1977), *Männerphantasien*, Frankfurt am Main: Stroemfeld/Roter Stern.

Theweleit, K. (2007), *Übertragung. Gegenübertragung. Dritter Körper. Zur Gehirnveränderung durch die Medien. Internationale Flusser Lecture*. Köln: Verlag der Buchhandlung Walther König.

Theweleit, K. (2013), "Früher Götter, heute Menschen. Ein Interview von Ulrike Fokken und Edith Kresta," *die tageszeitung*, October 5, 2013, accessed February 18, 2014, http://www.taz.de/1/archiv/digitaz/artikel/?ressort=hi&dig=2013%2F10%2F05%2Fa0039&cHash=f8c6fe9d7d5c9239aa20427d4d351697

Thompson, E. (2002), *Soundscapes of Modernity: Architectural Acoustics and the Culture of Listening in America, 1900–1933*, Cambridge, MA: The MIT-Press.

Thompson, M. and Biddle, I. (2013), *Sound, Music, Affect Theorizing Sonic Experience*, New York: Bloomsbury Publishing.

Thrift, N. (2008), *Non-Representational Theory. Space—Politics—Affect*, London: Routledge.

Tkaczyk, V. (2015), "The Making of Acoustics Around 1800, or how to do Science with Words," in *Performing Knowledge, 1750-1850*, edited by M. H. Dupree and S. B. Franzel, 27–55, Berlin: De Gruyter.

Thwaites, J. A., Koenig, G. M. and Ramsbott, W. (1963), "Die Fluxus-Leute. Interviews mit Jean-Pierre Wilhelm, Nam June Paik, Wolf Vostell und Carlheinz Caspari," *magnum—die zeitschrift für das moderne Leben* 47 (32–35): 62–7.

Tieck, L. and Wackenroder, W. H. (1797), *Herzensergießungen eines kunstliebenden Klosterbruders*, Berlin: Johann Friedrich Unger.

Tocotronic (2015), *Das Rote Album*, London: Vertigo Records.

Toop, D. (1995), *Ocean of Sound. Aether Talk, Ambient Sound and Imaginary Worlds*, London: Serpent's Tail.

Treib, M. (1996), *Space Calculated in Seconds: The Philips Pavilion, Le Corbusier, Edgard Varèse*, Princeton, NJ: Princeton University Press.

Ujita, N. (2028), *Sonische Zeitfragen I-IX*, Reykjavik: Jynweythek Publishers.

Valéry, P. (1957a), *Œuvres. Tome I—Édition de Jean Hytier*. Paris: Bibliothèque de la Pléiade.

Valéry, P. (1957b), *Œuvres. Tome II—Édition de Jean Hytier*. Paris: Bibliothèque de la Pléiade.

Valéry, P. (1957–61), *Cahiers, fac-similé intégral—vol.1-XXIX*, Paris: Centre national de la recherche scientifique.

Valéry, P. (1965), The Collected Works of Paul Valery, in Jackson Mathews, *Part V: Idee fixe. A Duologue by the Sea*, translation by D. Paul, preface by J. Mathews, introduction by Philip Wheelwright, Princeton, NJ: Princeton University Press.

Valéry, P. (2007), Cahiers/Notebooks 3. Translated by Norma Rinsler, Paul Ryan, Brian Stimpson, based on the French Cahiers edited by Judith Robinson-Valéry, Frankfurt am Main: Peter Lang.

Various Artists (1996), *Blech II: Blechsdöttir, mixed by DJ Food*, Sheffield: Warp Records.
Voegelin, S. (2010), *Listening to Noise and Silence: Toward a Philosophy of Sound Art*, New York: Continuum Publishers.
Voegelin, S. (2012), *Sonic Possible Worlds: Hearing the Continuum of Sound*, New York: Bloomsbury Publishers.
Volmar, A. (ed.) (2009), *Zeitkritische Medien*, Berlin: Kulturverlag Kadmos.
Volmar, A. (2014), "In Storms of Steel: The Soundscape of World War I and its Impact on Auditory Media Culture During the Weimar Period," in *Hearing Modern History: Auditory Cultures in 19th and 20th Century Europe*, edited by Daniel Morat, 227–55, New York: Berghahn.
Volmar, A. (2015), *Klang-Experimente. Die auditive Kultur der Naturwissenschaften 1761-1961*, Frankfurt am Main: Campus Verlag.
Wackenroder, W. H. (1971), *Confessions and Fantasies*. Translated and annotated with a critical introd. by Mary Hurst Schubert, University Park, PA: Pennsylvania State University Press.
Waldenfels, B. (2000), *Das leibliche Selbst*, Frankfurt am Main: Suhrkamp Verlag
Wallace, D. F. (1996), *Infinite Jest: A Novel*, Boston: Little, Brown and Company
Wark, M. (2015a), *Molecular Red: Theory for the Anthropocene*, New York: Verso Books.
Wark, M. (2015b), "The Capitalocene," in *Public Seminar*. New York: The New School for Social Research October 15, 2015. Online: http://www.publicseminar.org/2015/10/the-capitalocene/
Wark, M. (2015c), "Blog-Post for Cyborgs," in *Public Seminar*, New York: The New School for Social Research September 24, 2015. Online: http://www.publicseminar.org/2015/09/blog-post-for-cyborgs/
Wark, M. (2014), "Birth of Thanaticism," in *Public Seminar*. New York: The New School for Social Research October 3, 2014. Online: http://www.publicseminar.org/2014/04/birth-of-thanaticism/
Wark, M. (2007), *Gamer Theory 2.0*, Cambridge, MA: Harvard University Press
Westerkamp, H. (1974), "Soundwalking" *Sound Heritage* III (1974), No. 4 (also in: *Autumn Leaves, Sound and the Environment in Artistic Practice*, edited by Carlyle Angus, Double Entendre, Paris, 2007, 49).
Winthrop-Young, G. (2011), *Kittler and the Media*, Cambridge: Polity.
Winthrop-Young, G. (2002), "Drill and Distraction in the Yellow Submarine: The Dominance of War in Friedrich Kittler's Media Theory," *Critical Inquiry* 28 (4): 825–54.
Wittek, H. (2008), *Perceptual Differences Between Wavefield Synthesis and Stereophony*, PhD, University of Surrey.
Wulf, C. (ed.) (1997), *Vom Menschen. Handbuch Historische Anthropologie*, Weinheim & Basel: Beltz Verlag.
Wulf, C. (2013), *Anthropology. A Continental Perspective*, Chicago and London: Chicago University Press.
Zappa, F. (1989), *The Real Frank Zappa Book. With Peter Occhiogrosso*, New York: Poseidon Press.

TAK. DANKE. THANK YOU.

A book like this is written alone. Yet its thoughts and counterthoughts emerge in constant exchange, inspiration, in conflict, disagreement, in a collective, incessantly evolving, a dissipating improvisation with a myriad of people, environments, situations, and institutions over quite some time—and in loads of places, of discussions, of ramblings over coffee, on a walk, before an exhibition opening or after a concert performance. This book emerged over a timespan of roughly 15 years. I wish to thank the following humanoid aliens—in alphabetic order: You all contributed in one way or another to my work with your ideas, your sensibilities, and your dissent. Thank you:

Christine Amschler, Sam Auinger, Leah Babb-Rosenfeld, Sven Beckstette, Karin Bijsterveld, Susanne Binas-Preisendörfer, Carolyn Birdsall, Jochen Bonz, Georgina Born, Stefan Böschen, Candice Breitz, Caroline Buchheim, Hanna Buhl, Michael Bull, Thomas Burkhalter, Mark J. Butler, Marcel Cobussen, Christian Demand, Detlef Diederichsen, Diedrich Diederichsen, Kathrin Dreckmann, Melissa Van Drie, Anke Eckardt, Hajo Eickhoff, Katrin Emler, Veit Erlmann, Sabine Fabo, Sabine Flach, Monika Fleischmann, Golo Föllmer, Marcus Gammel, Felix Gerloff, Julia Gerlach, Antye Greie-Ripatti, Rolf Großmann, Ally Jane Grossnan, Günter Hack, Maria Hanáček, Karin Harrasser, Thomas Hecken, Thomas Hermann, Britta Herrmann, Bernd Herzogenrath, Rasmus Holmboe, Erik Granly Jensen, Kammerflimmer Kollektief, Anahid Kassabian, Christian Kassung, Daniel Kish, Marcus S. Kleiner, Ekkehard Knörer, Doris Kolesch, Ingo Kottkamp, Julia Krause, Jacob Kreutzfeld, Susanne Kriemann, Sanne Krogh Groth, Katja Kullmann, Meri Kytö, Brandon LaBelle, Tore Tvarnø Lind, Mo Loschelder, Thomas Macho, Carla J. Maier, Dirk Matejovski, Thomas Meinecke, Morten Michelsen, Satoshi Morita, Rahel Müller, Gisela Nauck, Bruce Odland, Jens Gerrit Papenburg, Malte Pelleter, Roland Posner, Olaf Schäfer, Matze Schmidt, Hans-Julius Schneider, Andi Schoon, Sebastian Schwesinger, Carsten Seiffarth, Erik Steinskog, Sharon Stewart, Ulrike Sowodniok, Georg

Spehr, Jonathan Sterne, Wolfgang Strauss, Søren Møller Sørensen, Achim Szepanski, Johanna Thompson, Christian Thorau, David Toop, Anselm Venezian-Nehls, Axel Volmar, Urs Walter, Peter Wicke, Thomas Wilke, Justin Winkler, Geoffrey Winthrop-Young, Jeremy Woodruff, Christoph Wulf, Zeitblom.

I wish to thank my dynamically generative tribe, who danced, sang, played, and traveled with me all these years around the writing of this book: Maren, Nanouk, Rasmus, and Pirkka.

INDEX

acoustemology 138, 139, 153, 154
Acoustics (Beranek) 23, 24
acoustics, physical 87
adequate listening 56, 57
Adorno, Theodor W. 110, 231
affordances 48, 207
Age of Capital 104, 106
agonism 109
alienation 191
Alphabet Symphony (1962) 37
Amacher, Maryanne 137, 140, 145, 224
 aural architecture 138
ambient music 33, 144, 145,
Animal Spirits 65
Anthropocene 104, 106
anthropology
 idiosyncratic 113
 negative 195
 of sound 8, 120, 132–5, 143, 146, 191
 of the senses 44, 64, 113, 182, 183, 189
 sonic 185
Apollo Amerika (Kriwet) 37
apparatization 57, 96
Apparatus Canto 94–5
 anthropomorphization of technology 98
apparatuses naturalized 172–8
 alien's sensibility 172
appellations 207
arousal 61, 62
Artaud, Antonin (French dramatist) 36

Arte Povera in Italy (movement) 36
artifacts 4, 42, 87
 acoustic artifacts 50
 artistic artifact 59
 audio artifacts 87
 auditory artifacts 9
 combinatoric artefact 38
 cultural artifacts 38, 87, 145
 humanoid artifacts 29, 64
 reduced artifacts 42
 sensory artifacts 81
 signal processing artifacts 87
 sonic artifacts 4, 40, 44, 138, 156, 166, 194, 216, 218
 technocultural artifacts 17
 technological
artificial intelligence 63
AT&T Bell Telephone Laboratories 17, 18
audile techniques 27, 151, 177
audio technology 47, 80, 87, 95, 145, 176
audiogame 133
audition 3, 6, 16
auditory dispositive 92
auditory processing 94
Aufführungspraxis 44–9
aural architecture 47, 138, 193, 225
auscultations 111, 157
Avid Technology 4

Bachelor Machine 101
Bahr, Hans-Dieter (Berlin researcher) 7
Baudry, Jean-Louis 39–44, 62, 98

INDEX

BB Talk (track)   220, 222
BBC Symphony Orchestra   32
Beloved Lady of Truth Inc.   63
Beranek, Leo Leroy   23–8, 213
  BBN Technologies   27
Black Mirror (Brooker)   166
Brecht, George   37
  Water Jam (1962)   37
Breton, André (French writer)   36
Brown, Norman Oliver (artist)   35

Cage, John (artist)   35
Californian Ideology (article by Barbrook and Cameron)   169, 197
capitalism, semiotic   128
capitalization   19, 22, 104, 105, 128, 175
Capitalocene   104, 105, 107
catharsis   61
Chthulucene, The   105, 106
City-Links (workgroup)   137
cohesion   147, 212–15
coincidentality   117
communication system   89–90
  channel   89, 90, 91
  destination   89, 90
  information source   89, 90, 91
  normative model   90
  receiver   89, 90, 91
  transmitter   89, 90, 91
Corbusier, Le (French architect)   28, 29, 30, 214
corporeal activity   149
corporeal epistemologies   120, 139, 151, 154–6
corporeality   147
corporealization of sonic experiences   57
  grounded fiction   71
corporeal listening   22, 27, 57, 88, 154, 228
corporeal phenomenology   144
corporeal reflexivity   138
corporeal science   122
corporeal sensibility   9, 150, 168, 180
corporeal state   204
corporeal technology   217

corporeal tension   204
corporeal thinking   73, 74
corpus in situ   140–5
corpus of vocal performer   219
corpus techné   217
corpus, sensory   159, 199
  skillful disruption   197
  xenocommon   196
Cressmann, Darryl   26
critical thinking   73, 75, 97
critique
  and analysis   168
  of cultural artefact   166
  syrrhesis   169
Cthulhu   107
Cyrus, Miley   225

dancing   55, 58
Dath, Dietmar (German author)   108, 118, 215, 216, 218
  The Abolition of the Species   216
  Im erwachten Garten   215
decolonization   202
Deleuze, Gilles (French philosopher)   36
deprivation, sensory   127
design   47, 76, 91, 155, 168
destroying instruments   31–3
Digidesign   4
digitalization   119
dispositive, auditive   207
dispositive, auditory   48, 96
dispositive's capitalization   101–7
dispositives   40–1, 49–53
Dolby 5.1 (sound reproduction technology)   51, 52
Duchamp, Marcel (avant-garde artist)   31

The Ear as an Organ of Knowledge (Kamper et al.)   7
echoing effects   23
echolocation   140
  see also human echolocation
emergence   206
empiricism   128
engineering culture   89, 92, 95, 96, 98, 103, 176

INDEX

enteroceptions 113, 181
epistemologies 150–6
  apparatus-based epistemologies 151
    new sensory materialist 152
    perceptual techniques 155
epistemologies, apparatus-based 151
epistemologies, auditory 151
epistemologies, sonic 134, 139, 151–4
erratic heuristics 196–200
  aleatorization 200
Eshun, Kodwo (music critic) 59, 95
Europeras (composed by Cage) 37
expanded site-specific rhythmanalysis 213, 214, 225
experialist 164, 166
Experience and the Creation of Meaning (Gendlin) 148

facial perception 139
fear 58, 75, 137, 203, 216, 229
Feld, Steven
  acoustemology 138
  reflective sensibility 139
Fletcher, Harvey 17–22, 213
Fluxus 36, 37
Fluxus, lessons of 39
4'33" 33
Freud, Sigmund 40
Fuckin Fucked Up (Cyrus) 220, 221, 222, 223

Gebauer, Gunter (Berlin researcher) 7
generative sensorium 145–50, 152
generativity 206, 217, 227–31
  personal 210
Gente 218
Gibson, James Jerome (psychologist) 48
globalization 36, 119, 174, 202
globalized security theater 85
golden mouth 64, 128
Goodman, Steve 48
Great Hall of the *Musikverein* in Vienna 23
Großmann, Rolf (German mucicologist) 47, 98

grounded fiction 68, 71
Guattari, Félix (French psychotherapist) 36, 77, 139, 205
gustatory sensation 53

hearing 15, 151, 187, 228
hearing loss 187
hearing perspective 9, 121, 122
Heartfelt Effusions of an Art-Loving Cloister Brother (Tieck and Wackenroder) 13
Heartstrings 134
Heider, Fritz (Austrian philosopher) 192
Hessel, Franz (German writer) 210
The Human 6, 8, 20, 49, 100, 101, 172–8
The Human Being 7, 8
human echolocation 137, 139, 151, 154, 155
humanoid aliens 6, 8, 44, 131, 132, 107, 108, 178, 184, 191
humanoid corpus 188
hypercorporealism 68, 159, 213
hypersensitization 76

iconoclastic laboratory instruments 14
idioplex 183–6
idiosyncrasies 117
idiosyncratic anthropology 113
idiosyncratic awareness of space 125
idiosyncratic biography 167
Im erwachten Garten (in the awakened garden) 215–19
IMAX-cinema 43
implex 113–20, 133, 152
Infinite Jest 199
Intelligent Life (workgroup) 137
Interdisciplinary Center for Historical Anthropology 7
Internationale Situationniste in France (movement) 36
intrinsic and idiosyncratic *jouissance* 201
invented tradition 76

jazz-rock   199

Kamper, Dietmar (Berlin researcher)   7, 119
Kant, Immanuel   12
  Kantian categories   167
  Kantian concept   14
  Kantian epistemology   14
  Kantian suspicion   167
kinesthetics   53, 72, 118, 139
Kirchner, Barbara (German author)   118, 215
Kish, Daniel   139
Kittler, Friedrich   98, 99
  engineering genius   100
  The Expulsion of Spirit from the Humanities   98–9
Klavierstück XI (Stockhausen)   37
knowledge   33, 34
  auditory knowledge   34
  embodied knowledge   152
  epistemological knowledge   44
  individual knowledge   34
  tacit knowledge   152, 180
Kollektief, Kammerflimmer (German author)   215, 216, 225
  Im erwachten Garten   215
Kresge Auditorium, Massachusetts Institute of Technology   23

laughing persona   156
Le Corbusier (architect)   28, 29, 30
Lefebvre, Henri   144
Les Cinq Sens—The Five Senses (Serres)   62
listeners' precision of sensibility   226
listening   3, 4, 17, 57, 66, 80, 81
  apparatization of   96
  materialize listening   57
listening body   156–9
  auscultations   157
  corporeal physics of existence   158
listening practices   155
listening, corporeal   228
listening, deep   105, 138, 139, 145, 154, 155
listening, idiosyncratic   184
listening, inadequate   57

listening, substance of   219
logocentrism
  logocentric angst   152
  logocentric cultural forms   129, 155
  logocentric interpretation   150, 153
  self-destructive logocentric confederation   64
The Lord (ultimate reference in Christianity)   97
loudspeakers   79, 82
  machinic deep listening   105

Machine Célibataire (Duchamp)   100
macropolitics   164
magnetic induction   92
Marcuse, Herbert (German-American philosopher)   35
material culture   44
material migration   67
material percept   136–40
materialism
  sensory   82, 126
  sonic   81
materialization   31, 42, 53
  of listening   22, 53, 214
  of senses   153
  of sound   24, 30, 53, 112
A Mathematical Theory of Communication (Shannon)   89, 90, 92
Maverick Concert Hall   33
media technology   41, 42, 43, 63, 87, 94, 97
Mediaset (TV network)   170
mediatization   202
Merleau-Ponty, Maurice   124
metaphors   17, 67, 70, 76, 121, 199
microphones   5, 85–8, 89
militarization   91
military-industrial-communication-entertainment complex   101, 166, 176, 216
monism   146, 148, 149
Moore, Jason W.   104
Morgan, John Pierpont   18, 19
Motor Vehicle Sundown (crucial performance of Fluxus, 1960)   37

MP3 format 17, 51, 177
Müller, Georg Elias (psychologist) 14

Nancy, Jean-Luc 66–75, 143
nanopolitics 163–6
networked sensorium 136
new sensory materialism 79–82
noise abatement 195
noise as presence 200–5
noise making 201
non-anthropocentric anthropology 49
non-humanoids 27, 79, 131, 184, 218
non-persona perspective 168
non-responsiveness 190–6

olfactory sensation 40, 53, 137, 167, 181
Oliveros, Pauline 138
otoacoustic sounds 138

Paik, Nam June (composer) 31
    Etude for Piano 31, 33
The Pale King (Wallace) 229
Panacousticon 50
perception 140
perceptual material 137
perceptual politics 164
perceptual techniques 44, 51, 137, 139, 142, 155, 164
Perniola, Mario (Italian philosopher) 20, 169
persistent materialities 112
persona resista 206–11
persona, gustatory 156
persona, kinesthetic 156
persona, medial 170
persona, mimic 156
persona, olfactory 156
persona, sensory 132, 133, 156, 184, 206, 207, 220, 222
persona, visual 156
persona, vocal 156
personae, multitude of 156
perspectivization 122
petit perceptions 182
    proprioceptive perception 180
    sensing 180
petite perceptions 33

phenomenon of hyperrealism 41
Philips Corporation 30
    Philips Pavilion 28
Philips Pavilion 28
phonautograph 5, 6, 16, 51
Photek (a.k.a. Parkes, Rupert) 212, 213
pitch 134
    deep pitch 219
    high pitch 49
    low pitch 210
    progression of 16
pitch 16
plane of immanence 158
plasticity 75, 114, 118, 126, 179, 216, 217, 221
Plato 71
    Heaven of Ideas 97
    history of philosophy 65
    Symposium 70, 78
Poème électronique (Varèse) 29
practices 144
pragmatics 70, 164, 198, 199
precision of sensibility 178–83
Pro Tools 3–6
processing sensory data 63
pronomos 123
proprioceptions 113, 148, 180, 181
prosopon 123

radical empiricism 128
radiophonic art 133
radiophonic recording 86, 87
ready-felts 170, 172
ready-thoughts 170
receptivity 41, 62, 219, 227
    sonic receptivity 183
    tactile receptivity 88
reproducibility 96, 97, 152, 154
resistance 137, 192, 203, 205
reverberation time 25, 26, 138, 154
rhythmanalysis, expanded site-specific 213
rhythmic event 55
Ritter, Johann Wilhelm (psychologist) 14

Sabine, Wallace (physicist) 25
Sanctuary of Asklepios at Epidaurus 23

INDEX

Schwitters, Kurt (avant-garde artist)   31
scientific reification   16
second tongue   64
Seitter, Walter (Austrian philosopher and Michel Foucault scholar)   158
semiosis   58, 69, 70, 95, 148, 150
sensation, visual   53
sensibility   62, 139, 210
sensing sound   15, 142
sensologia   20
sensology   20, 169, 172, 177, 189
   Perniola's theory of sensologies   171
sensorial materialities   112, 113
sensory anthropology   72, 79, 121, 141, 181, 183
sensory corpus   157, 227
sensory critique   52, 53, 166–72, 179
   corporeal sensibility   168
sensory data processing   63
sensory deprivation   113, 127
sensory ethnography   52, 113
sensory experience   7, 8, 11, 58, 63
   generative sensorium   145
   of humanoids   15
   imminent sensory immanence of   122
sensory fictions   183
sensory materialism   126, 210
sensory perception   24, 40, 62, 63, 123, 140, 155
sensory signal data processing   5
sensory syncope   219–24
   concept of commodified sound   221
   dispositive of pop   222
sensualism   128
Serres, Michel   58–66
servomechanism   49, 178, 195
Shannon, Claude   80, 90, 93, 194
shannonist concept
   of instrumentalizing   177
   of signal processing   175–6, 194
shannonist thinking   91
signal processing   63, 77, 88, 95
signal transduction   14, 47, 87, 92, 94, 95

singing   41, 65, 218, 223, 228
   way of dancing   58, 231
Six Pieces   212, 214, 220
slow scholarship   64, 130
social fiction, dystopic   192
social generativity   55, 200
sonic actors   52, 98
sonic affect   53
sonic affordances   50
sonic anthropology   185
sonic bodies   27
sonic choreographies   138
sonic dominance   58, 109, 120
sonic epistemology   139
sonic experiences   3, 81, 93
sonic explorations   80
sonic fictions   11, 79, 95, 126, 185
   fictionalized   230
   generated from syrrhesis   218
sonic flux   143
sonic generativity   120, 183
sonic materialism   81, 82, 127, 142, 152, 225
sonic nanopolitics   166
sonic persona   120–5, 156, 158
sonic skills   27, 34, 44, 151
sonic thinking   73
sonic traces   111–13, 123, 132
sonic-actor-network   49
sonification   120
The Son of God   69
sound art   32, 37, 47, 50, 80
   performing sound art   78
   site-specific sound art   151
sound engineer   34, 46, 48, 85
sound in flux   33–9
   aleatorization   38
   anesthetic measure   38
sound of responsiveness   192
sound processing software   78, 87
sound source   194
sound studies   48, 191
sound waves
   distortions by   55
   material carriers of   142
   in public places   23
   scientific concept of   27, 28

sounding   20, 81, 96
　listening and   20
　see also listening
soundscape   32, 117, 121, 158
Soundwalking (Westerkamp)   209, 210
Soupault, Philippe (French writer)   36
Space Boots (track)   221
space-time continuum   78, 81, 150
spatial sound reproduction   52, 53
spatiality of position   124, 125, 142
spatiality of situation   124, 125, 142
Speech and Hearing (Fletcher)   17
Spreading Membrane (Müller and Amschler)   9
stereo hi-fi   97
stereo speakers   50
Stockfelt, Ola (Swedish musicologist)   56
　adequate listening   57
Stumpf, Carl (psychologist)   14
subject-centered philosophy   143
subjectivity   62, 114, 219
　Western subjectivity   63
Synaptic Island   224–7
　dispositive of sound reproduction   226
　ocean of sound   225
　sensory critique   226
　sonic arena   224
syrrhesis   64, 68, 99, 169, 183
Szepanski, Achim   104

tacit knowledge   152, 180
technological fetishization   122
technology   80
　anthropomorphization of   98
　audio technology   47, 80, 87, 96, 145, 176
　computer technology   82
　media technology   43, 87, 94, 97
　military technology   27
　network technology   27
　of sound production   4, 87
　phonautograph   16
tension of attention   203
textile persona   156
thanaticism   64, 101, 103, 228

Thanatos   193
Theweleit, Klaus (cultural theorist)   46, 49, 207, 208
third mouth   64
third tongue   64, 130
thoughtprobes in music   60, 64, 68, 82
tone sensations   14, 24
touchscreen   165
transitions of experience   129
transmission   87, 88, 93
Tudor, David (performer)   33

ubiquitous listening   144
ubiquitous reflexivity   138
Uncle Meat (album)   199
utopia   213, 216

Varèse, Edgard (composer)   29, 30, 214
varieties of experiences   127
varying experientiality   126–32
vibrational nexus   48
vibrations   23
　actual vibrations   53
　vibrational nexus   52
video cameras   89, 97
violent uprisings   67
Virtual Electronic Poem   28–9
The Virus of Control (Burroughs)   58
visceroceptions   113, 181
vocal skills   85
von Helmholtz, Hermann   9–16, 213
　anthropocentric concepts   15
Von Neumann architectures   97
Von Neumann-machine   116
von Webern, Anton   212, 213

W.A.N.T. (Weaponized Adorables Negotiation Tactics)   163
Wallace, David Foster   107
Wark, McKenzie   103, 163
Water Jam (crucial performance of Fluxus, 1962)   37
waveform synthesis (WFS)   43, 50, 51, 52
WEIRD (Western, Educated, Industrialized, Rich, and Democratic)   21, 43, 195

weird and WEIRD   195
Western research cultures   21
Western subjectivity   63
  theories of sensory perception   63
Western Suprematism   7
White, Hayden (historian)   35
The Wider Role of Bodily Sense in Thought and Language (Gendlin)   148
Williams, Emmett   37
  Alphabet Symphony (1962)   37

Wulf, Christoph (Berlin researcher)   7, 119
Wundt, Wilhelm   14

Xenakis, Iannis (composer)   28, 29, 214
  Xenakis' pavilion   30
xenocommon   196

zeige deine Wunde (show your wounds)   187–90
zoon acousticon   123